D0467420

Can I Get a Witness?

CAN I GET A WITNESS?

Thirteen Peacemakers, Community Builders,
and Agitators for Faith and Justice

Edited by
Charles Marsh, Shea Tuttle,
and Daniel P. Rhodes

WILLIAM B. EERDMANS PUBLISHING COMPANY
GRAND RAPIDS, MICHIGAN

Wm. B. Eerdmans Publishing Co.
4035 Park East Court SE, Grand Rapids, Michigan 49546
www.eerdmans.com

25 24 23 22 21 20 19   1 2 3 4 5 6 7

ISBN 978-0-8028-7573-0

Library of Congress Cataloging-in-Publication Data

A catalog record for this book is available from the Library of Congress.

For these thirteen witnesses,

and for the cloud of witnesses
too great to know, too numerous to name,

so broad as to occasion holy surprise and reforming delight.

May these stories honor you.

Contents

CONTENTS

Acknowledgments

This book represents a collaboration of theologians, writers, and editors over two successive years in Charlottesville and Chicago, who were seeking to retrieve and celebrate the tradition of Christian social progressives in the United States. The editors are grateful to each of the contributors for bringing this rich cast of characters to life and for answering the question "Can I get a witness?" with a resounding yes.

We owe huge thanks to Jessica Seibert, the project manager at the University of Virginia's Project on Lived Theology. Her brilliant organizing made the meetings happen, and she continued to offer limitless support and smart editorial advice in the months since. Koonal Patel and Gosia Czelusniak, the excellent team at Loyola University Chicago's Institute of Pastoral Studies, assisted Jessica in invaluable ways in preparation for our meeting at the Water Tower Campus.

Editor extraordinaire Lil Copan shepherded us through the drafting and first revision of the manuscript with her sharp eye and generous intelligence. We are grateful to David Bratt, Anita Eerdmans, Holly Knowles, Jeremy Cunningham, Leah Luyk, Alexander Bukovietski, and the whole Eerdmans team for their attentive and encouraging partnership. We are delighted this book landed in their exceedingly capable hands.

The Project on Lived Theology exists thanks to the generosity of the Lilly Endowment and theological vision of Jessicah Duckworth and Chris Coble. We are ever so grateful to count them among our cloud of witnesses.

Introduction

Charles Marsh and Shea Tuttle

When Dietrich Bonhoeffer came to Union Theological Seminary in Manhattan as a visiting student and postdoctoral fellow in the late summer of 1930, he was a straight-arrow scholar whose star was rising. His sights were set on a lifetime of academic accomplishments and the rich rewards of the guild. He didn't think there was anything he could learn from the American Protestant churches who worshipped a god tailored for their middle-class tastes and preferences.

But when he left New York ten months later, he left with a dramatically transformed perspective on social engagement, faith, and historical responsibility. He began to put aside his professional ambitions and look for resources in the Christian (and increasingly in the Jewish) tradition that could inspire and sustain dissent and civil courage. A technical terminology that had distinguished his writings and teaching before 1930 began to fade, and in its place emerged a language more direct and expressive of lived faith.

In Tegel prison in 1944, incarcerated for his role in a plot to assassinate Hitler, Bonhoeffer recalled the first American visit as one of the decisive and transformative influences in his life. "I don't think I've ever changed very much," he wrote, "except perhaps at the time of my first impressions abroad. . . . It was then that

I turned from 'the phraseological to the real.'"[1] Something had happened in America, as Bonhoeffer's best friend and biographer Eberhard Bethge later wrote.

Over the course of that transformative year in the United States, Bonhoeffer encountered the strange and unfamiliar world of radical Christianity, represented at the time by the Protestant social theology taught and practiced at Union Seminary; the American organizing tradition, flourishing in New York and in an ever expanding network of progressive Christian activism; and the African American church, where he said he finally heard the gospel of Jesus preached with power and conviction. Five months into the school year he told a friend that he had come in search of "a cloud of witnesses."

The cloud of witnesses that he found comprised the largely forgotten tradition of a confessional left: activist theologians, Bible-wielding labor organizers, social gospel reformers, and African American preachers—which is to say, the cast of characters foregrounded in *Can I Get a Witness?* Bonhoeffer's encounter with this tradition transformed his sense of vocation, enabled him to do theology closer to the ground, and set him on the difficult road that would ultimately lead to Flossenbürg concentration camp.

*   *   *

The stories of the church's peacemakers, community builders, and inside agitators, those who "refuse to remain spectators of the panorama of injustice,"[2] can be difficult to hear—and to find. These people are like wild and crooked trees. They are gnarled and weathered, their very flesh bearing the marks of storms, persistent droughts, and long winters. They don't care if they're growing in inconvenient places; they grow where they are. They are unrepentantly unruly. They live in the freedom of Christ with open hearts and minds. These peculiar people aren't good for church growth or the accumulation of political power. They don't make anybody any money. Yet we are confident that their examples will outlast those of the multitudes scrambling to see who can bow down first to country, or party, or profit, or another reigning idol of the day. It is a good time to remember the peculiar people, dissidents, misfits, and malcontents who sing strange and beautiful songs of God's peaceable kingdom. Being peculiar has never been easy, but in this second decade of the twenty-first century, amid the violent convulsions and linguistic political confusions of Christian witness in the United States, the testimonies of dissidents take on new urgency. These are challenging days for those who affirm the integrity of the global, ecumenical church; read the Bible against the principalities and the powers; and dare to speak against the day.

Peculiarity is not a quality intended to highlight the feeling of specialness, as in the conceited notion that we are peculiar because *we are God's chosen ones*. The stories of Scripture make clear that much is expected of those who call on or claim relationship with God. Being "peculiar," a "royal priesthood," a "holy nation," means being a people who practice mercy and seek justice. Only the nation that defends the defenseless, establishes equity, and relieves the oppressed is "chosen." This is the message of the prophets of the Hebrew Bible.

Many of the earliest writings on the identity of the people who call themselves followers of Christ convey bewilderment at the new moral habits of the Christian community. They live in the cities and countries of the empire but as sojourners; "they bear their share in all things as citizens, and they endure all hardships as strangers." Yet they display "a wonderful and confessedly striking method of life."[3] They live in the tension and torque of being in the world but not of the world, refusing, as the earliest Christians did, "to honor the emperor by offering a pinch of incense before his image."[4]

Living as strangers in a strange land, as the peculiar people in this volume vividly attest, is not about withdrawal from the world or resignation to injustices. It is rather about learning to act and to think, to read and to interpret, to organize and to vote in the new light springing from the teachings and life of Jesus. It means bearing witness to the authenticity of our faith and building hope in the practices we keep: showing hospitality to strangers and outcasts; affirming the unity of the created order; reclaiming the ideals of beauty, love, honesty, and truth; and embracing the preferential option for nonviolence. It means participating in the world in such a way as to affirm it as God's good creation—and to labor to make it ever more so. It means living in the expectation of God's ongoing advent among us to make all things new.

"These things I have spoken to you," Jesus says in Saint John's Gospel, "that in Me you may have peace. In the world, you will have tribulation; but be of good cheer; I have overcome the world" (16:33 NKJV).

*　　　*　　　*

Can I Get a Witness? tells the stories of thirteen peculiar people who worked to transform American culture based, at least in part, on their religious convictions. These narratives are not comprehensive, cradle-to-grave biographies, nor are they characterized by staid rehearsal of facts; rather, this collection strives for vibrant storytelling and research-enriched narrative to bring these figures to life. The chapters illumine aspects of the historical figures' religious experience and conviction as well as the work they did in the world, all the while exploring how their convictions shaped their work and how their work refined their convictions. These narratives are written by authors chosen for their unique abilities to tell these very particular stories.

The notion of *witness* is not limited to a personal testimony or an altar call. As one of our authors says, witness is what we do. The thirteen religious figures in this book can be witnesses for our time only if we can see what they did: how they lived, what they gave, and whom they accompanied. These narratives offer readers the opportunity to peer into history and witness these witnesses' lives. So many longings, hopes, and struggles are wrapped up in this question—Can I get a witness?—and, for this reason, we ask it with fear and trembling. We entrust the work of faithful response to story because we believe in the power of story to illustrate complexity, to illumine truth, and to reach into minds and hearts. In the black church tradition, the question "Can I get a witness?" is asked in anticipation of an "Amen!" Our "Amens" are these stories: holy and hopeful.

Ultimately, the question Can I get a witness? is answered with a resounding *yes*. You *can* get a witness, and you can get witnesses writing about those witnesses: writers and subjects together creating not a single unison strain but a polyphony of voices—women and men; Catholics and Protestants; white, Latino/a, African, Asian, and Indian Americans; clergy and laity; gay and straight—all grounded in the *cantus firmus* of the incarnate Word.

"The Church has an obligation not to join in the incantation of political slogans and in the concoction of pseudo-events," Thomas Merton wrote in a 1966 essay, "but to cut clear through the deviousness and ambiguity of both slogans and events by her simplicity and her love."[5] Biblical religion cuts through propaganda, deception, and idolatry with the double edge of heavenly discontent and disarming love. The good news in this book is that the spiritual vision that animated these thirteen witness—that inspired their moral imagination and civil courage—remains a vital source for the present age. May we accept that vision as gift and guide in the uncertain years ahead.

Cesar Chavez

(1927–1993)

Cesar Chavez portrait, Forty Acres Headquarters, Delano, CA, 1969. Photo: Bob Fitch Photography Archive, Department of Special Collections, Stanford University Libraries.

In the Union of the Spirit

Cesar Chavez and the Quest for Farmworker Justice

Daniel P. Rhodes

To all appearances, Cesar Estrada Chavez was a rather unimpressive figure. Diminutive in stature, he had a boyish face, a wide, faintly aquiline nose, chestnut skin, and thick onyx-colored hair often neatly parted low on the left side and combed back and to the right across his head. He was handsome but forgettable. That he would organize the first farmworker union in a struggle for justice that took on the industry of agribusiness scarcely seemed possible.

The differences could not be starker between Chavez and the heroes of popular Westerns playing during the time that he was organizing farmworkers in southern and central California. Next to a Roy Rogers or a John Wayne, he surely would have seemed unintimidating and even unremarkable. Compared to the great orators of the day—such as Malcolm X or Martin Luther King Jr.— he would have seemed prosaic. Only his eyes offered a clue: they were captivating and intense. He was hobbled by chronic back pain much of his life as a result of years spent working bent over in the fields, bone depletion, and one of his legs being slightly longer than the other, something that would be diagnosed later in his life. Yet this physical fragility and meekness was nearly eclipsed by the calm, fortified nature of his presence. One journalist biographer described him as a person of "density" who "walks as lightly as a fox."[1] He had a sharp sense of humor, and though he was kind, he could also be acerbic. As a kid he had been a *travieso* (prankster), and this disposition served him well throughout his life.[2] Many photographs of Chavez capture his wry smile framed by a look of determination; he was a man pitted against the odds, and he seemed to enjoy it.

Chavez was a shrewd union and community organizer who, with gritty creativity, sustained a quest for justice among farmworkers. His aim first and foremost was to forge solidarity among migrant laborers. This goal grew out of his own personal and spiritual yearning to belong, and the farmworker movement he led was built on these relationships and connections. Rarely does solidarity take the shape of a life, but it did in the person of Cesar Chavez; it was the single objective that infused and consumed him.

His people recognized it. As Luis Valdez, the innovative founder of El Teatro Campesino, wrote, "Here was Cesar burning with patient fire, poor like us, dark like us, talking quietly, moving people to talk about their problems, attacking the little problems first and suggesting, always suggesting—never more than that—solutions which seemed attainable. We didn't know it until we met him, but he was the leader we had been waiting for."[3] In him and his fellow leaders, farmworkers found their own capacity to transform their plight through the formation of a union that could challenge the power of agribusiness.

Chavez always understood the movement to be about more than wages or contracts; it was a spiritual campaign. For him, the work of the union was woven inextricably into a fabric of religious significance. Jesus was with them, and in their struggle and sacrifices they were a part of his kingdom, his people. It was nearly sacramental—eucharistic.

This sacred quality of Chavez's work registered for me at church one Sunday. As our priest made the sign of the cross over the eucharistic elements, she asked God to sanctify them to be "the holy food and drink of new and unending life" and to sanctify us to receive them as a new people. Then, just before we were to pray the Lord's Prayer and receive the elements, she said, "All this we ask through your Son, Jesus Christ. By him, and with him, and in him, in the unity of the Holy Spirit, all honor and glory is yours, Almighty Father, now and forever. Amen." During this prayer of consecration, I caught a glimpse of how Chavez understood the union. Here, the very life of the Godhead gathers and joins humanity in the creation of a new people, a people *in the union of the Spirit* suffused with transformational grace, binding love, and hopeful endurance. Through much suffering and difficult labor, Chavez and his people were being gathered in a sanctified union for a society in need of transformation. Their search for justice was inscribed with God's own life. Suffused with this calling, Chavez came to embody their spiritual quest for a new reality.

*   *   *

Prior to the 1965 grape strike where, as his mentor Fred Ross said, he "walked into history," Cesar Chavez himself trod the destitute road of the migrant laborers he later began to organize.[4] It was an experience that profoundly shaped him. The Chavezes were never wealthy, but when Cesar was a child the family resided on a farm near Yuma, Arizona, on the eastern side of the arid North Gila Valley in the foothills of the Laguna Mountains. This farm was a 160-acre plot that his grandparents carved out of the rocky Arizona countryside. The valley's name, Gila, came from a Native American word meaning "river that runs salty."[5] The surrounding area was a makeshift arrangement of rough canals and fields planted with grasses or whatever crops could withstand the desert heat and brackish soil. Foreshadowing what was to come, Cesar's parents, Librado and Juana, had relocated to the ranch in 1929 after their own small business venture fell into debt and was foreclosed. The young family took up residence in a large storage room attached by a breezeway to the main adobe house at the center of the compound built by his grandfather and namesake, Cesario, or Papa Chayo as they called him.

His grandfather had died by the time they moved to the homestead, but one of Cesar's aunts and his elderly grandmother, Dorotea, affectionately called Mama Tella, still lived in the main house.[6] More of Cesar's aunts and uncles lived just up the adjacent canal. Here Cesar, with his older sister, Rita, and younger brother, Richard, enjoyed the relative security, stability, and community that he would always associate with home.

They were a tight-knit family and, as Cesar recalled, "I had more happy moments as a child than unhappy moments."[7] This fond and familiar life, however, soon came to an end. The county, likely influenced by a neighboring banker eager to acquire the ranch, took possession of the property in the late summer of 1937 when Cesar's father could not make up the back taxes he owed. Though they were allowed to stay for another year while they appealed the seizure, they eventually lost the farm, which was auctioned to their banker neighbor for a mere $1,750, a total of less than half of the taxes they owed.

Intense sorrow must have consumed Chavez as his family packed into their Studebaker the following spring while a bulldozer leveled their fields and horse corral. "When we left the farm," he recalled, "our whole life was upset, turned upside down. . . . We had been uprooted."[8] From that point on he carried with him an abiding homesickness. "I bitterly missed the ranch," Cesar recollected. "Maybe that is when the rebellion started. Some had been born into the migrant stream. But we had been on the land, and I knew a different way of life. We were poor, but we had liberty. The migrant is poor, and he has no freedom."[9] The loss scarred him deeply.

Loss was not the only thing that shaped Chavez's character as an organizer and his hope for the farmworkers. His devoutly Catholic family, especially the strong faith of his mother and grandmother, also deeply formed him. His grandmother, Mama Tella, was an orphan raised in a convent, where she learned to read and write both Latin and Spanish. She catechized Cesar and his sister, Rita, preparing them herself for First Communion. She taught them about the saints, and as Cesar stated, "I remember her, she was always praying, just praying."[10] Cesar's primary apprenticeship in the faith, however, came by way of his mother, Juana. With no church near their home, she taught them their prayers, taking up where Cesar's grandmother had left off. He recalled, "As we didn't have a church in the valley and it was very difficult to go to Yuma, it was my mother who taught us prayers. Throughout the Southwest and Mexico where there were no priests for a long time, the amazing thing was that people kept the faith. But they were oriented more toward relics and saints. My mother was very religious without being a fanatic, and she believed in saints as advocates, as lobbyists, to pray to God for her. Her patron saint was St. Eduvigis."[11]

A Polish duchess, Eduvigis had given all her possessions to the poor when she converted to Christianity. As a boy, Chavez recalled his mother always reaching out to those in need in imitation of this saint, modeling for him the spirit of charity. Within their home, instruction in the faith often also took the form of his mother's *dichos* (proverbs) or *consejos* (advice). These "sermons," as Cesar related, were his first trainings in nonviolence, selflessness, honesty, and other virtues long before he would read St. Francis, Catholic social teaching, or Gandhi. She frequently wrapped these teachings in stories that included miracles and magical realism, opening young Chavez's imagination to the possibility of holy surprises.[12] Deep spirituality shaped the Chavez home just as it would saturate his work with farmworkers later. As he stated, "I don't think that I could base my will to struggle on cold economics or on some political doctrine. While most people drawn toward liberalism or radicalism leave the church, I went the other way. I drew closer to the church the more I learned and understood."[13] He grew in wisdom and stature under the influence of his mother's *religión casera* (homespun religion), so characteristic of devout Mexican Catholics, and it permeated all of life.[14] This faith formed the core and basis for a moral vision not only of individual piety but even more of human community and society.

Faith and family sustained Cesar even as both of these put him on a path of hardship. The Chavezes were well acquainted with suffering. One of Cesar's younger sisters, Helena, died at eleven months old of dysentery, a condition likely engendered by the dilapidated state of their living quarters. His siblings and he suffered constant marginalization in school, where they were not allowed to speak Spanish. (Cesario, his given name, became the Anglicized Cesar.) But once the family was forced off their Arizona homestead, life took a more difficult turn as they experienced a new level of poverty and discrimination as a result of their dislocation. In his new schools, students taunted him for wearing the same gray V-neck T-shirt every day, and his teacher regularly insulted his Mexican heritage. He recalled, "when I came to class, I was frightened. I didn't know the lesson. I was given a seat, and the next morning I wasn't sure if that was really my seat. I was so frightened I was afraid to even ask the teacher for permission to go to the restroom. I didn't dare ask very often, as the kids laughed at my accent, the way I talked."[15] He attended more than a dozen different schools before finishing the eighth grade, when he quit so he could work full time for the family in the fields.

Merchants in the new towns they passed through refused to serve them, and they faced segregated seating in movie theaters and restaurants.[16] As new migrant workers, they also struggled to learn the system, often arriving too late to gain work or falling prey to con men and crooked managers. Working their way northwest through the Imperial Valley and the Central Valley, they finally reached San Jose and the impoverished and flood-prone eastside barrio of Sal Si Puedes, which means "get out if you can." There, they moved into a resident's vacant garage, the only place they could find to live. As they traversed the state working the fields, exploitation by labor contractors and growers was a constant. The family often inhabited barns, shacks, or labor camps, or slept under a tarp near ripening crops, inhabiting unfamiliar and often hostile places. Chavez became familiar with being an outcast. He also became intimate with the oppression of working the fields, symbolized by *el cortito*—the short-handled hoe, the use of which required a bent, subjugated posture. Of the terrible jobs Chavez was forced to work, one of the worst was thinning lettuce. Laboring as fast as possible because pay was piece rate, or by the row or acre, *los lechugueros* (lettuce harvesters) had to work stooped over in a tireless rhythm of pulling and chopping. "It was really inhuman," Chavez recounted. "Every time I see lettuce, that's the first thing I think of, some human being had to thin it. And it's just like being nailed to a cross. You have to walk twisted as you're stooped over, facing the row, and walking perpendicular to it. You are always trying to find the best position because you can't walk completely sideways, it's too difficult, and if you turn the other way, you can't thin."[17]

Beyond the excruciating and humiliating labor, as Chavez knew from experience, the entire system was saturated with prejudice and injustice aimed at dehumanizing the workers. Farmworkers could not afford to purchase the very produce they harvested. They had no protections and no insurance. They were frequently exposed to poisonous pesticides. Growers pitted one ethnicity against another in order to solidify their dominance and curtail any resistance from the workers. Reflecting later on the impact of these experiences, Chavez relayed, "There are vivid memories from my childhood—what we had to go through because of low wages and the conditions, basically because there was no union. I suppose if I wanted to be fair I could say that I'm trying to settle a personal score."[18] The life of farm labor was difficult, but they survived and resisted its dehumanization as a family, only deepening their devotion to one another. In their loss and struggle, as

Chavez learned, they found new fibers of solidarity and strength, building a sense of home among one another.

It's only fitting that, years later, his small home in Sal Si Puedes was the place where Chavez heard his spiritual call to organize farmworkers. The calling came during a house meeting scheduled by Fred Ross, who had come north after being hired in 1946 by Saul Alinsky and his Chicago-based Industrial Areas Foundation to organize Mexican Americans in Los Angeles. A practice launched by Ross, a house meeting was an organizing tool for beginning to turn anger and seeming impotence into power and possibility through collective engagement. A tall, thin figure, refined, articulate, and tedious, Ross was also somewhat unorthodox. Years later, Ross's eulogist would reiterate his philosophy of organizing with one of his favorite sayings: "A good organizer is a social arsonist who goes around setting people on fire."[19] He had been trying to organize in the area for more than five years by the time he met Chavez, but his efforts had borne little fruit.

It was the early summer of 1952 when the local priest, Fr. Donald McDonnell, along with the parish nurse, Alicia Hernandez, suggested the two meet. At that time, Chavez was working in a lumberyard when he wasn't in the fields. Initially suspicious of the gringo outsider, Cesar and his brother, Richard, eventually acquiesced to meeting with Ross after Helen, Cesar's wife, refused to continue to deflect Ross's attempts to make contact. That evening of Monday, June 9, 1952, as Chavez recounted years later, "He [Ross] changed my life."[20] Amid a rugged group of workers intentionally gathered by Chavez to intimidate him into leaving them alone, Ross made his pitch, suggesting that even the most powerless could change things if enough of them worked together.[21] Unexpectedly, Chavez found himself ignited by Ross's message, which converted him to organizing.

Still, Chavez was an unlikely leader. Rather meek in affect and not prone to grandstanding, he did not fit the typical stereotype of the head of a movement. Initially, he was even petrified of his own house meetings. He often circled the neighborhood several times before entering the house. Once inside, he would hide in the corner, only to finally pipe up when someone asked, "Where's the organizer?"²² Nevertheless, he kept at it because he found life in building community. Chavez envisioned the apostle Paul as an organizer who, similarly, admitted to being no eloquent rhetorician or extraordinary personality (1 Cor. 1) but found strength in the power of the community-gathering spirit of the gospel. Like the apostle, Chavez went to the people, and from the grassroots began to build the connections essential for fashioning a new future.

The choice to organize farmworkers and to subject his family to the challenges they faced was not easy for Chavez. But it was a call he could not escape. For four years he contemplated the move. "More than anything else, I wanted to help farm workers," he recalled. "Only my financial security had me tied up and kept me from moving. There was my wife, Helen, and I knew it would be asking a lot of her to give up what we had." At the time he had a decent job with a regular paycheck, and the family had been able to put away some savings. They had eight children to care for. "Helen and I discussed the problem from many angles," he recounted. "There were the risks, the odds against success, and the desperate needs we saw daily around us. Helen, naturally, was very worried about our children. If I quit, who knows what would happen? Where would the money come from for food and clothes and housing? I could only point to my own childhood where, despite our struggles and bitter experiences, ours was a very close and happy family. I was sure our children could endure."²³

Finally, Cesar and Helen decided that they could not organize farmworkers the way they wanted without first liberating themselves. As Chavez stated, "I realized that I couldn't do what I felt must be done without first giving up one of the best jobs I'd ever had."²⁴ What made the decision so difficult was that Chavez was already working as a professional organizer on farmworker issues with the Oxnard-based Community Service Organization (CSO). But, as is so often the case with top-down approaches, he quickly realized that while he could achieve small changes this way, a larger co-creative effort to change the system itself was necessary. And he saw that the only way to do this was to commit fully to live with and among the people.

Chavez learned this lesson while working under Ross at the CSO, where he was constantly frustrated with leaders who became complacent and focused on their own comfort. Another source of frustration was the desire for immediate results, which meant work toward real, hard change was aborted. Venturing out on his own to organize differently, Chavez did not want to repeat those mistakes. Instead, he sought to build off of the tradition of *mutualistas* (the informal mutual assistance programs) that Mexican immigrants in the Southwest had been self-organizing for years. Consequently, he did not even call the new organization a union but the Farm Workers Association, and he initially focused on setting up cooperative service-provisions.[25]

Organizing this way was a family enterprise, and as Helen and he had anticipated, it required sacrifice and dedication. Often the family went without food or other basic necessities. Helen juggled many responsibilities, picking crops while running a nascent credit union, administrating a co-op, and caring for their growing family. Together, they embodied the ethos and spirit of the organization.

Chavez's method was simple and direct, resulting in a deep commitment from early members of the organization. One of these early members was Manuel Rivera, who sought Chavez's help after his family was left destitute as a result of a dispute with a dishonest labor contractor. Chavez and Helen welcomed the Rivera family into their small home and loaned them one of their cars while working to help them get back on their feet and resolve the issue. Rivera never forgot this sacrifice and genuine charity. Even after he was struck by a truck while on a picket line years later and rendered lame, he remained stolid in his dedication to the movement and to Chavez.[26] Such incidents testify to the powerful character of Chavez's grassroots style of leadership. Chavez's gifts were not exactly recognizable on the surface, and neither was the potency of the movement he organized. But he was able to see his own story in others' stories, and he saw in this connection the possibility of writing together a new one. Such a path was never straightforward, but it was the path of real change, for, as he cheerfully believed, "God writes in exceedingly crooked lines."[27]

Suffering alone under the cruel hand of agribusiness, farmworkers were left to a life of pain, misery, and despair. But suffering together, Chavez believed, they might begin to translate this pain, anger, and alienation into a powerful movement for change. As the "Plan of Delano," an early summation of their cause, stated:

> We have suffered, and we are not afraid to suffer in order to win our cause. We have suffered unnumbered ills and crimes in the name of the law of the land. Our men, women, and children have suffered not only the basic brutality of stoop labor, and the most obvious injustices of the system; they have also suffered the desperation of knowing that the system caters to the greed of callous men and not our needs. Now we will suffer for the purpose of ending the poverty, the misery, and the injustice, with the hope that our children will not be exploited as we have been. They have imposed hungers on us, and now we hunger for justice. We draw our strength from the very despair in which we have been forced to live. WE SHALL ENDURE.[28]

The organizing movement, forged in a spirit of solidarity, constituted something of a new people borne in and through hardship and maltreatment. These bonds would form the base of all that was to come.

*   *   *

In the spring of 1962, Chavez left the CSO and struck out on his own, moving his family to the small central-California town of Delano, located at the southern end of the San Joaquin Valley. Here Chavez sought to establish a base for his union among the residential farmworker community.[29] It became the epicenter of a radical farmworker movement.

The bed of an ancient inland sea, the San Joaquin Valley stretches two hundred miles down the spine of central California and is some sixty miles wide. Set between the Sierra Nevada Mountains to the east and the coastal mountain range to the West, it was the heart of the agribusiness industry and would become the battlefield of *La Causa* (the movement). Massive irrigation projects rendered the fertile soil one of the most productive regions in the world; a quarter of the United States' fruit and vegetables grew in its fields. Vast farms dominated the area geographically, and the growers, along with the transnational corporations connected to them, dominated its political and socio-economic landscape.[30] As an industry, agribusiness was immensely powerful and well coordinated. Large conglomerations with farms of 50,000 to even 100,000 acres were not uncommon.[31] Only the largest and most cutthroat of family farms survived, as they adopted the monopolistic "best practices" of their industry competitors.[32] The growers clearly had the upper hand, and the workers had little traction against such aggregated power.

The structure of this food basket of the country was that the growers owned the land, reaping the rewards of its bounty, while migrants provided the labor. It was an arrangement established early on in the industry to the great benefit of the growers. John Steinbeck vividly depicted the exploitations of this burgeoning industry in his epic *The Grapes of Wrath*. But such practices did not end after the Great Depression. One such strategy was the implementation of the Bracero Program. Braceros were seasonal work-

ers imported from Mexico for the purpose of filling the labor short-
age created by World War II. A program instituted by Congress in
1942, braceros worked under tight regulations and at set wages.
Their temporary contracts left them open to wage theft. Housing in their labor camps was deplorable. As aliens, they suffered
racism, lived under the thumb of growers who could have them
deported without cause or notice, and were forced to overpay for
necessities they could purchase only through their sponsors. The
program was so popular among the growers that they lobbied for
its extension well past the conclusion of the war. A surplus, com-
pliant labor force of imported workers was extremely useful for
the growers in breaking strikes and holding down wages.[33] The
program was discontinued by Congress in 1965, but the practice
of importing workers to dilute the workforce and suppress wages
remained regular among growers. To maintain their position of
power, the growers knew it was important to ensure that the workers remained insecure and isolated.

Though the situation in Delano was difficult, Chavez realized
that the town provided some advantages as a place to begin. He
had family in the area, providing a natural support network and
safety net for the precarious venture. It was also one of the few
communities in which workers resided nearly year around, as the
temperamental vines of the table grape trade required tending
even when the fruit was not in season.[34] While there were still
many migrants flowing through the area, Chavez rightly estimated
that the somewhat settled population would be crucial for getting
the organization off the ground. Furthermore, though they were
rather large, family-owned companies controlled the town's lucra-
tive table-grape industry.[35] This fact was not inconsequential, as
the proprietary nature of these farms made them more susceptible
to strikes and boycotts than their corporate kin, most of which
were part of national or multinational conglomerates. Nevertheless, the work of building an indigenous movement was slow, tedious, and filled with risk and failure.

Early on, for instance, a private foundation offered Chavez a $50,000 grant to jump-start the organization, no strings attached. Though the infant movement's finances were tenuous at best, he turned it down. His reasoning for doing so was integrally connected to his vision for the movement itself. He argued that if they accepted the money, they would feel the need to work faster than is consistent with building the kind of trust-based, grassroots organization he envisioned. As Chavez recognized, the membership itself had to invest in the organization instead of relying on outside resources that would always be subject to external expectations and could be withdrawn at any time.[36] This was no small decision for Chavez, as his own salary was drawn from the union's scant budget. At the time, he was the only farmworker leader in the nation who depended on dues for his salary.

At last, in September of 1962, after a summer of endless relational and house meetings, the Farm Workers Association (FWA, and later NFWA, adding National to its title) held its first convention with a modest 150 delegates in attendance. It elected its first officers, adopted its symbol in the black eagle flag, and embraced its motto: *Viva la Causa.* Dues were set at $3.50 per month,[37] though collecting these dues was a constant struggle. The organization was small and ragtag. But by its second anniversary, the intentional work began to bear fruit, and the union had gained one thousand dues-paying members associated with fifty local affiliates throughout the valley.[38] Attempting to build momentum by focusing on winnable issues, Chavez was selective about the FWA's actions even as he recognized that it needed to start delivering for the workers. He wrote to Ross in early 1965, saying, "We need a fight right now."[39] But the workers themselves, though loaded with grievances, were still reluctant to engage.

The union chose for its first contest the rose industry in McFarland, California. There were some advantages for them here. The workers were skilled and therefore tough to replace with scabs, or strikebreakers. Additionally, the delicate nature of the plants made the work time sensitive. Agreeing by vote ahead of time, they struck on May 3, seeking a raise in wages. Union leadership, beginning with the feisty Delores Huerta, cofounder of the movement, nearly had to coerce the workers into sticking to the plan. To prevent the workers from sabotaging their own strike, she parked her truck in one worker's driveway, pinning in his car to keep his crew from reporting to work.[40] Though the workers were unwilling to press for full contracts, the movement claimed its first win with a small increase in pay. A similar small victory that summer over rent hikes in a labor camp near Porterville, California, allowed the organization to gain experience and build confidence. These campaigns also allowed them to make vital allies, not the least of which was the California Migrant Ministry led by Reverend Chris Hartmire. They were maturing into a real union.

The first true contest for the organization came with the 1965 grape harvest, commencing an all-out struggle with the powerful growers of the table-grape industry. This struggle—a five-year campaign in which Chavez's farmworkers were overmatched in every category—set the tenor and trajectory of Chavez's movement. As the war in Vietnam flared up under the newly resolved Johnson administration, the sparks of protest began to fly in the California fields. The renewed use of braceros by growers along with racially disparate pay structures intensified tensions and frustration, pushing workers to the brink. In May, in the Coachella Valley of Southern California, the Filipino-led Agricultural Workers Organizing Committee (AWOC, an affiliate of the AFL-CIO) responded with a strike, earning limited raises for Filipino and Mexican workers bolstered by the area's brief, but intense, harvest season. As the harvest season jogged north into the heart of grower power in the San Joaquin Valley and the city of Delano, however, even small victories became more difficult. Here, the farmworker movement clashed with entrenched growers.

On September 8, Filipino workers walked out of the vineyards, protesting wage discrimination. The move was met immediately by grower force; growers evicted these workers from labor camps while colluding with police to harass them. Faced with such backlash, Larry Itliong, the Filipino head of AWOC, reached out to Chavez and his young union for assistance. Chavez knew they were grossly underprepared and underorganized for such a fight. "All I could think was, 'Oh God, we're not ready for a strike,'" he later recalled.[41] The union members would have to vote, deciding for themselves what to do. On September 16, Mexican Independence Day, some five hundred union members squeezed into the warm meeting hall at Our Lady of Guadalupe church in Delano. Chavez remembered:

> We first talked about the Filipino brothers, about solidarity and the need to have a general strike. When my turn came, I recalled a little story.
>
> 155 years ago in the state of Guanajuato in Mexico . . . a padre proclaimed the struggle for liberty. He was killed, but ten years later Mexico won its independence. . . . We are encouraged in another struggle for the freedom and dignity which poverty denies us. But it must not be a violent struggle, even if violence is used against us. Violence can only hurt us and our cause.[42]

Their quest too had to embrace the spirit of nonviolence and sacrifice. Members voted enthusiastically to strike with their fellow AWOC workers, shouting "Viva la causa!" and "Huelga, huelga!" (Strike, strike!).[43] Ready or not, the time for them to act had come.

The farmworker union was no normal union, and this would be no standard union struggle. It was a struggle that reached all the way down to their values, their spirits and faith—something Chavez understood and from which he drew. In fact, his first act after the vote was to gather his family and pray a Hail Mary for each grower.[44] Incessant prayer and regular Mass permeated the movement. Like any war, it came with suffering, but such suffering for the cause found meaning in the religious culture and spirituality of the union. As Father Jim Drake described it, "Mexicans believe that from suffering you get strength rather than death. This is expressed in penitential acts and especially in the Eucharist," where they connect not with the conquistador mentality but with the suffering servant. He continued, "When we celebrate the Eucharist in a field or beside a picket line, with real grapes and real bread, it has the kind of earthly meaning that it had in the Indian villages before all the cathedrals were built."[45] This theological outlook pervaded even their view of time. Chavez himself had learned an old Mexican *dicho* from his mother: "Hay mas tiempo que vida" (We have more time than life), and this mantra guided his work. The growers may have had the money and the political, legal, and police power that came with it, but the farmworkers had the trajectory of the cosmos on their side.[46] The long view of justice gave them more freedom and hope, and allowed them to be more patient amid a struggle the growers wanted to end quickly.[47]

Tensions around the Delano grape strike quickly escalated. *El Malcriado* (Bad Boy, or Outcast), the union's bimonthly paper, reported regular incidents of growers intimidating strikers by driving at them with their trucks, spraying them with poisonous sulfur, and physically assaulting them.[48] These acts of violence were not without effect, and soon strike efforts began to flag. In response, Chavez expanded the union's tactics, launching a national boycott of grapes with the help of United Auto Worker president Walter Reuther. This move not only drew publicity to the situation but also offered a way for sympathetic consumers around the country to participate and support the effort. Production slowed with the shrinking market, angering growers as they watched their fruit shrivel on the vine or were forced to dump it off to wineries. They hit back. In one instance, they had the police apprehend forty-four farmworkers and clergy, loading them into a paddy wagon where they sat for hours in the baking midday sun. Then, after humiliatingly searching them, the officers booked the protestors in the Bakersfield jail. Eight of those arrested were mothers, whose thirty-eight children had to fend for themselves for the three days their mothers were held. When police refused to allow the children to see their parents, the union members and clergy gathered on the jailhouse steps to pray and sing.[49] Slowly, the farmworkers' witness in the face of such aggression by the growers began to tilt the position of the church, which had to this point remained rather conservative in its view of the struggle. Finally, a farmworker Mass was hosted in Delano in honor of St. Joseph the Worker with top church officials presiding, providing leverage.[50]

At this time, Chavez turned to another controversial and radical practice to act against the growers' system. With the beginning of the Lenten season in 1966, Chavez's union orchestrated a march, or what Chavez called the *peregrinación* (pilgrimage) of penance and revolution. Embarking from Delano, they would proceed up through the San Joaquin Valley until they reached the state capitol in Sacramento. They timed their arrival for April 10, Easter Sunday, and their route stretched some three hundred miles. As with other civil rights marches, this pilgrimage was intended to build solidarity and to pressure officials and growers by lifting the plight of the farmworkers onto the national stage.

As a pilgrimage, however, it was not solely protest. A pilgrimage is drama, a public performance of an alternative and deeply significant story. To walk the road of pilgrimage is to participate in a narrative, usually connected with the life of Christ or a saint. This kind of journey invites those involved to reorient themselves through physical exertion and repentance in order to solidify their devotion. Chavez understood that this was exactly what the farmworkers needed. This act of embodied prayer called them back from the temptation of violence and reoriented them to the core commitments and spirit of the movement. It also reaffirmed their devotion to the cause, functioning as a kind of ascetic training for the struggle ahead.[51]

The pilgrimage publicly transformed the framework of the movement, setting the cause of the farmworkers dramatically within a theological story. In the process Chavez was able to integrate the fragmented groups of farmworkers as participants joined in the journey. And he discovered that as an organizing tactic, it allowed them to shift the field on the growers by locating the movement in a sacred history.[52] As people on a pilgrimage, they weren't merely laborers; they were sojourners on a spiritual quest of liberation, making their way out of the oppressive system of agribusiness. As Chavez stated, "There's something about a march that is very powerful. It's a powerful weapon, a powerful organizing tool, and it has a powerful influence on those who participate. . . . [It] picks up its own cadence, its own spirit, its own history."[53] Penance and pilgrimage were not standard organizing procedure. They were certainly not part of the Alinsky or Ross community organizing playbook. Chavez stated his own reason for the march:

> Throughout the Spanish-speaking world there is another tradition that touches the present march, that of the Lenten penitential processions, where the *penitentes* would march through the streets, often in sack cloth and ashes, some even carrying crosses as a sign of penance for their sins, and as a plea for the mercy of God. The penitential procession is also in the blood of the Mexican American, and the Delano march will therefore be one of penance—public penance for the sins of the strikers, their own personal sins as well as their yielding perhaps to feelings of hatred and revenge in the strike itself. They hope by the march to set themselves at peace with the Lord, so that the justice of their cause will be purified of all lesser motivation.[54]

Chavez himself encountered suffering on this path. He developed severe blisters on one of his feet that left him unable to walk. His foot became infected, and the infection spread upward, swelling his leg. He broke out in a fever. His nurse forced him to ride in a station wagon alongside marchers for two days. Then Chavez resumed the walk, limping on a cane. Through such suffering, however, the pilgrimage only seemed to pick up momentum. A banner depicting the Virgin of Guadalupe headed the procession, followed by the black eagle flag. The marchers were bolstered by constant prayer and evening programs that included singing, theater performance, and dramatic readings of the "Plan of Delano." The mood was religious and revolutionary. Chavez saw that, as pilgrims, "the farmworkers in the union—the strikers and boycotters—were themselves the Church-in-the-world, showing the way for many Christians who yearned for a better world."[55]

Pressure from the pilgrimage eventually began to weigh heavily on the growers. As the progression reached Stockton on April 3, where a crowd of nearly five thousand festive workers and their families greeted them, Chavez received a call from Sidney Korshak, a representative of the Schenley Corporation, a multinational company and one of the main players in Delano grape industry. Korshak said Schenley was ready to recognize the union and to sign a contract, a message that Chavez took to be a prank and that prompted him to abruptly hang up. Korshak, however, persisted in calling back, and that night, Chavez and Chris Hartmire drove from the procession to Beverly Hills to negotiate, arriving at one o'clock in the morning. Even then, no easy resolution came. But after hours of back and forth with the company and other players, they finally reached an agreement. Schenley would formally recognize the union and give the workers a raise of thirty-five cents per hour. The company also accepted the union's hiring hall and its credit union.[56] The remainder of the contract was to be worked out in the next sixty days. A few days later, as the rain fell on Easter Sunday, some ten thousand marchers amassed in front of the capitol in Sacramento, celebrating the end of the pilgrimage and the new work contracts between the union and Schenley. Aside from a small victory for pineapple workers in Hawaii, this was the first time in US history that an agricultural laborers union had gained recognition by a corporation.[57] It was to be only the beginning.

*   *   *

With Schenley contracts in hand, the union turned its attention to the DiGiorgio Corporation, the largest of the Delano growers and a family-owned business headed by the patriarch, Robert DiGiorgio. No minor opponent, the DiGiorgio Corporation was the inspiration for the infamous Gregorio ranchers in Steinbeck's *Grapes of Wrath*. They had been ruthlessly blocking strikes since the 1930s.[58] The movement was about to commence a new chapter in its five-year battle with the grape industry.

One thing the union learned in the struggle with Schenley was how powerful a boycott could be. It was the losses associated with the boycott that really got Schenley to the negotiating table. The union now sought to bring the same tactic to bear on DiGiorgio, calling for a national boycott of their products after the company refused to allow its workers to vote for union representation. Again, success seemed unlikely as the well-connected and powerful company dug in. Company guards threatened picketers with guns, pushed them to the ground, assaulted them, and colluded with police to have them arrested.[59] These acts of intimidation were merely the start. At the behest of DiGiorgio, police grew increasingly abusive. Similarly, as other growers came to DiGiorgio's side, the corporations and their employees became more hostile to the workers. On October 15, 1966, Manuel Rivera was run over by Lowell Schy, a Goldberg Packing Company salesman. Rivera was on a picket line outside the vineyard entrance when an exasperated Schy commandeered the truck of a reluctant driver and proceeded to ram through demonstrators. Rivera was caught in the wheels, his broken body left lame as a despondent Schy locked himself in the truck's cab. A riot nearly ensued and was only avoided because Chavez intervened to keep angry picketers from mobbing Schy.

DiGiorgio also used the notorious Teamsters union to derail the farmworkers. DiGiorgio cut sweetheart deals with the Teamsters in order to argue that there was already union representation in the fields. It also hired Teamster goon squads to harass and rough up strikers. Meanwhile, DiGiorgio filed a litany of suits against the union, attacking the organization itself and entangling it in court disputes. Playing its political leverage, DiGiorgio was able to win a court order restricting pickets, severely hamstringing the union.

In the eyes of many of the farmworkers, the tactic of nonviolence seemed to be failing, provoking a fairly tense meeting of union members at the American Legion Hall in Delano. Pressure within the union was building to respond to DiGiorgio's actions with force. While the union agreed to continue nonviolently, Chavez admitted he was "out of ideas of things to do" but that he was willing to trust in members to find the answers. They concluded the meeting with things still up in the air.[60]

The turning point came, Chavez recalled, from a burst of holy creativity. "A couple of hours later," he recounted, "three ladies said they wanted to see me." Chavez expected them to ask for money, and he knew he would have to refuse, since the union was broke as a result of the long strike. Nonetheless, he invited them into his office. He reported,

> First they wanted to make sure that I wouldn't be offended by what they wanted to tell me. Then they wanted to assure me that they were not trying to tell me how to run the strike.
>
> After we got over those hurdles, they said, "We don't understand this business of the court order. Does this mean that if we go picket and break the injunctions, we'll go to jail?"
>
> "Well, it means that you go to jail, and that we will be fined," I said.

"What would happen if we met across the street from the DiGiorgio gates, not to picket, not to demonstrate, but to have a prayer, maybe a mass?" they asked. "Do you think the judge would have us arrested?"

By the time they got the last word out, my mind just flashed to all the possibilities.[61]

After this meeting, Chavez asked his brother, Richard, to outfit his old station wagon as a small, portable shrine. Richard installed a picture of the Virgin of Guadalupe, candles, a cross, some flowers, and a flag bearing the union eagle, and union leaders held a vigil just outside the entrance to the vineyards. Soon they added a daily Mass to the twenty-four-hour prayer meeting. The practice gained steam. "Every day we had a mass, held a meeting, sang spirituals, and got [the workers] to sign authorization cards," Chavez relayed. "Those meetings were responsible in large part for keeping the spirit up of our people inside the camp and helping our organization for the coming battle." Like Joshua facing the formidable walls of Jericho, they confronted DiGiorgio with active, prayerful observance, looking for God to work. "It was a beautiful demonstration of the power of nonviolence."[62] Not part of the typical organizing manual, it originated with the workers, and, drawing on their faith, it continued to build the unique character of the farmworkers movement. The pressure from the campaign along with the negotiation of a shrewd merger with the Filipino AWOC union positioned Chavez's union to win elections at DiGiorgio ranches, securing recognition from the company.[63] But it also bolstered Chavez's own spiritual devotion, re-centering the cause within his own connection to God.

The victory in the struggle with DiGiorgio led to another fight. On August 3, 1967, the union challenged the Giumarra Corporation, the largest provider of table grapes in the country. Short on money and struggling to maintain morale, the union was truly outmatched by such a Goliath. After weeks of strikes, again Chavez turned to the boycott to contest Giumarra, initiating what became the largest and most hostile confrontation between the union and the growers to that point. Giumarra vigorously retaliated, filing court injunctions, hiring braceros, intimidating picketers, and bringing in the Teamsters. In order to defang the boycott, Giumarra colluded with other growers to share labels, making it impossible for consumers and distributors to distinguish the boycotted products from others. This move prompted the union to call for a comprehensive boycott of all table grapes, ramping up the confrontation.[64]

As the fall of 1967 gave way to the winter and spring of 1968, the entire country seemed embroiled in conflict, giving way to what would be one of the most violent years of the nation's history. Student protests of the Vietnam War erupted on campuses across the nation, and images of police beating back demonstrators filled the evening news. Sit-ins at lunch counters ignited violent white reactions across the South. Before summer, Martin Luther King Jr. and Robert Kennedy would be assassinated, bringing strained racial relations to a boil and sparking uprisings from Chicago to Los Angeles. Similarly, tensions rose between the union and the growers, and more and more members began to think violence was necessary. Facing escalating actions from Giumarra and other growers, workers began to resort to more aggressive tactics, displaying weapons at picket lines and setting fire to packing sheds.[65] As Chavez noted, the temptation mounted to resort to the "dangerous short cuts" of violence.[66] "I thought that I had to bring the Movement to a halt, do something that would force them and me to deal with the whole question of violence and ourselves. We had to stop long enough to take account of what we were doing."[67] After Giumarra won a contempt citation against him, charging that the union had harassed and intimidated company employees, sabotaged their trucks, and illegally picketed, Chavez turned to another holy practice that would also be one of the most controversial actions of his life. On Valentine's Day, Chavez quietly began to fast.[68]

As with the pilgrimage, the fast was a spiritual discipline that would galvanize the movement, forging deeper solidarity and recommitment to nonviolence. The fast was part of Chavez's spiritual sense of the transformative mission of the movement.[69] He would explain later, "I undertook the fast because my heart was filled with grief and pain for the sufferings of farmworkers. The fast was first for me and then for all of us in the union. It was a fast for nonviolence and a call to sacrifice."[70] For Chavez, the means of the struggle could not be divorced from its goal; on a deeply religious level, he believed that the union had to embody an alternative to the growers' violence and dehumanization.[71] As knowledge of Chavez's fast leaked out, it began to impact the workers profoundly. It served to bring them together. Each evening, a Mass was celebrated at Forty Acres, the union headquarters where Chavez had taken up residence, and farmworkers from across the region converged on the site. As the media caught on, it also gained national attention, drawing Senator Robert Kennedy's involvement in the ongoing labor dispute. As something of a "time out," this faithful improvisation on organizing allowed the workers to recollect themselves and to bond together. It also invigorated their belief in the truth of their cause.

Many viewed it as a stunt, a distraction, or an ego trip. Some organizers intentionally avoid such actions, taking them to be moral manipulation, ineffective, and utopian. But for Chavez, I think there was more to it. The fast was a way of focusing his entire person—body, mind, and spirit—on a cause that went well beyond contracts or raises. It was a refining of his desire for a new country. He was a fan of the Spanish phrase *"encaprichado a vencer"* (dead set, or hellbent, on victory).[72] He could be stubbornly single-minded. Indeed, his doggedness was a trait that tragically impacted the union years later when close friends and longtime leaders were pushed out as his leadership took a dictatorial turn.[73] The fast signaled to the growers the depth of his dedication, renewed despite all their antics. His spiritual resilience would be essential for the strenuous years ahead.

The fast racked Chavez's body. He lost forty pounds. His kidneys suffered severe damage, and his already ailing back was rendered frailer from nutrient depletion. On March 10, 1968, an enervated though saintly looking Chavez joined with over eight thousand farmworkers and supporters to break his fast. Joined by Senator Robert Kennedy, a mile-long procession of priests, minsters, nuns, farmworkers and their children, and union officials followed the image of the Virgin of Guadalupe and the union flag, arriving at a makeshift altar on a flatbed truck where Chavez waited. The people carried boxes of *semita* (Mexican peasant bread) for the Mass.

Too weak to speak, Chavez asked the union's vice president, Julio Hernandez, and Reverend Jim Drake to read his speech first in Spanish, then in English. It was brief and to the point, articulating the basic credo of the farmworker movement.[74] "We are a family bound together in a common struggle for justice. We are a union family celebrating our unity and the nonviolent nature of our movement," it said. "It is my deepest belief that only by giving our lives do we find life."[75]

The struggle with Giumarra and the grape industry crested in the spring and summer of 1970. Pressure had been mounting on the growers throughout the intervening year, as the nation began to awaken to the farmworker's situation. "Gradually, it became a national moral issue not to eat grapes," due in no small part to the boycott efforts in cities such as Boston, New York, Chicago, and Detroit.[76] With losses amounting to $25 million, the growers made a last-ditch effort to challenge the union, turning again to the Teamsters. They also entreated Governor Ronald Reagan to intervene. Reagan took to national television, denouncing the boycott. Growers also persuaded the sympathetic President Richard Nixon to vastly increase the Defense Department's purchase of table grapes. But the boycott proved too durable, compelling Giumarra and the industry to the negotiating table. A committee of Catholic bishops arbitrated.[77] Desperate to cut a deal, John Gi-

Helen Chavez, Robert F. Kennedy, and Cesar Chavez breaking the fast, March 10, 1968. Photo by Richard Darby. Walter P. Reuther Library, Archives of Labor and Urban Affairs, Wayne State University.

umarra, the owner and company president, summoned Chavez to room 44 of the Stardust Motel in Delano at 2 a.m. on July 26. By daybreak, Giumarra leveraged his influence to assemble all the growers at the local parish school auditorium to meet with union leadership for what became an intense two-day-long interchange. At last, on July 29, an overflow crowd gathered in the hall at Forty Acres, and Giumarra dramatically signed off on the contracts, throwing up his hands in mock surrender.[78] The other growers then followed, though not with such a flourish.

In the midst of the celebration, Chavez—ever mindful of the deeper reality of these events—spoke thoughtfully, saying, "The strikers and the people involved in the struggle sacrificed a lot, sacrificed all of their worldly possessions. . . . Ninety-five percent of the strikers lost their homes and their cars. But I think that in losing those worldly possessions they found themselves, and they found that only through dedication, through serving mankind [sic], and, in this case, serving the poor and those who were struggling for justice, only in that way could they really find themselves."[79]

Within this statement is the spirituality of Chavez and the movement he led. A sojourner who found his home among the farmworkers, Chavez sought in solidarity with them to challenge the unjust system of agribusiness. But he also believed that justice would come only by peaceful means, for only the work of nonviolence could transform the country and create the home he sought. Such was his unflinching commitment to the unity of the Spirit, the illuminating theme of his life.

As I came to read about his life, I grew to see Chavez as an icon of what faith-based organizing can do. His life is a reminder of the kind of country for which Christians long. But it is also a tangible example of the way there. In his spirituality, I can see what solidarity and nonviolence mean and how they lead to the justice we desire. Nothing may capture the arc of his witness like these words from his "Prayer of the Farmworkers' Struggle," where he pleads: "Show me the suffering of the most miserable / So I will know my peoples' plight / Free me to pray for others. . . . Help us to love even those that hate us / So that we may change this world."[80] Praying with him, I hope we will yearn for the same union of the Spirit that he sought and that our sacraments celebrate.

HOWARD THURMAN

(1900–1981)

Howard Thurman, July 18, 1964. Photo by Dick Darrell / Toronto Star / Getty Images.

Solomon's Son

The Wise Tenderness of Howard Thurman

Donyelle C. McCray

He was always so tender, always knew the right thing to say in the face of their insults. He kept a good quip ready—not a scathing one but one that would hold a mirror up to them. But not this time. This time all he had was a stream of expletives. When the stream slowed, he would have space for a wordless prayer and room for silence to fill his mind. But only in fits and starts.

Still a student at Colgate Rochester Seminary at the time, Howard Thurman had been invited to speak at a white church that Sunday night, and the evening began with dinner at a church member's home—a feat in itself for Rochester in 1927, a Ku Klux Klan haven.[1] Thurman knew they wanted him to be relaxed and happy, grateful for the opportunity to sup with them. As soon as he took off his coat, he befriended the family's five-year-old daughter. A fast friend, she insisted on sitting next to him at the table.

It was one of those courteous meals with lots of smiling and giggling. The mood was so light that he almost didn't believe it when he heard it, the child's faint whisper, "Stop, nigger, stop!" He thought he must've been mistaken. The conversation sparked up again but beneath the laughter and the clink of forks on porcelain, the whisper broke in again, "Stop, nigger, stop!" He was sure of it this time. Under the hum of the conversation he could hear the child's mother, "Why don't you take him out into the kitchen, and be sure to close the door so he can't come in and bother us."[2] At that, the little girl reached under the table, picked up a large black cat, and bounced off to the kitchen. The glad table carried on, clueless.

If Christian faith forced him to swallow his horror along with the meal, it was toxic. If faith demanded that he speak out, but gently and apologetically or pedagogically, so as to preserve the dignity and the feelings of his hosts, then that faith was a tendril of white supremacy. He had no use for a faith that denied him rage in a moment like this one.

What other man would've let his guard down? What other *black* man would've even come to dinner at a white stranger's house, let alone with any expectation of friendship? But Howard had a softness that would not stay tucked away. Its continuous unfurling was a radical thing in a world where only the numb survived. Sometimes his tenderness opened doors to genuine conversation and other times it left him vulnerable to eating with white folks and their nigger cats. The worst thing about their sick mix of scorn and affection for blackness was how familiar it was—familiar, that is, in the way one's own vomit is familiar. He was glad to rise and walk away from that table.

That Howard became so tender in the first place is a miracle. There were many reasons to let calluses grow on his soul and protect himself from the stoniness of life. And there was every reason to believe tenderness was a virtue reserved for elves or fairies or other creatures with recourse to a more enchanted world. Yet throughout his life, Howard intentionally claimed his tenderness. With this central piece of his humanity intact, he became a pathbreaking teacher of spiritual life.

Convinced that the practice of Western Christianity was corrupted by white racism, Howard Thurman practiced what he called the "Religion of Jesus." With his sharp and searching mind, he preached with such authority that some of his listeners experienced him as a mystic or prophet. A theologian and religious philosopher, he taught courses in theology at Howard University and lectured widely. His writings, over twenty books in all, reveal a man with unusual vitality. His vibrancy cut through the numbness that was so prevalent in twentieth-century America. As a respected pacifist, he became a leading voice in the civil rights movement and inspiration for Dr. Martin Luther King Jr., who cherished Howard's celebrated book *Jesus and the Disinherited*. Howard cofounded the Church for the Fellowship of All Peoples, the nation's first intentionally interracial and interfaith church. A pastor at heart, he also held esteemed roles as dean of Howard University's Andrew Rankin Memorial Chapel and dean of Marsh Chapel at Boston University, where he also hosted a radio show and regularly appeared on a local television show, *We Believe*. Throughout his journey, Howard was usually discerning enough to see his titles and accolades as empty shells, and he focused instead on his core vocation: caring for souls. For this task, exceptional clarity was required.

*   *   *

Howard's tenderness began emerging in boyhood, when the hours he spent playing alone in the woods grew into full days. In the stillness of the woods, he found company in orange blossoms and honeysuckle vines and especially trees.[3] The trees could listen to a black boy's fears and dreams without wincing. The bald cypress, the mahogany, and the southern magnolia had all been there for him from time to time but nothing like his live oak. The live oak had been true. His oak was patient and reserved enough to let him lean back and trace one question after another until all was said and he could finally wander back to the house, content for the night.[4]

The live oak heard all his griefs: how schoolmates had laughed at his pigeon-toed gait, how tired he was of eating field peas, how he felt like he was being punished for his blackness, but why?

Why? In the silence, the live oak always seemed to give Howard some of its ease. And beneath its shade, he grasped the essence of the old Ignatian proverb: "I come from God. I belong to God. I am destined for God." And it was at the foot of the live oak that he began healing after the death of his father.

Private moments between Howard and his father had been rare. Saul Solomon Thurman laid railroad tracks along the route from Jacksonville to Miami. Visits home took place every two weeks. When home, Saul got a haircut, a shave, and lost himself in a book. At times he'd stare off into the distance for long stretches. Howard would slip into the silence with him. Standing out of Saul's field of vision, Howard would study his father's face. He waited for a head tilt or a blink. Sometimes he'd crawl under the porch and watch his father through the slats.[5]

But when Saul came home in the middle of one work week, feverish and barely able to walk, Howard could not gaze from a distance. This time he watched from the bedside with his mother. They took turns cooling the beads on his brow hour by hour until Saul started gasping in a haunting rhythm. They had five straight days together and up close. Howard was snugged on a corner of the bed when the last groan came.[6]

At his Grandma Nancy's urging, he rose to pool money from the neighbors. The family couldn't afford a coffin and would need all the help they could get. Asking was shameless and expected. The neighbors knew full well that Saul's able body was the only cushion the Thurmans had against starvation. With no local undertaker who served black people and no means to get Saul to a neighboring town, Howard helped his mother bathe and dress the body for burial.

But Saul left his curious boy a precious thing. Saul's brooding silence and the apparent respite he found in it was a map to a form of wholeness that could only be found on the shores of the temporal world. Because of Saul, Howard knew there was such a thing as safety. There were whole regions in space and time where full personhood was possible. And even if the soul could only spread out for a few hours, the very existence of territory that green was a path to life. In the days following Saul's death, Howard would go to that psychic land and emerge sane. Grief still beckoned but didn't drown him. He had a beachhead in the spiritual world.

Church could not offer a comparable solace. This lesson came quickly and with searing clarity. Saul had not been a religious man, at least not in a way that counted for Daytona Baptists, so the pastor had outright refused to preside at the funeral. If Grandma Nancy had not pressed the deacons at Mount Bethel Baptist, there wouldn't've been a funeral for Saul inside a church at all. It happened only because an itinerant evangelist, a Reverend Sam Cromarte, volunteered to preach.[7]

Huddled on the front pew between his mother and Grandma Nancy, Howard clung to his memories. If there was compassion in the sanctuary that day, if there was empathy for the now-fatherless boy, Howard did not feel it. The funeral became a spectacle of damnation, and Saul, wood for the fire. There were no wonderings about what Saul found in the long silences on his porch and no tears for the son who cherished him. In damning Saul, Reverend Cromarte proved church was a place where beauty was burned. Howard decided never to go back.

At that charade of a funeral, the church folk taught him hatred. They called it obedience and respect for sound doctrine, but he knew the truth. As he foraged deeper into the woods and deeper in thought, he saw how leprous hatred was, how first it was theirs and now his, spreading into memories of his father, taking up more and more room in his mind. Would he have to hate them every time he remembered his father? Was hatred more alive in him than love for his father? It was a wound that the woods healed but one he never forgot. Even much later, after he found himself back with Jesus and compelled to talk about loving his enemies and turning the other cheek, he could not forget that hatred. Experience had taught him that demands for cheek-turning and enemy-loving were forms of assault. Neither could happen without sealing hatred in. First there had to be a miracle—a planting of *desire for* the desire for something other than hatred.[8] Then, a cheek might turn without compromising the dignity of a maimed soul. Howard faced this dynamic more than once.

Like the time he hired himself out to rake leaves. He was maybe eleven or twelve that year. He remembered the nice white man and the broad lawn and the hours he spent raking the leaves into little piles but making no progress. The man's young daughter kept skipping from one pile to the next digging for pretty leaves. Flecks of yellow, crimson, and maroon called to her from the bottom of the piles and she could not resist their beauty. Each of her dives drew Howard back to rake the discarded leaves that didn't fascinate her. Asking her to stop proved futile in the face of that wonder. So he had to pierce her enchantment, "I'm going to tell your father about this when he comes home." Incensed, she pulled a straight pin out of her little white apron, ran over to him, and jabbed it in his hand. When Howard flinched, she was indignant, "Oh, Howard, that didn't hurt you! You can't feel!"[9] There was something monstrous in her refusal to face the wound she had inflicted, in her insistence on innocence. He couldn't shrug off her grisliness as childish ignorance. He looked at her and wondered who she would become.

Mindful that he couldn't correct her without exposing himself to more of her hatred, he let his own outrage well up. Even as an adolescent, he knew this anger was a sign of personhood. Turning the other cheek required that he first be in touch with this hurt. Then, after he felt the rage flood his body, from his pierced hand down to his feet, then maybe he could receive that heavenly gift: *desire for* the desire for something other than hatred. It wasn't an automatic thing.

Howard needed interior resources in order to survive his early years in Daytona, and in this respect he was helped by the women in his life, who set the rhythms of home after Saul's death.

There was Mamma, Grandma Nancy, older sister Henrietta, and younger sister Madeline, for whom Howard was a babysitter. He learned the patience only a toddler can teach when he changed her diapers, dressed her, braided her hair, and learned the art of soothing her when she was distressed. He figured out how to be calm and still when she was seated on his lap until her crying turned to dozing. Madeline's needs also made Howard more inventive, prompting him to cut little leg holes in a lined crate and attach it to the handlebars of his bike so she could ride along with him.[10]

Madeline wasn't his only teacher. Mamma's lessons were endless. She spent long hours as a laundress and cook in white households but reserved her masterpieces for her own family. Howard watched the pressures of the day wane under the spell of her thick lemon pies, homemade doughnuts, and chicken perlo.[11] He'd rise from the table convinced that there was much to savor in life.

The quiet intensity of Mamma's prayers was a template for Howard, too. One time, he came into her bedroom without knocking and found her kneeling in prayer.[12] When she turned around, Howard was the one who was startled. Her face was radiant and her body shrouded in calm. Another time, he heard her praying aloud in church at a weekly prayer meeting. In the ether of prayer her voice shifted—so much so that it took Howard a moment to recognize who was speaking. He was struck by the way she "spread her life out before God," lifting up her longings for her children and her hopes for who they'd become alongside her own fatigue.[13] In both her words and the tenor of her voice, Howard heard her express things that could not be boiled down or mixed into conversation.

Largely because of his mother, Howard had the character and inner scaffolding he needed to flourish. She was not able to recognize the fullness of her influence on him. When Howard graduated as valedictorian of his class at Morehouse College, she greeted the president, Dr. John Hope, by saying, "I just want to thank you for what you've done for my boy." "Oh, no," he replied, "it was done by you, long before he ever came here."[14]

And then there was Grandma Nancy. She, perhaps more than any other person, revealed the delicate nature of the soul and showed how great its capacities are for bearing light. Born into slavery near Madison, Florida, Grandma Nancy had seen things human eyes shouldn't see. Howard knew very little of the details but sensed that some piece of her core had been chipped away by the experience. At times she'd go to a cordoned-off place in her mind to reflect on things that he, having never been the property of another human being, could not fathom. The most he could do was be a witness to her suffering and respect her needs for space and sustenance.

Often the sustenance came through reading Scripture. Psalms and biblical stories were her manna. Denied the opportunity to learn to read as a child, she especially enjoyed listening to Howard read. But there was a condition: she was unwilling to listen to anything written by the apostle Paul. She made a small exception for his short passage on love in 1 Corinthians 13, but her ears were otherwise closed. Having heard, "Slaves, obey your masters" as an enslaved child, she had promised herself that she would never hear it again if she became free. Howard helped her keep that vow, but more than that, he developed admiration for her resolve. She built a moat around her spirit as an act of self-respect and preservation. In the years that followed he learned to do the same.

Despite her rigid rule concerning the apostle Paul, Grandma Nancy was a soft woman who could be trusted with fearful things. Howard ran crying into her arms one night when events from earlier in the day shook him up. He and Henrietta were on their way home when they heard that a woman had been murdered in a neighboring town. They'd walked the twelve blocks to see for themselves. But Howard was not ready for what he saw: blood streaming on the sidewalk, lifeless eyes still open, panic frozen on the face. He had seen a dead body before, but this was different.

This time he saw that "death by human hands violates and ravishes the spirit, that it is unclean, that the mind recoils from it."[15] Though he and Henrietta had made a pact not to speak of what they'd seen or even to mention their venture into the neighboring town, he folded. The memory of the dead woman's face haunted him. He poured out the whole story in the safety of Grandma Nancy's arms, and she understood. Terror never had to be explained to her.

* * *

Later, Howard would say spending the first twenty-five years of his life in Florida and Georgia left deep scars on his spirit.[16] Some parts of him were only nearly mended. Long after he left the South, racial division still quickened disgust in him. The memory of it could be triggered easily. In 1935, Howard went on a pilgrimage to India, Burma, and Ceylon, and during a stay in Colombo, he dined with a teacher. Midway through the meal, Howard felt the man's anger on the rise. There was something about the tightness of the man's body and the violent way he poked at his fish. The tension at the table spiked when he finally threw down his fork, his knife, and the whole conversation in outrage. "Boy!" he yelled over his shoulder to the cook (a grown man with a name). "Boy! Bone this fish!"[17] The venom in his tone, the habit of treating another adult like a perpetual minor, the cowered body of the cook—all of it felt like Florida.[18]

In witnessing this episode, Howard saw more than a man tormenting another man. What he saw was the vacuity of that which passed as Christianity. Questions pressed him: "What adjustment could be made to accommodate the ethic of a religion like Christianity to the political and economic demands of imperialism? What is the anatomy of the process by which the powerful and the powerless can draw their support and inspiration from the worship of the same God and the teachings from the identical source?"[19] He would not claim a faith that handled souls so violently, or conversely, required adherents to remain silent and defenseless under daily humiliation. If a faith was worth having, it had to be a support for the one who "stands with his back against the wall."[20]

Howard had long since differentiated between Western Christianity and the Religion of Jesus, but now he did so more openly. He saw Western Christianity as an anti-faith, a belief system molded out of violence, racism, and imperialism. All three took on creedal significance and functioned as the heart of the faith despite the denial or obliviousness of its followers. Christian precepts were selectively applied to dignify self-aggrandizement rather than stir genuinely ethical action. And more, Jesus's role as the "hope of the disinherited and the captive" was "carefully overlooked."[21] In contrast, the Religion of Jesus centralized Jesus's experiences of bodily fragility and scorn and understood them as mandates for minimizing human suffering whether physical, psychological, or spiritual. Howard saw the Religion of Jesus as both a comfort and a catalyst for people like the berated cook in Colombo.

In fact, the memory of that humiliated cook haunted him for years afterwards. The predicament of the cook and his black brethren in the United States led Howard to pen *Jesus and the Disinherited*. In part, the book was an attempt to reclaim Christian teaching by gathering Jesus's messages to oppressed people. In doing so, he explained the Religion of Jesus and challenged the normative vision of Christianity, one that propelled and glorified whiteness. One foundational aspect of counterfeit Christianity that Howard challenged concerned comfort. He did not hold a vision of faith that prioritized one's own comfort, safety, or respectability. A piety that led to such ends was thinly veiled narcissism in his view, and he had no interest in stroking self-righteous egos.

Instead, he wanted to commune with people who continually bore unbearable burdens, and rather than offer Jesus's words as salve alone, he sought to spark pride and resistance. He wanted to stir their long-dormant hopes for freedom—to awaken in them a desire for some sense of alternative.[22] The reader was called to face the brutality of white supremacy and stand as one who was "pressed to the wall, dying, but fighting back!"[23] This fight was to be waged nonviolently with the sobering knowledge that catastrophic loss of life was inevitable. Coming to terms with one's mortality and the likelihood of an unnatural death was an essential dimension of the Religion of Jesus.

Howard wanted their readiness for death to match his own. Even as a younger man he seemed ready to die. It was this readiness as distinguished from mere resignation that made him so believable when he spoke about fear, love, and truth. He was utterly convinced that death was something that happened *in* life, that there was within him an essence that would not die.

When he and his wife, Sue, sailed across the Atlantic on the way to India in September of 1935, they faced a rough ride. Violent waters drew panicked gasps from passengers, but Howard was in bliss. He knew the ocean was tossing the ship, trying to expel it from her waters, but this dramatic struggle prompted nothing but awe in him. At one point, part of the ship squeaked and cracked under the pressure, sending waves of terror through the ship. Howard smiled—he was no more afraid of death than the ocean was. He believed that he and the ocean were one. They were roaring with life, refusing to be dominated. And while the heaving waters left most of his fellow passengers with nausea, Howard didn't miss a single meal during the journey.[24]

If the Atlantic could not subdue Howard with the threat of death, neither could a white man. He wanted his readers, students, and parishioners to feel the same freedom and outwit this scheme of white supremacy. They had to be willing to die if they were to engage in meaningful dissent against racist structures. Dissent also required ridding themselves of the passivity that false Christian teaching so often nurtured. And that was a second aim of *Jesus and the Disinherited*. He hoped to pierce the fantasy of a Christianity that shielded believers from the very vulnerability and unity with humankind that God intended. Once exposed to the bankruptcy of Western Christianity, Howard hoped people would seek a more authentic religious identity. If Christianity had any hope of unmasking the powers and principalities of the age, it would need to become a religion where people could be unmasked before themselves, their neighbors, and God.

*   *   *

Howard's demand for an authentic faith was sometimes difficult for others to accommodate. Wedded to his inner compass, he could be unyielding when pushed to violate it. Once, as a guest at a Four-Square Gospel church, he was asked to give the altar healing prayer. Howard refused, "I don't feel the pull of that now." Disregarding this response, the pastor announced that Howard would indeed offer the healing prayer. Howard sat motionless and after several awkward minutes, the pastor went ahead and offered the prayer himself. Looking back on the encounter, Howard had no regrets, "Religion (and religious experience) is too vital to have it tampered with by hypocrisy and by insincerity. . . . When you pray in public, <u>pray</u>, and if you can not pray, do not get up and 'spoof.'"[25]

Whether in public or alone, when Howard prayed he dove into the Great Deep. His prayers revealed utter dependency and abandon. Once, in San Francisco around the time that he was forming the Church for the Fellowship of All Peoples, he offered the opening prayer at a convention for cooks and stewards. Summoned to the podium, he spoke in that merlot baritone that carried all of the emotion and solemnity of one addressing the omnipotent God. His opening line, "Let us pray," seemed to rise from the center of his being. And he continued with palpable intensity, as was his custom. On the way back to his chair, the president of the organization stopped him, grasped his hand, and looked him in the eyes. "Hell, that was good."[26]

In Howard's voice one heard the simple clarity of a person who was at home with himself. Something about Howard's lack of pretension made him a fuller, gentler presence. This serenity seemed to abide whether he was before the throne of God or talking with friends. And "friends" also included trees. Well into his fifties, Howard was still chatting with trees. If he saw one looking particularly majestic on the Boston University campus, he'd stroll over and say, "You're doing a fine job." Fuller conversations would sometimes raise the eyebrows of people in earshot, but he was unfazed. This, too, was part of Howard's authenticity. He'd found a companion in a Daytona live oak, hadn't he? And they had shared a longing for God and love of silence and helped each other survive. Why pretend otherwise? Trees had become part of the landscape of Howard's prayer life. They offered him a testimony about the providence of God and a reminder that the entire creation relied on divine care.

More than that, trees—and his Daytona live oak in particular—helped Howard claim his identity as a human being and relish his body. Anyone who spent a meaningful amount of time with Howard knew that he was a man *in* his body delighting in its sensorium. An enticing aroma, food, or melody could leave him spellbound and wondering why others didn't experience the same degree of ecstasy. If they were just more present, he surmised, if they were just a little looser, they would also be swept up. When he pastored the Church for the Fellowship of All Peoples, he made sure worship appealed to a range of senses. Parishioners regularly found themselves gazing at paintings, listening to vocalists or instrumentalists in concert, or moved by liturgical dance.[27] Howard helped them understand that part of the soul's work was to soak in beauty and deepen one's capacity for joy. He was convinced that their capacity for joy could outmatch their capacity for suffering if they let it. And watching Howard lose himself on the dance floor or over a plate of chicken à la king suggested that such a miracle was possible.

When members of the congregation saw him so enchanted, they were also getting a lesson in prayer, and they were compelled to seek God in new ways. In this respect, Howard was a spiritual midwife for them. Much like his Grandma Nancy, who was a real midwife, he saw himself as one who helped the soul's potential surface and then placed it screaming and squirming in the bearer's arms.

His prayers, whether formal or informal, spoken aloud or danced, had the mark of one who knew human actions carry cosmic consequences. By sheer will, he could stir the universe's well of hope, peace, and love, and faithfulness demanded that he do so. One of the elders at his home church in Daytona hinted at this level of spiritual maturity in a conversation she and Howard shared one day. Howard fell while fishing and hit his head on the seat of the boat. He wasn't seriously injured, but the pain prompted a "spectacular series of profanities" that brought him to tears when he remembered that he'd recently been baptized in those very waters.[28] He spent the rest of the day weeping. "Let that be an object lesson to you," the church elder warned. "Satan is always waiting to tempt you to make you turn your back on your Lord." Thurman charitably interpreted her comment, taking it to mean that his choices in life mattered on a cosmic scale.[29] Action and intention carried a new gravity after that encounter, and the years spent living with that consciousness bore fruit in places like the Church for the Fellowship of All Peoples.

*   *   *

Given Howard's fidelity to delighting in God, not many people would have assumed that physical pain was a constant for him. By October of 1954, the packed days began to take a toll on his body. He was 213 pounds, heavy for his five-foot-ten-inch frame, which worried his physician, John Sisson.[30] In regular letters, Dr. Sisson urged more rest, exercise, and a 1,400-calorie diet.[31] Long walks and dinners at home with Sue helped, but the deanship at Boston University made it hard. He had not fallen prey to administrative minutiae. Just the opposite. The crisis in Western Christianity kept him at his desk studying and writing sermons, meditations, and lectures (often scribbling in longhand before typing). How would he nurture human souls in such delicate times? How would he teach nimbleness and freedom to people so estranged from the ways of the Spirit? The existential questions were so urgent that he didn't hear his body's first warnings to slow down.

Howard had been nursing pain in his right wrist for years. The wrist would awaken him at night and throb until he cradled it under a pillow. Lifting his right hand became increasingly hard. Writing triggered sharp pain, and bouts of fatigue made the pain worse. It was an old injury. When he was nine years old, he and a group of other boys were chased by a dog. Howard tripped and fell into a gully, breaking his wrist. The pain had been so bad that he was convinced that he was being punished. The wrist was set in a cast but didn't heal well. By college the wrist was unusually sensitive, and gripping anything with the right hand was a chore. Now, with sermons and speeches to write and essays to edit, the wrist was failing. X-rays revealed a lump on his right ulna. The old broken bone irritated other bones in the wrist.

Rather than bring his schedule to a halt, Howard opted for a leather wristlet. It did not provide total relief, but the sturdy bands gave him enough support to fulfill his weekly duties. Now he could shake the hands of a stream of parishioners after Sunday's worship service without pangs of agony, and he knew his soft hand was saying as much to some of them as the sermon. With the wristlet, he could also hold a pencil again for hours at a time and maintain his writing commitments. The irony of writing about healing with an aching hand was not lost on him. Whenever the twinges erupted, he thought of them as conduits to the pain that churned in the universe and found himself energized. In tiny increments he felt he was being stretched for divine purposes. Yet he had no fantasies about the wrist getting better. Believing as he did in sowing and reaping and in natural law, he knew the wristlet was just buying him time before he faced sharper pain or, more frightening, immobility.

The decision to keep working at such a hectic pace was not a sign of masochism or martyrdom but an indication of Howard's acceptance of bodily fragility. He recognized the limitations of his body but wouldn't allow those limitations to be determinative. At the end of the day, he was convinced that some things were just more important than his own comfort. Sensitizing people to the divine love stirring at the heart of the universe and giving them a compass for spiritual life were holy tasks that made wrist pain, even debilitating wrist pain, pale in comparison.

It is striking that Howard could see the need for limits and rest in others. For instance, Howard's most important piece of advice for Martin Luther King Jr. was to get a deep rest for his mind and body. The two had watched the New York Yankees play the Brooklyn Dodgers in the 1953 World Series while they were both at Boston University, but otherwise had little contact in person.[32] But one Friday afternoon in the fall of 1958, Martin was mysteriously on Howard's mind. Howard would occasionally have "visitations" or moments when a feeling of urgency, physical sensation, or familiar face would arrest his consciousness.[33] This time it was Martin's face, and Howard knew Martin was in Harlem Hospital recovering from a stab wound. The following day Howard went down to New York to visit. He sensed that the demands of the civil rights movement were pressing in on Martin and urged rest, suggesting that he extend the doctor's convalescence by two weeks in order to return to work refreshed.[34]

In less than a decade, Howard would be eulogizing Martin. All through the night of April 4, 1968, Howard's remarks echoed on Los Angeles' KPFK radio station in regular intervals, "May we all remember that the time and the place of a man's life on the earth are the time and the place of his body, but the meaning of his life is as vast, as creative, and as redemptive as his gifts, his times, and the passionate commitment of all his powers can make it."[35] The same might be said of Howard. While his version of "passionate commitment" did not provoke an assassin's bullet, health and wellness took a back seat to mission.

In ministry, Howard found "the fullest expression" for his life, or at least that is what he told Thomas Hardmon, a high school freshman from Bowling Green, Virginia.[36] Back in November of 1934, Thomas sent Howard a vocational questionnaire, and Howard had taken particular pleasure in writing back.

1. Why did you become interested in Ministry?

I became interested in the ministry because I felt that I could find the fullest expression for my life in that field.

Throughout the survey Howard offers Thomas candor as well as wit:

7. Is your vocation over-run?

Depends upon your point of view.

8. Does the pursuit of this vocation require a large amount of capital?

No. Just sense.

9. What advice have you to give me as one who might enter this vocation?

Don't be in too big a hurry to make up your mind. Enter this vocation only if you feel you have no other choice for complete fulfillment.

10. Is this vocation interesting?

Thrilling.

Letters like the one from Thomas taught Howard the most about the art of mothering souls. When he read them, he took off his administrative hat and remembered what it felt like to be fourteen. And more, he saw letters like Thomas's as holy invitations to pray for the inquisitiveness of a teenager. By age fifty-five, he was all the more grateful for the people who had provided a nest for his younger self. Without his Mamma and Papa, his Grandma Nancy, his kindergarten teacher, Miss Julia Green, Dr. John Hope and Dean Samuel Archer at Morehouse, his mentor Rufus Jones, and so many others, he wouldn't have become an empath or learned to tune into his own interior life. Still, there was much in him that needed incubation and nurture.[37]

The great spiritual writer Julian of Norwich says that no Christian grows beyond childhood in this life.[38] Julian was emphasizing human vulnerability but also revealing a deep respect for children that Howard shared. In children, Howard saw the human personality without the defenses that came with success; he wanted to bask in that softness. Playful as he was, he still needed reminders not to take himself too seriously. How could he model the relationship an individual ought to have with the divine if he could not play? If he could not laugh or be at home with all that he did not know?

It wasn't until age sixty that Howard really grasped the spiritual freedom of being a child. His awareness was awakened when he began taking clarinet lessons. He sounded awful at first—*awful!* When using words, he could readily find the means to express the subtleties of his thought, but not so with the clarinet. He found himself grappling with a new language, and the struggle brought a new depth of humility. Self-discipline and practice took him far, but not farther than his sense of humor. Without laughter, the hours of rehearsal would have been unbearable. His hard work seemed to make only a minimal impact on his sound, but other aspects of his life were noticeably smoother. Little by little, he was losing a preoccupation with mastery—an obsession he hadn't noticed in himself. To his delight, he was becoming more gentle and alive.

That Howard, talented as he was, did not succumb to the gods of mastery, money, and limelight, is a remarkable thing. Pressures to be a spokesperson for black America persisted through much of his life. And while he was keenly aware of the rationale for this pressure, he would not allow these forces to rob him of inner freedom. In this respect Howard was a different kind of luminary—one who was as committed to interior thriving as he was to structural and relational justice.

Rather than lead a movement, Howard's call was to stay in touch with the cosmic pull toward justice. He was most joyful when he felt carried along by a divine current. On August 28, 1963, he was, as one might expect, on the National Mall at the March on Washington. But Howard was not on the dais. He was down in the crowd, breathing his own buoyant hope into the multitude and allowing the energy of the masses to flood his soul. Looking back, he said, "Perhaps the ultimate demand laid upon the human spirit is the responsibility to select *where* one bears witness to the Truth of his spirit."[39] His model of gentle, contemplative activism was as revolutionary then as it is now.

Yuri Kochiyama

(1921–2014)

Yuri, founder of the Crusaders, with two girls at the Jerome camp in Arkansas. Japanese American National Museum (Gift of Yuri Kochiyama, 96.42.5).

SETTING THE CAPTIVES FREE

Yuri Kochiyama and Her Lifelong Fight against Unjust Imprisonment

Grace Y. Kao

In 1939, when Mary Yuriko Nakahara ("Yuri") was a youthful eighteen, she penned the following creed:

> To live a life without losing faith in God, my fellowmen, and my country; to never sever the ties between any institution or organization that I have been a small part.... To never humiliate or look down on any person, group, creed, religion, nationality, race, employment, or station in life.... To always keep in mind that any opportunities, achievement, or happiness I have had, I owe to someone else.... To love everyone; to never know the meaning of hate, or have one enemy.... This creed ... I will sincerely try to keep.... It is my philosophy of life. Dear Heavenly Father—Help me live it.[1]

By her own admission, Yuri had thus far lived a comfortable, "all-American" life. As a middle class *Nisei*, or second-generation Japanese American, she had been popular among her public high school classmates (she was the first girl elected to student council in her school's history), active in the Presbyterian church and other community service organizations (Girl Scouts, Red Cross, YWCA), and a poetry and sports enthusiast who had worked as

61

a volunteer journalist for the local paper, the *San Pedro News Pilot*. Not long after that Pollyannaish creed was penned, however, Yuri's fate would change for the worse on December 7, 1941—the date then-President Roosevelt declared would "live in infamy."

Within hours of Japan's attack on Pearl Harbor, three agents from the FBI appeared at Yuri's home where she lived with her twin brother, Peter, older brother, Art, and Japanese immigrant parents in a white neighborhood in a coastal town near Los Angeles, California. The FBI said they were looking for her father, Seiichi—a fisherman and small business owner who sold fish and supplies to American and Japanese ships that sailed between Japan and the West Coast. Yuri told the agents he was sleeping, as he had just returned from the hospital a day earlier after having undergone an ulcer operation. The FBI nevertheless brusquely rifled through the family's belongings, demanded that Seiichi get dressed in a bathrobe and slippers, and quickly whisked him away to an undisclosed location without even giving her a chance to say goodbye. What the Nakaharas didn't know was that Seiichi was one of more than seven hundred Japanese American fishermen, business leaders, farmers, produce distributors, Shinto and Buddhist priests, Japanese-language school teachers, and consular officials who were being detained on fears of possible espionage— all within twenty-four hours of the Pearl Harbor attack.[2]

Though the specific reasons for Seiichi's arrest were not then disclosed, a lawyer friend found out several days later that he had been taken to a federal penitentiary on neighboring Terminal Island. When Yuri's mother, Tsuyako, saw his health decline over a short period of time during her visits (he was diabetic, had respiratory problems, and was still recovering from surgery), she sent desperate telegrams to anyone who might possibly be in a position to intervene, pleading with them to attend to his urgent medical needs before turning to the matter of his arrest.[3] Perhaps due to her persistent efforts, Seiichi was eventually transferred to a hospital several weeks later, though he was placed in a room full of recovering US merchant marines with a sheet around his bed and a sign that read "Prisoner of War."

Yuri and her brother, Peter, were finally permitted to visit their father on January 13, 1942, after he had been moved to a private room for his safety. Seiichi seemed to them very weak, emaciated, and disoriented. He cowered when he saw Peter, who, as a new enlistee, had come proudly dressed in his army uniform, and said in Japanese, "You are not my son. You came to interrogate me."[4] Seiichi recognized Yuri but worriedly asked her, "Who beat you up?" even though there was nothing about her to suggest a recent assault. The family saw him again in an even worse state a week later when he arrived home from the hospital in an ambulance. Yuri recalled: "He couldn't talk. He made only guttural sounds and we didn't know if he could hear. We put our hands over his eyes to see if he could see; there was no way even to know if he could see. All he did was to make guttural sounds until he passed."[5] By the next morning, at age fifty-four, he was dead.[6]

Less than two months later, Yuri would be imprisoned as well—along with approximately 120,000 other West Coast Japanese Americans—in a "penal" regime involving "armed guards, barbed wire, [and] roll call."[7]

*   *   *

In ways no one could have anticipated, that self-described naive, carefree, and apolitical young adult would go on to become one of the most prominent activists of Asian heritage in US history. The White House officially honored Yuri's legacy following her death in 2014 with this tribute:

Today, we honor the legacy of Yuri Kochiyama, a Japanese American activist who dedicated her life to the pursuit of social justice, not only for the Asian American and Pacific Islander (AAPI) community, but all communities of color.

Mary Yuriko Nakahara was born in 1921. . . . She and her family spent two years in an internment camp in Jerome, Arkansas, during World War II, and the similarities she saw between the treatment of Japanese Americans during World War II and African Americans in the Jim Crow South inspired her to dedicate her life to activism on behalf of marginalized communities. In the early 1960s, Yuri . . . enrolled in the Harlem "freedom schools" to learn about black history and culture. Soon after, Yuri began participating in sit-ins and inviting Freedom Riders to speak at weekly open houses in the family's apartment. She was a strong voice in the campaign for reparations and a formal government apology for Japanese American internees through the Civil Liberties Act, which President Ronald Reagan signed into law in 1988.

Yuri leaves behind a legacy of courage and strength, and her lifelong passion for justice and dedication to civil rights continue to inspire young AAPI advocates today. I am moved by her leadership and her unwavering commitment to building coalitions to improve the quality of life and opportunities for all Americans, regardless of background.

As Yuri stated at a press conference outside the Federal building in downtown San Francisco in 2002, "An injury or injustice to one is an injury and injustice to all."[8]

Two years later, on what would have been Yuri's ninety-fifth birthday, the popular internet search engine Google gave her a "Google doodle" (a temporary alteration of their logo) to commemorate her lifelong "fight for human rights and against racism and injustice," deep involvement with "African American, Latino, and Asian American liberation and empowerment movements," and "tireless intensity and compassion" in the midst of her dedication to still other causes.[9] Yuri's activism was remarkable even when judged from an international perspective. In 2005 she was nominated for the Nobel Peace Prize through the

1000 Women for the Nobel Peace Prize Project.[10] She was not, however, universally revered, as her sympathies for and work alongside dissidents and revolutionaries rendered her more suspect than beloved in some quarters.[11]

Whatever the reception, public profiles of Yuri outside of Asian American circles have typically emphasized the longevity of her activist career and the remarkable, cross-racial solidarity she showed with others in numerous campaigns. While such portraits are technically correct, they remain incomplete insofar as they leave out two key aspects of her biography. The first is the role religion, specifically a service-oriented and this-worldly form of Christianity, played as a motivating force in her life. The second is the explicit identification of unjust imprisonment as the issue Yuri felt most passionate about.[12] Indeed, Yuri's steadfast commitment to persons wrongfully languishing behind bars runs throughout her lifelong pursuit of social justice.

To be sure, the shock of her father's arrest and premature death was not sufficient to transform Yuri into the full-fledged reformer and revolutionary she later became. Rather, as the White House proclamation suggests, she first had to be conscientized—a slow process that involved her grasping the realities of institutionalized racism some years after her own racially motivated incarceration and then vowing to do something about it. In an ironic twist of fate, her wartime "internment"[13] by the federal government provided her with not only a personal reason (beyond the memory of her father) to later champion the causes of other prisoners but also invaluable experience in community organizing to know how to advocate on their behalf.

*   *   *

On February 19, 1942, President Roosevelt issued the now-infamous Executive Order 9066: Resulting in the Relocation of Japanese (1942), which authorized the eviction of anyone from certain designated military areas for the sake of securing "every possible protection against espionage and . . . sabotage" in the course of prosecuting the war.[14] Approximately 120,000 Japanese Americans, two-thirds of whom were native-born US citizens, were singled out because of their ancestry and involuntarily displaced from their homes and communities. Without being formally charged, told how long they were to be detained, or even informed that their first place of exile would only be temporary, Japanese Americans were warehoused in repurposed fairgrounds or racetracks euphemistically called "assembly centers" (i.e., detention sites) while the ten permanent "war relocation" (i.e., concentration) camps were being built in the desolate landscapes of seven states. Yuri's family was sent to the largest of these, the "Santa Anita Assembly Center" (formerly racetrack), and made to live in a converted horse stall.[15] The harsh living conditions were difficult for everyone, but Yuri remembered the hay and lingering stench of horse manure especially aggravating her older brother's asthma.

One surprising result of the mass incarceration was the newfound pride Yuri developed for her community's resilience in the midst of great upheaval and suffering. She acknowledged that while some Japanese Americans were mentally ill and others "became so" through the ordeal they had endured following the attack, the majority carried on and effectively ran the temporary detention centers and, later, the inland camps, as they essentially operated their own schools, religious services, post offices, canteens, mess halls, and hospitals.[16] Yuri was especially heartened by the resourcefulness of the women who fashioned chairs and tables out of cardboard boxes and other leftover construction material, decorated the drab walls of the buildings, planted gardens outdoors, and created more privacy both in the bathrooms and in the sleeping areas by making curtain dividers out of fabric purchased through mail-order catalogs. In her own words: "Seeing the camp folks work together, confronting problems, overcoming difficulties, I couldn't help but admire their industriousness, their perseverance, and their creativity. It may sound strange—but I fell in love with my own people there."[17] Further, "My own people . . . do things, even little things such as serving tea and crackers, with such artistry. In camp, under duress, the best and worst came out. I think it was mostly their strengths that came out. I was really proud to be Japanese."[18]

Yuri worked officially as a nurse's aide, but her biggest contribution to community life came through boosting morale. Just as she had taught Sunday school to middle schoolers prior to the onset of war, so she continued, first at Santa Anita and then at Jerome, Arkansas, where her family was later sent. Her teaching philosophy is reflected in her (self-composed) Sunday school teacher's creed:

> I will keep in mind first that "what I am will speak louder than what I say." Therefore I will strive to live in such a way that what I do, how I think and what I say, will inspire them in a Christian faith [rather] than to destroy it. . . . I will try to make the girls realize, that no matter how much Bible Text-book learning and memorizing they may do, they must LIVE the life of a Christian, not merely STUDY it. They must . . . in short, "do unto others as they would have others do unto them."[19]

Yuri's pedagogy echoed what she herself had learned at the Los Angeles Presbytery in a three-week course on how to work with children—it is "more important what you teach a child to *love* than what you teach a child to *know*."[20] According to former student Dollie (Nagai) Fukawa, everyone "loved" her "wonderful" classes because in lieu of having them study the Bible, Yuri "related biblical concepts to how to live our lives as good Christians," kept their faith in God and humanity alive despite their mistreatment and suffering, and pressed upon them the importance of "not wast[ing] time" and "livi[ng] up to [their] potential" even in the midst of adversity.[21]

The major project Yuri spearheaded in her Sunday school class to enact the "Gospel mission to be of service to our fellow human beings" not only grew the class's membership from about five or six girls to almost ninety in a short period but also served as a foretaste of her activist, community-organizing future.[22] Yuri coordinated what quickly became a massive letter-writing campaign to help (indirectly) with the war effort and to lift the spirits of all those evicted, forcibly removed, and incarcerated by the Executive Order, since most of her students had brothers or other relatives serving in the army.

She led her class, self-named the Crusaders, to correspond with the Nisei soldiers serving in the segregated, all-Japanese-American 442nd infantry regiment—the same regiment that would later become the most decorated unit for its size and length of service in US history. In addition to sending letters of encouragement, the Crusaders mailed cards five times per year at major holidays, along with the occasional small gifts of chocolate or dried shrimp. The cards themselves often contained Christian themes, as seen in the Crusaders' Easter message, reprinted below:

> May Easter seep within you
> And give you strength to dare.
> For when our Lord and Savior
> Descended to the sky,
> He left in body only,
> His spirit is still high.[23]

Yuri's role in the American GI letter-writing campaign was pivotal. In addition to leading the Crusaders, she helped to organize two spin-off groups for the younger kids eager to participate. The work of all of these groups had lasting effects beyond their detention at Santa Anita, as individual Crusaders organized their own letter-writing campaigns at the permanent camps to which they were later sent, including in Arizona, Wyoming, Utah, and Arkansas. In short, Yuri had inspired her fellow inmates to write the letters, collected the names and addresses of the soldiers, written sample cards and poetry her students could copy, contributed her entire monthly salary to purchase postcards ($8 from her nurse-aid job could purchase eight hundred of them), and composed numerous personal letters herself—essentially "she [had] provided leadership."[24] Equally impressive were the staggering numbers of soldiers reached. At Jerome alone, where Yuri helped to found the Nisei United Service Organization, the Crusaders and their supporters corresponded with some thirteen thousand soldiers over the course of eighteen months. And one of the most grateful recipients of voluminous mail was a certain Bill Kochiyama—Yuri's future husband.[25]

As traumatic as the forced removal and incarceration was for Japanese Americans, these years were also a time of great personal growth for Yuri. The period following America's entry into World War II marked the beginning of her political awakening, for she slowly began to shed her uncritical "red, white, and blue" thinking and "banana" identity (of being "yellow on the outside, white on the inside") and see the "world and America with entirely new eyes—Japanese American eyes."[26] Not only had Yuri's time behind bars taught her the power and pride of the communal imagination, but the GI letter-writing campaign had also helped her to hone the skills she would need to become an effective activist outside of the camps: how to recruit volunteers, motivate people around a common cause, and handle logistics.

*   *   *

Yuri became passionately engaged in multiple social justice struggles during the decades she spent working in what she has called "the Movement." When mobilizing against unjust imprisonment, she explicitly drew on her community's trauma of mass incarceration in a smaller subset of cases, including in her advocacy in the late 1960s for the repeal of Title II of the 1950 Security Act, her solidarity with Iranian Americans during the 1979 Iran hostage crisis, and her participation in the 1970s and 1980s in the redress movement for Japanese Americans for their wartime exile and imprisonment.

The anti-Communist Cold War legislation of Title II of the Internal Security Act of 1950 allowed the federal government in an emergency to preventively detain—without due process—anyone who *might* engage in espionage or sabotage.[27] Popularly known as either the Emergency Detention Act or McCarran Act for its sponsor (Patrick McCarran), it was nicknamed the "concentration camp law" by its critics. Its provisions permitted the designation in 1952 of six potential detention sites, one being the Tule Lake site that had formerly held Japanese Americans. While the Emergency Detention Act was never in actuality invoked, Yuri and other Japanese Americans pushed for its repeal in the late 1960s because they feared it could someday provide legal cover for a governmental roundup of activists considered subversives or dissidents in the socially turbulent times of the civil rights, black power, antiwar, radical student, and various people's liberation movements. Title II was ultimately repealed in 1971 by the Non-Detention Act, and since momentum for the repeal first developed among Japanese Americans, this victory was widely regarded as a precursor to the national movement for redress for the Japanese American community.[28]

With several others, Yuri and her husband, Bill, went on to co-found Concerned Japanese Americans (CJA) in response to the surge in anti-Iranian sentiment following the November 1979 seizure of the US embassy in Tehran. The Iranian student-led takeover, which involved more than fifty American hostages and lasted an astounding 444 days, occurred in the aftermath of the Iranian revolution that had toppled the US-backed Shah when the revolutionaries demanded the Shah's extradition after the United States had granted him medical refuge. While the hostage crisis saw no signs of abating, CJA members observed an "alarming similarity between the hysteria against the Iranians in the US which called for their deportation . . . and the panic that led to the incarceration of Japanese Americans during World War II."[29]

When various US politicians entertained deporting or once again incarcerating an entire ethnic group (this time Iranian Americans) because of their shared ancestry with a foreign enemy, Yuri and other CJA members strenuously objected to these proposals in protests, demonstrations, and panels with fellow Iranian American community activists. Fortunately, Iranian Americans were not imprisoned en masse, as Japanese Americans had been decades before.[30] The crisis ended after the Iranian revolutionaries released the remaining hostages in January 1981, only minutes after the American presidency officially passed from Jimmy Carter to Ronald Reagan.

The CJA turned next to the growing redress movement for Japanese Americans, wherein both Yuri and Bill went on to assume leadership roles.[31] Congress had established the Commission on Wartime Internment and Relocation of Civilians (CWIRC) in July 1980 to review the facts and circumstances surrounding Executive Order 9066 (1942), consider the impact on those affected by its mandate, and recommend appropriate remedies. To raise public awareness of and support for redress, CJA organized its first official Day of Remembrance commemoration in New York in 1981, featuring Yuri as their keynote speaker. When Washington, DC, was the only East Coast site originally scheduled for one of the CWIRC's hearings, CJA applied considerable pressure for the CWIRC to hold an additional meeting in New York. According to fellow CJA member Leslee Inaba-Wong, their success was due in large part to the Kochiyamas' extensive experience with grassroots organizing: "Yuri and Bill played an absolutely pivotal role. . . . It was their contacts, their mailing list, their history in the community. . . . They gave us an in into the Japanese American community."[32] When the New York CWIRC hearing finally took place on November 23, 1981, Bill, among others, provided dramatic testimony, while Yuri marched with others in front of the commissioners and held up political placards as a "visual expression of [Bill's] feelings"—thereby increasing the media coverage of the event.[33]

When the CWIRC presented their official report to Congress in 1983, they concluded Executive Order 9066 was not justified by "military necessity" as previously maintained for generations and even upheld by the Supreme Court in *Korematsu v. the United States*, 323 U.S. 214 (1944).[34] Rather, its true causes were "race prejudice, war hysteria and a failure of political leadership."[35] In acknowledging that a "grave injustice" had been done to Americans of Japanese ancestry during World War II, the national conversation decisively turned from *whether* a wrong had been committed to what now should be done to *remedy* it.

On August 10, 1988, President Reagan signed the Civil Liberties Act into federal law, which provided a $20,000 tax-free payment to those internees still alive, established a public education fund, and issued an official apology. The long road to redress no doubt required the collective efforts of countless individuals to compel the federal government to finally, in President Reagan's words, "admit a wrong . . . [and] reaffirm our commitment as a nation to equal justice under the law."[36]

*   *   *

Yuri did not take her first steps in political activism combatting unjust imprisonment. Rather, her initial forays in the Movement began with participating in various civil rights sit-ins and boycotts. For instance, her protest with the Congress of Racial Equality over racially discriminatory hiring practices of construction workers against blacks and Puerto Ricans at the Downstate Medical Center in Brooklyn in 1963 ended with her arrest. Later that year she demonstrated with the Harlem Parent's Committee on several

campaigns for better schools and safer roads for their children.[37]
As Yuri's prophetic political consciousness expanded beyond civil
rights to embrace black nationalism and self-determination for
other peoples,[38] she turned to prison support work as so many
of her "brothers" and other "comrades" were being jailed. In
response to the need, Yuri provided a compassionate ministry
of presence to those in prison through frequent visitation. She
also organized rallies for their defense and composed articles
for Movement publications, editorials in local papers, and even
Kochiyama family newsletters (mailed annually to three thousand
people) replete with details and updates on their cases.[39]

To be sure, her fellow activists were not just facing harassment
and incarceration by the local police but also infiltration and detention by the FBI under what the American public would later
discover was its secret counterintelligence program (COINTEL-
PRO) to suppress political dissent by monitoring—with the aim of
discrediting—the likes of Dr. Martin Luther King Jr. and civil rights
organizations; the Black Panthers and other black nationalists;
Puerto Rican independence groups; anti–Vietnam War activists;
and the American Indian movement.[40]

Yuri thus joined the National Committee for the Defense of
Political Prisoners (NCDPP) and threw herself fervently into the
work. As fellow NCDPP member Nyisha Shakur recounts: "Yuri,
out of all of us, was in touch with people the most. People would
call her relentlessly, just all the time—frequently collect. And
somehow she never refused them. . . . She was the one seemingly
writing and visiting most of [the] political prisoners and really
staying on top of it. . . . Yuri literally worked until two or three in
the morning every night."[41] Ahmed Obafemi, a black separatist
leader who was himself targeted by COINTELPRO and imprisoned for a period in the 1970s offered a similar portrait of Yuri's
dedication: "Anybody that got out of prison, they'd go right to Yuri.
She would know where they were staying and would let everybody
know. She had everybody's address and had memorized most peo-

ple's phone numbers. I don't know how many numbers she had up in her head. She was very efficient, very dedicated, very committed, particularly around the issue of the prisoners."[42] Puerto Rican activist Richie Perez concurs that Yuri advocated ceaselessly for those imprisoned "in almost every community" and that she approached each case "amazingly with the same enthusiasm as if they were people from her own community."[43] It is no wonder that her activist contemporaries, reflecting back on the heightened activity in those years, dubbed her "the Internet in those days."[44]

What could explain Yuri's unwavering loyalty and dogged work ethic on this score? There was, of course, a personal dimension: given her own politically motivated wartime imprisonment decades earlier, she could empathize with fellow activists the authorities had branded as dangerous. Yuri had earlier also drawn great satisfaction from imagining Nisei soldiers receiving letters from her Crusaders thousands of miles away and had herself experienced the tremendous morale boost from receiving mail from loyal friends.[45] Perhaps these reasons inspired her to so faithfully care for persons behind bars decades later through regular correspondence and personal visits where possible, sometimes for years on end.

No doubt Yuri's religious convictions also served to support her work. As with her Sunday school teaching pedagogy, Yuri believed the mark of Christian discipleship lay more in love and service to others than in the instilling or proselytizing of doctrine. In fact, well before turning to prison work, Yuri practiced an ethic of radical hospitality—arguably the opposite of "unjust imprisonment"— by housing and feeding nearly anyone in need, first in her family's small, government-subsidized, three-bedroom apartment in Midtown Manhattan (1948–1954) and later in their four-bedroom, housing project apartment when they moved to Harlem in 1960. She took in mothers and children with nowhere else to stay, military service personnel and veterans, vacationing friends, fellow Movement activists, local college students, persons with medical needs, and even strangers.

74

That the Kochiyamas would provide hospitality to others for weeks or months on end—even if it required their children to double up in their beds or give up their rooms entirely to guests, and even if they had to improvise by putting someone on a mattress in the bathtub when they ran out of floor space—resulted in their home being nicknamed "Grand Central Station."[46] In essence, Yuri's Christian faith had taught her that she could not in good conscience look after her husband and six children only, particularly when the needs of others were great and when she believed she had the means or social capital to alleviate them. Her eventual realization that prison is "not a place of rehabilitation . . . [but] a place for punishment, isolation, and humiliation" thus influenced the shape of her service to others in that direction.[47]

Yuri called political prisoners the "heartbeat of struggle" and dedicated several chapters of her memoir and countless speeches, publications, marches, and other events to them and their causes.[48] While the definition of "political prisoners" is itself contested, for Yuri they were minimally those who have been locked up by the authorities because their actions, beliefs, or associations with others threatened the established political order.[49] What follows below are brief descriptions of three campaigns among the dozens Yuri championed, each drawn from a different minoritized community.

*   *   *

One of the most dramatic events Yuri took part in was the nonviolent takeover of the Statue of Liberty on October 25, 1977, to draw attention to the plight of Puerto Rican political prisoners. As the only Asian American among twenty-eight other (mostly Puerto Rican) activists, Yuri worked alongside the New York Committee to Free the Five Puerto Rican Nationalists, the Young Lords, and other *independentistas* (supporters of Puerto Rican independence) to hold the Statue of Liberty for the balance of the day while dramatically draping the Puerto Rican flag across Lady Liberty's crown. As Yuri, who had done her part by moving furniture around to block off doors, recalled: "We could hear the police helicopters overhead and boats coming to the statue and then police landing. I mean, it was exciting! We had planned to give up peacefully when the police came. But we seized the statue for nine hours. We made our point."[50]

By taking over this icon of America's freedom, the activists sought to symbolize Puerto Rico's control over its own destiny while pressuring the federal government to release the five who, by 1977, "were the longest-held political prisoners in the Western Hemisphere."[51] Oscar Collazo had been imprisoned since 1950 following a failed assassination attempt on President Truman, and the four others—Lolita Lebrón, Rafael Cancel Miranda, Andres Figueroa Cordero, and Irving Flores—had been locked up since opening fire on the Capitol on March 1, 1954, and wounding five members of the House of Representatives when the House was discussing the matter of Puerto Rico. From the perspective of Yuri and fellow activists, these five *independentistas* had received excessive sentences (the then-average was nine years for *convicted* murderers and Lebrón was given fifty-six years for *attempted* murder) because their actions had been motivated by their opposition to the ongoing colonialism of their homeland: the island was ceded to the United States in 1898 as a result of the Spanish-American War and treated later as commonwealth following a 1952 plebiscite.

Yuri's longstanding rapport with the diasporic Puerto Rican community is what allowed members of the Young Lords Party to trust her enough to invite her to participate in their risky, nonviolent direct action. She had worked and lived alongside Puerto Ricans (and blacks) at various low-paying waitressing jobs and as neighbors in low-income, government-subsidized apartments in New York since 1946. She had been corresponding with the ringleader of the 1954 Capitol shooting, Lolita Lebrón, since the late 1950s, with the two even exchanging words of comfort about the

Yuri being arrested following her participation in the Statue of Liberty take-over on August 25, 1977. Photo by Mike Lipack. © Daily News, L.P. (New York). Used with permission.

premature deaths of two of their children: Lebrón, who had lost a son under suspicious circumstances in July 1954 while she was imprisoned, sent "profoundest condolences" to Yuri in November 1975 following the suicide of her oldest son, Billy, telling her that

"Your son liveth in the infinite love and glorious happiness of our Creator. . . . I understand and participate in your pain."[52] Yuri had been such a strong ally and advocate for Puerto Ricans that she had been invited to serve on the board of directors for two Puerto Rican organizations in the mid-1970s.[53]

On September 6, 1979, President Jimmy Carter commuted the sentences of four Puerto Rican nationalists to time served, having earlier granted clemency to the fifth, Andres Figueroa Cordero, on humanitarian grounds because Cordero was dying of cancer.[54] Following the attorney general's advice, President Carter's executive clemency was partially based on "each of the four ha[ving] served an unusually long time in prison" and "humanitarian considerations militat[ing] against retaining in custody persons who have served (according to Bureau of Prison records) prison terms of far greater length than the terms normally served by those convicted of equally or even more heinous offenses."[55] In this presidential commutation of sentences came an implicit acknowledgment and vindication of Yuri's and the *independentistas'* belief that the state had indeed punished the five more severely for political reasons.

*   *   *

On July 13, 1987, an all-white jury convicted David Wong of second-degree murder for the stabbing death of a fellow prison inmate, Tyrone Julius. At the time of the murder, Wong was a twenty-three-year-old immigrant and Chinatown busboy two years in to a three-year sentence for his role in an armed robbery against his boss. While there was neither physical evidence nor an obvious motive linking Wong to Julius's death, the testimonies of two prosecution witnesses were apparently damning enough to get him sentenced to an additional twenty-five years to life.

Yuri caught wind of his case sometime after a fellow Chinese inmate, Tse Kin Cheung, began writing to outsiders about Wong's

78

innocence. As Yuri came to understand the matter, Wong's case had all the markings of "racism, anti-immigrant sentiment, prosecutorial misconduct and poor defense."[56] The Mandarin-speaking translator assigned to him neither had worked before as a translator nor could speak his native Fuzhou dialect, thus leading to Wong's confusing testimony at trial. A corrections officer testified that Wong had been acting suspiciously near the scene of the crime, though the officer's vantage point was 120 yards away in an eighty-foot tower with approximately seventy to one hundred other prisoners in the same vicinity wearing identical clothing. The second prosecution witness, fellow inmate Peter DellFava, received a favorable parole recommendation for identifying Wong as the attacker, but the jury was not informed of DellFava's deal with the prosecution and thus unable to factor in his incentive to cooperate.[57]

After personally visiting Wong in jail in 1990 and recognizing that "he was a guy who had been unjustly treated and . . . needed support," Yuri formed the David Wong Support Committee (DWSC).[58] She mobilized the DWSC for more than a decade to write letters to Wong in prison, speak to college groups and Chinese government officials about his case, and hire lawyers to handle his appeal. To generate money for his support, Yuri donated honoraria she received from speaking engagements and organized fundraisers, such as one 1999 Chinatown banquet that attracted more than two hundred supporters and garnered more than $8,000 in donations.[59] Incredibly, none of the core members of the New York DWSC, including Yuri, had a prior relationship with Wong. But Wong came to regard some of them as his "best friends" through their correspondence, exchanges of small gifts by mail, and visitation. In his own words, "I have no concept before I come to prison that if I suffer or have pains, others will feel pains and suffer with me. . . . I [am] happy [now]. I don't feel bitter."[60] Indeed, Wong was no longer measuring victory in terms of a successful appeal, but was already counting his blessings for being able to work with "these wonderful people" to "make the system a little bit better."[61]

The tide began to turn for David Wong in the late 1990s and early 2000s when his legal team uncovered new evidence. Peter DellFava admitted he had lied about seeing Wong brutally attack Julius because he had cut a deal with the prosecution to get out of prison. In addition, more than a dozen other current and former prison inmates were willing to name Julius's rival, Nelson Gutierrez, as the real killer after Gutierrez had died from a drug overdose shortly after finishing out his sentence.

Eighteen years after being sentenced for a crime he did not commit, David Wong was finally released in 2004 when a state appellate court overturned his conviction and a judge dismissed the charges. Because of his undocumented status, however, he was immediately sent to a Homeland Security detention facility and ultimately deported back to Hong Kong in 2005 at the age of forty-three. Though the DWSC was not successful in their efforts to allow Wong to stay in the US given all that he had endured, they were nonetheless essential to facilitating his jailhouse transformation (from bitterness and isolation to hope) and exoneration.[62]

*   *   *

Mumia Abu-Jamal has lived more of his life behind bars than he has on the outside as a free black man. He even spent twenty-eight years on Pennsylvania's "death row" and survived two execution dates (August 15, 1995, and December 2, 1999) before his sentence was commuted, in December 2011 after a series of court proceedings, to life without parole.[63] While Mumia was convicted of first-degree murder in 1982 at the age of twenty-seven for the shooting death of white police officer Daniel Faulkner, Mumia and his supporters have consistently maintained his innocence. The facts not in dispute are that Mumia had been working as a part-time cab driver, saw Faulkner in a physical altercation with his brother (William Cook, age twenty-five) and intervened, and became seriously wounded from a beating and a bullet after an exchange of gunfire in a chaotic scene involving several others that ultimately left Faulkner dead.

Today, Mumia is regarded as an unrepentant "cop killer" by his critics but frequently hailed as "America's most internationally renowned political prisoner" by the media and also as the "voice of the voiceless" by his supporters.[64] Throughout the decades since his sentencing, a diverse coalition of educators (including Cornel West, Mark Lewis Taylor, and Toni Morrison), heads of state (including Archbishop Desmond Tutu), members of the US Congress (including the Congressional Black Congress), and city governments (Detroit and San Francisco) have pushed for stays of execution when his execution was imminent, demanded a new trial, and in some cases publicly stated their belief in his innocence.[65] Supporters familiar with Mumia's case allege a list of wrongs that include prosecutorial witness tampering, police fabrication of a purported confession, withholding of evidence from the defense, inadequate defense representation at trial, racial bias in juror selection, and the trial judge's racial bias. Amnesty International conducted an extensive review of his case in 2000 and concluded, without taking a position on Mumia's guilt or innocence, that "justice would best be served" if he were granted a new trial, since his original one was "irredeemably tainted by politics and race and failed to meet international fair trial standards."[66]

For Yuri, Mumia is not simply an innocent man wrongly convicted. Rather, he is a bona fide political prisoner because his grassroots organizing with the Philadelphia Black Panther Party from the age of fifteen and his vocal support as a radio journalist of MOVE, a black liberation group that had had two violent (and fatal) conflicts with the police, had made him "a threat to the powers-that-be in Philadelphia."[67]

While Mumia has garnered legions of supporters in the US and abroad, Yuri began corresponding with him in the 1980s, well before he became a national and international cause célèbre. Through correspondence, Yuri discovered to her delight their shared love of a playwright and Mumia's ability to write in Japanese (Hiragana). As their friendship developed, she founded Asians for Mumia with Gloria Lum and therein helped to mobilize the Asian American community to support him. In speeches and press conferences, Yuri commonly linked Mumia's plight to the "struggles of nearly all other marginalized and oppressed groups and their political prisoners."[68] She frequently wore her "Save Mumia!" T-shirt around town, wrote "Save Mumia! Save Mumia!" at the bottom of her Christmas cards, and sported no less than four "Save Mumia!" stickers on the walker she used in her old age.[69]

Most beautiful about Yuri and Mumia's relationship was their reciprocal admiration. To Yuri, Mumia was an inspirational "phenomenon like Malcolm X"—someone who, more than any other political prisoner, successfully "galvanize[d] support for himself" and others across the world and whom she came to know multidimensionally as a "father, grandfather, an articulate speaker, an eloquent journalist, and an extraordinary political activist."[70] She counted meeting him in prison in Waynesburg, Pennsylvania, as one of the "ten most significant moments in [her] movement life."[71] Mumia, in turn, paid tribute to Yuri upon her death in 2014 in a radio broadcast entitled "Yuri Kochiyama: A Life in Struggle"; he described her as a "strong supporter of Malcolm X," a "freedom fighter," an "icon of the Black Freedom and Asian American rights movements," and as someone who, after ninety-three summers, had become an "ancestor."[72]

*   *   *

Up until her eighties, Yuri continued giving speeches, attending protests and marches, sending letters with small $10 and $20 gifts to friends and comrades behind bars, and visiting at least one prisoner, Marilyn Buck, monthly. According to Yuri's granddaughter, Akemi Kochiyama-Sardinha, Yuri would ask for nothing for Christmas other than postage stamps, and would get mad if family or friends gave her something for herself instead.[73] In the epilogue to her award-winning memoir, *Passing It On*, Yuri thanked "all political prisoners in the U.S., past and present" who taught her the meaning of "struggle and sacrifice fighting against racism, inequalities . . . and restrictions," and who gave her the hope that "freedom, justice, truth, human dignity, and basic needs" could one day be experienced by all.[74] Her closing tribute to political prisoners is a fitting bookend to the personal creed she penned at age eighteen, for Yuri's deep love and solidarity with others in need regardless of "group, creed, religion, nationality, race, employment, or station in life" can be clearly seen in her lifelong fight to set the captives free.

One common, but arguably inaccurate, perception of Yuri is that she gradually moved away from her Christian faith the more she grew in her political consciousness and Movement activities. Admittedly, Yuri had faithfully taught Sunday school in her teens and twenties and continued to do so when she moved to New York, first at the Japanese American Christian church and then at a predominantly white Presbyterian church, but stopped sometime in the early 1960s.[75] What is more, Yuri practiced Sunni Islam from 1971 to 1975 and traveled biweekly to the Sankore Mosque in Greenhaven prison in Stormville, New York, to visit with imam Rasul Suleiman, a former security guard for Malcolm X and member of Malcolm's Muslim Mosque, Inc.

Whatever the content of Yuri's confessional religious beliefs or understanding of her own religious identity, it is worth noting that she neither lost her connection to the institutional church nor ceased rendering the service to others the Christianity of her youth had first taught her to provide. She continued to volunteer at soup kitchens and homeless shelters in various New York City churches and also taught English conversation to international students at Riverside Church in Harlem for most of the 1980s through the mid-1990s.[76] Following Bill's retirement in the early 1980s, she took her first full-time job—as a secretary for a Presbyterian church—since they had their first child. She next worked in a clerical position for the United Methodist Committee on Relief, a job that for nine years allowed her to "see the church in a different light. . . . [It] was there for people all over the world, especially after disasters; also for refugees and those suffering from starvation."[77]

For these and other reasons, Yuri's official biographer ultimately interprets her as having lived a "humanitarian" form of Christianity in her embodiment of Hebrews 13:2-5 (NRSV): "Do not neglect to show hospitality to strangers, for by doing that some have entertained angels without knowing it. Remember those who are in prison, as though you were in prison with them; those who are being tortured, as though you yourselves were being tortured. . . . Keep your lives free from the love of money, and be content with what you have; for he has said, 'I will never leave you or forsake you.'"[78]

Insofar as Yuri's Christianity was never principally about dogma but about the "Gospel mission [of being] of service to our fellow beings," it is thus inaccurate to characterize Yuri's Christianity as having been stronger or more faithful in her youth or early adulthood than in her more mature, politically active years. After all, the teaching of Matthew 25:31-46 would suggest that Yuri's actions are to be counted as overtly theological, not just "humanitarian," for in that passage Jesus likens ministering to others, such as by visiting "the least of these brothers and sisters" in prison, as acts of love to *God* Godself.[79]

HOWARD KESTER

(1904–1977)

An undated photograph of Howard and Nancy Kester. Howard Kester Papers #3834, courtesy of Southern Historical Collection, Louis Round Wilson Special Collections Library, University of North Carolina at Chapel Hill.

Dreaming and Doing

Howard Kester and His Search
for Prophetic Christianity

Peter Slade

Howard Kester looked out from the pulpit in Miller Chapel across the massive polished communion table at the seminary students and professors packed into old upholstered pews.[1] It was his second semester at Princeton Theological Seminary, and he was going to tell them exactly what he believed God needed them to hear. Though only twenty-one years old, Kester was already an experienced public speaker. His slow Virginia drawl shook with passion as he read the assigned passage from the Gospel of John: "Jesus saith unto him, If I will that he tarry till I come, what is that to thee? follow thou me" (21:22 KJV). This was the call of Jesus to his disciples to do the work of establishing God's kingdom here on earth. And this reckless young man in the pulpit that spring day in 1926 believed the mainline Protestant elite gathered before him needed to hear the call, especially those among his fellow students who "belonged to the Klan" and his professor who "was on the lecture circuit defending child labor."[2]

Howard Anderson Kester—"Buck" to his friends—came of age in the South: a region drenched in the Sunday-school piety of the Bible Belt and built on the intertwined injustices of racial discrimination and the exploitation of labor. As a child, in the tobacco fields and farms of Martinsville, Virginia, Kester learned the social etiquette of benevolent paternalism and white supremacy. As a teenager in the coalfields of Beckley, West Virginia, he saw the poverty of miners and their strikes for better pay and conditions. Then as a student on a ministerial scholarship at Lynchburg College, he became acquainted with a wider world.

In the spring of 1923, the YMCA invited him to travel through Europe as one of fifteen students on a "Student Pilgrimage of Friendship."[3] He visited the battlefields of Europe and witnessed the "brutal scars left by the Great War."[4] He witnessed anti-Semitism in Poland that opened his eyes to the treatment of African Americans in his own country.[5] The YMCA sought "a curriculum devoted to Jesus' teachings . . . [as] the direct means of developing students with 'prophetic personalities.'"[6] Kester certainly fit this profile and he learned the lessons well. "It occurred to me that Jesus was speaking to me and my generation and that what he had to say was just as pertinent now as when spoken to the early Christians," he later explained. "The teachings of Jesus seemed to be particularly pertinent to the world with which I was beginning to be acquainted."[7]

Returning from Europe a pacifist and an opponent of white supremacy, Kester determined, "I was a gentleman and a Virginian and I thought it proper to begin to try to be a Christian."[8] "Sure you've got to believe in the Gospel," he would say, but being a Christian meant "you've also got to *do* something about it."[9] Doing something about it for Kester meant challenging the systems of racism, injustice, and violence.

While his Presbyterian parents—particularly his father—struggled to understand their son's strange new religious commitments, they were proud when he announced he was going to Princeton Theological Seminary.

But Kester and Princeton were not a good fit. "I thought that I could get the kind of training that I needed for the ministry at Princeton. Well, I got everything else but that."[10]

Kester went to the seminary, his faith shaped by the progressive social gospel of the YMCA, on a personal quest to discover "the true essence of Christianity."[11] But when he arrived in the fall of 1925, the seminary's faculty were caught up in the doctrinal debates generated by the war raging in Protestant mainline churches between the fundamentalists and modernists. The professor of New Testament, J. Gresham Machen, one of the intellectual leaders of the fundamentalist movement, was determined to keep Princeton a bastion of "doctrinal purity" from those who held less than a literal understanding of the virgin birth, miracles, and resurrection of Jesus.

Kester could not identify with the debates raging around him: "I was neither a 'modernist' . . . [n]or a 'conservative.' . . . I was just an ordinary American boy in search for something I knew I did not have but must have if my life was to be meaningful."[12] Locked in this intractable contest of their own, the professors had little time for Kester's quest.

The professor of practical theology, William J. Erdman (the fundamentalist Machen's nemesis on campus) was no practical help at all. Erdman rejected the prophets of the "so-called 'social gospel' which discards the fundamental doctrines of Christianity and substitutes a religion of good works."[13] Issues of economics, labor relations, and race relations—the matters concerning his young student—were, as Erdman explained, the job of the state and not the church. "It is for the state to secure social reconstruction . . . and the establishment of justice," he taught the ministers-in-training. The church, on the other hand, "is to secure, on the part of individuals, wholehearted devotion and allegiance to Christ. . . . The real blessedness of the Church and of the world awaits the personal return of Christ."[14]

Kester, of course, had no intention of leaving the state to deal with injustice while he waited for the second coming. More importantly, he didn't believe Jesus did either. "Jesus saith unto him, If I will that he tarry till I come, what is that to thee? follow thou me." Kester understood the text assigned to him by the faculty "as a challenge straight from the Almighty" not to remain silent.[15]

In Miller Chapel, a Presbyterian meeting house built in 1843 and designed for the faithful to hear the Word of God, with students and faculty arrayed in the pews directly in front of him, Kester let them have it. "I talked about all the things on my mind—war, child labor, exploitation of the poor, churchmen and the Klan, racism—and I was very specific at points, naming names."[16]

Some students were incensed. There was talk of throwing him in the lake. A couple of Kester's friends smuggled him out the side door to avoid the ducking.[17] Following this pointed display of prophetic zeal in the chapel, the college president, J. Ross Stevenson, invited Kester to his home that evening for dinner and a chat. In the spring of 1926, Stevenson was fighting to keep the seminary faculty from flying apart from doctrinal acrimony, and so his meeting with Kester was equal parts pastoral concern and damage control.[18] He listened to Kester share his convictions and anxieties, and then, together with his wife, prayed with the seminarian in crisis. At one point in their conversation Stevenson suggested, "My friend, you are rejecting eighteen centuries of Christian thought and practice."[19]

Back in his room, Kester couldn't sleep; Stevenson's words echoed through his mind. Was he really rejecting eighteen centuries of Christian thought and practice? Since his days at Lynchburg College, Kester found himself drawn to a verse in Acts: "Now when they saw the boldness of Peter and John, and perceived that they were unlearned and ignorant men, they marvelled; and they took knowledge of them, that they had been with Jesus" (4:13 KJV). This passage seemed to point toward the very thing for which he searched: "the kernel, the heart, the power of that simple, unalloyed faith that shook, overwhelmed, and for a time overcame the world."[20] In the middle of the night he came to a resolution. "I decided that if I was to find the answer, it was not to be found in scholarly treatises but in the lives of common men and women."[21] The next morning he left Princeton.[22]

*   *   *

Fleeing the disorienting world of Princeton, Kester continued his theological education at the Vanderbilt School of Religion in Nashville, an institution more open to consider the lives of common men and women. He found a way to cover the cost when the school agreed to hire him as an associate secretary of Vanderbilt's YMCA.

Before moving to Nashville in the fall of 1926, he traveled to the Appalachian Mountains of North Carolina for the YMCA's southeastern colleges summer conferences.[23] There he met Alice Harris, a student in the YWCA camp, from Wesleyan College in Macon, Georgia. As Kester neatly summarized: "In three weeks we were engaged, in eight months married; and the pilgrimage of life with a true friend, comrade and co-worker had begun."[24]

*   *   *

In the mining town of Wilder, Tennessee, a crowd gathered outside the company store on Sunday evening, April 30, 1933. Barney Graham lay in the dirt street, dead. Deputies and mine guards—hired thugs of the Fentress Coal and Coke Company—stood around the body. They were nervous. The miners were armed with guns and dynamite, and recently they had shown they were not shy in using either.[25] When the guards finally received orders to hand the body over, the miners found their union leader riddled with bullets and his head caved in: a broken pistol butt lay on the ground beside him.[26] They took Barney Graham to the funeral parlor in Livingstone, where a doctor, not in the pay of the company, examined his corpse. He found ten bullet wounds, four in his back. No one believed Shorty Green and Doc Thompson's claim that the killing was self-defense.[27]

That night Alice and Howard Kester heard the news of Graham's murder. Howard had been with him only the day before:

along with Alva Taylor, the professor of social ethics at Vanderbilt School of Religion, he had driven the union leader from Wilder to Jamestown to go to the Red Cross office.[28] Kester had planned to see Graham the following week for a trip to Washington, DC, for the Continental Congress on Economic Reconstruction; instead, in the middle of that Sunday night, he and his wife gathered up some groceries in a box and drove east on Lee Highway 130 miles from Nashville to Wilder.[29] Driving into Fentress County in the small hours of the morning, the road turned to gravel, and then, when they reached the company town of Wilder, they made their way slowly through the rutted dirt streets to Graham's home.[30] Barney and Daisy Graham lived in one of the company houses with their three children.[31] It looked like all the other houses in Wilder. A simple four-room framed house with walls, floor, and ceiling of unpainted pine planks: the only concession to architecture was the wide front porch. The water came from a pump at the end of the row. A small "ancient kitchen stove" cooked the food and provided the heat in the winter.[32]

When they arrived, the Kesters found Daisy in no condition to care for the children. Alice knew she was suffering from pellagra and was prone to epileptic seizures.[33] Barney Graham had stepped out the night before to try to get his wife some medicine from the store—the errand from which he did not return. In the house with Daisy were Graham's twelve-year-old stepdaughter, Della Mae, five-year-old Bertha, and two-year-old Barney Jr. As he carried the groceries into the kitchen, Howard noticed that there was no other food in the house.[34]

Despite his familiarity with the miners' living conditions in Wilder—he and Alice had been running the Wilder Emergency Relief Committee since November—the poverty they met still stunned and angered him.[35] Miners worked for two dollars per sixteen-hour shift. Before the depression hit Tennessee, they had worked five or six shifts a week—a modest wage for this backbreaking and dangerous work. Then, with the economic downturn, they had been reduced to three shifts a week. Most of what they earned never left the pockets of the company: their wages were garnished to pay the debt incurred from the rent of their houses, the use of the company bath house, and the groceries bought at the company store. The miners even had to buy their own tools and the blasting powder for use in the mine.[36] That previous summer the company had announced a 20 percent cut in wages. Facing starvation, on July 8, 1932, the miners went on strike, led by forty-six-year-old union leader Byron F. "Barney" Graham. Nine months later, the strike had left his family malnourished and sick, his wife a widow, and his children orphans.

That Monday afternoon, the day after the murder, Howard Kester met with his friend Don West. West, recently ordained, had been a fellow student with Kester at Vanderbilt and was now working with the radical Myles Horton, a graduate of Union Theological Seminary, to establish the Highlander folk school in Tennessee.[37] West was trying to arrange the first funeral he ever conducted. The problem was that the one church building in Wilder was owned by Fentress Coal and Coke, and the company had no intention of allowing the family and striking miners to use it for the service.[38] After discussions with representatives of the union and the family, they decided to have a small ceremony at the house and then proceed to the cemetery.[39]

Alice and Howard chose to stay with Daisy Graham and her children that night. A burning cotton wick in a Coca-Cola bottle half-filled with kerosene provided the only light in the room. There was nowhere for them to sleep; the cabin didn't even hold enough beds for its regular inhabitants, let alone for visitors. The couple settled themselves for the vigil in a couple of straight-backed chairs. "It was an awesome and terrible night as sobs of grief came from Mrs. Graham and the children," Howard recalled.[40] Neighbors came in through the night "to sit on the pine wood floor to talk in subdued tones about their troubles." One group of visitors proved most striking. "Uncle Ed, a devoted union man and mountain preacher, came with his three boys. They brought their guns. There were tears in Uncle Ed's blue eyes and one could feel that smoke had already begun to curl out of the end of that long mountain rifle."[41]

As the Southern Secretary of the Fellowship of Reconciliation (FOR), Kester had supported the organization's doctrinaire embrace of pacifism, but recently his newfound Christian socialism had caused him to question its presuppositions.[42] "It is . . . of paramount importance that the Fellowship exert every ounce of strength it possesses in demonstrating the effectiveness of aggressive pacifism for social and economic revolution," he had written in a recent report. While still a faithful employee of the FOR he wanted them to know that "I am not so emotionally wedded to the idea of pacifism that I am blind to the possible benefits of violence in certain situations."[43] Now sitting across from the "devoted union man and mountain preacher" and his rifle, Kester imagined he saw the embodiment of the prophetic religion he and his colleagues hoped to find when they came to Wilder.

Uncle Ed and the other mountain preachers backing the union were not peddling the pie-in-the-sky revivalism so prevalent in pulpits throughout the South. Theirs was not an opiate for the masses. "They believed Jesus and God and all the forces of righteousness were on their side and eventually they'd win—not a seat in glory on the other side of the grave but a living wage for a day's work and a world fit for men to live in."[44]

Don West conducted the funeral that Tuesday afternoon. Howard Kester, and a Rev. H. S. Johnson, who was a miner and local preacher, assisted him. Over seven hundred people met the hearse that brought Graham's body back to Wilder. Processing single file, they followed it down into town, pausing at the spot in the street where he had been gunned down, then on to the cemetery.[45]

Daisy was too sick to get out of the car to go to her husband's graveside.[46]

"I have heard many eloquent sermons and many stirring speeches on social justice," Kester later claimed, "but never have I been so moved as I was by the words of Preacher Johnson."[47] The words Kester recorded coming from Johnson's mouth evocatively summarize the radical turn Kester's theology took after Wilder: a turn toward a prophetic religion of the laborers, and the farmers, and the miners that shakes the world, fights for justice, and establishes a new economic order.

Kester left Princeton Seminary looking for "the true essence of Christianity . . . in the lives of common men and women."[48] He went looking for the bold faith in Jesus of those first apostles: those "unlearned and ignorant men" (Acts 4:13). And he believed he found it in Wilder in the mountain preacher's eulogy:

Barney Graham was murdered by the bosses because he wanted us to get a full day's pay for a full day's work, because he wanted us to have better houses in which to live, because he wanted us to be men and not slaves. He was tired of seeing men go into the pits with nothing in their buckets but bread and water and sometimes molasses, he was tired of seeing our children go barefooted in the snow, he was tired of hearing our babies cry for bread and us all the time working our hands off digging coal. He was tired of the dirt, the filth and the poverty we are forced to live in. They killed him because he wanted to change all this. It was the same kind of people—coal operators, thieves and robbers of women and little children, company thugs, and hired gunmen—that murdered Jesus Christ. They crucified Jesus Christ because he was a friend to the poor man and because he stood up against the rich and powerful men of his day. Jesus wanted to change things in his day and they killed him. They killed Barney Graham because he wanted to change things in Wilder Hollow.[49]

"This is not the end; it is only the beginning."

"This is not the end," and a thousand voices echoed, "Amen."[50]

*   *   *

After the funeral, Howard and Alice threw themselves back into the work with the strikers. Alice continued distributing food and clothing to the starving families, and Howard secured a lawyer for the predictably futile prosecution of Barney Graham's murderers.[51] This made Kester a marked man. The miners heard rumors that the company's gunmen were threatening to blow his brains out, and they thought it prudent to protect him.[52] "I was definitely considered company enemy number one," he wrote in his report to the FOR in October. "When I went to Wilder thereafter I was always guarded. When going into the camp I was usually met by a group of the strikers who accompanied me until I left."[53]

In Kester's annual report to the FOR he wrote, "it seems to me . . . that within the framework of capitalistic society any attempt to build a decent world is a dream and illusion." He felt compelled to join the "revolutionary movement . . . until capitalistic society is uprooted." "In doing this we have merely accepted the historical position of Jesus who definitely recognized the class struggle and set his face steadfastly against the oppressors of the poor, the weak and the disinherited."[54]

He had glimpsed the coming kingdom of God and the demise of capitalism. It was exhilarating.

"While the year has been marked by tragedy and madness," he wrote in his October report, "it has been for me the most satisfying period of my life for I have felt that I was helping to prepare the bier of a dying civilization and sharing in the birth pangs of a society struggling to be born."[55]

Reinhold Niebuhr, the well-known theologian and chairman of the FOR, read Kester's report with approval, but his talk of revolution and the mention of armed miners guarding the Fellowship's secretary alarmed others. Kester's report from Wilder fueled an already raging debate going on in the Fellowship. With its pacifist principles formulated to oppose international wars, it wasn't clear

Howard Kester with striking miners, Wilder, Tennessee, 1933. Howard Kester Papers #3834, courtesy of Southern Historical Collection, Louis Round Wilson Special Collections Library, University of North Carolina at Chapel Hill.

to many how this purist form of pacifism could accommodate its secretary's participation in "the Class Struggle."[56] In November 1933, the FOR polled its members on "how far the F.O.R. should go ... as to the struggles of workers or other underprivileged groups."[57] It transpired that Howard Kester along with Reinhold

Niebuhr were prepared to go much further than the majority of the members felt comfortable. They both agreed that "In case the legal owners of the essential industries resort to armed force" against striking workers, they would "consent to the use of armed force if necessary to secure the advantage of the workers, but regretfully and only while the necessity for it continues."[58]

Howard Kester had actually persuaded the miners at Wilder not to engage in violent attacks against the company, but being forced to take this hypothetical stand in a mail-in survey cost him his job. It also lost the FOR its chairman. At the start of 1934, the cover of the *Christian Century* announced "The Pacifist's War." In his article "Why I Leave the F.O.R.," Niebuhr explained to the Protestant establishment why he quit: "It is only a Christianity which suffers from modern liberal illusions which has ever believed that the law of love could be made an absolute guide of conduct in social morality and politics."[59] He followed up this public pronouncement by writing letters to "a number of persons who have been deeply impressed with Kester's work who will want to continue to support it."[60] And so, to the great relief of Alice, Howard had a job with an income as the sole employee of the Committee on Economic and Racial Justice (CERJ). With the iconoclastic Reinhold Niebuhr as chairman, CERJ existed for one purpose, "the support of Howard Kester's work in the South."[61]

*   *   *

The mood was troubled on campus Saturday night, November 3, 1934, when Howard Kester arrived at Florida Agricultural and Mechanical College in Tallahassee. The college's president, J. R. E. Lee, had warned the faculty to have nothing to do with the white man who was coming asking questions about the lynching that occurred over in Jackson County. They all knew about it. The newspapers and radio stations had all reported the murder of the white Lola Cannidy and the arrest of her African American neighbor Claude Neal, and had even advertised his lynching before it had taken place. "Mob Plans Fiery Death for Killer" announced the *Florida Herald*, "Place of Attack on Girl Is Scheduled Scene of Reprisal."[62]

Thousands of whites from across the region had converged on Marianna on Friday, October 26. Walter White, the executive secretary of the NAACP, sent telegrams to the governor of the state calling on him to intervene, to no avail.[63] Now White wanted a detailed report of the killing and the race riots that had occurred the previous weekend in Marianna to shock the nation and swing public opinion behind the Costigan-Wagner anti-lynching bill. He had sent a telegram to Kester on Wednesday asking him to go to Marianna to investigate.[64]

White's request came at a bad time for Kester. He was busy organizing a conference of the Younger Churchmen of the South taking place the next month in Chattanooga, organizers of the newly formed Southern Tenant Farmers Union (STFU) were expecting to see him in Memphis in a couple of weeks, and Alice was struggling at home with their six-month-old baby, Nancy.[65] But he wired a reply to White saying he would go.[66] Kester dropped everything and drove south on Highway 31 into the heart of America's darkness.[67]

Walter White sent letters introducing Kester to his NAACP contacts in the region, describing him as "a first-rate young white man, who is absolutely right on the race question" and asking them to afford him any assistance he might need in his investigation.[68] President Lee of Florida A&M had received such a letter. His college was the only black school in Florida supported by state funds, and he understood exactly what would happen to that support if state legislators suspected the school was helping the NAACP. Lee ordered his faculty to have nothing to do with Kester.[69]

When Kester arrived at the college, there was a dance in progress. Looking around the crowded hall he caught sight of a woman on the faculty who he knew from his work with the "colored"

YMCA and YWCA.[70] Kester was careful never to reveal his contacts, and so we do not know her name, but when he went over to talk to her, the professor explained that it was more than her job was worth to be seen talking to him. As Kester turned to leave she caught his arm and quietly said, "Go outside and you stand at the far corner of the porch, and I'll see if I can do anything to help you." A few minutes later she returned and introduced him to a "young man," a student who was the pastor of a black church in Marianna. "He might be able to help you," she said and left.[71]

Kester asked the pastor if he would introduce him to members of the African American community in Marianna. The young man, anxious for his own safety, was reticent. Kester pushed. "Will you meet me at the church? Would you meet me at the church maybe with some of your elders, or just by yourself on next Sunday afternoon?"

"I'll try to be there."[72]

When Kester checked into Marianna's Chipola Hotel, this friendly, well-dressed man appeared to be just another one of the many white folks breaking the journey between Tallahassee and Mobile to see the limestone caverns and the site of the Civil War battle.[73] The Chipola was a large, modern hotel just a short stroll from the town square, or "the Plaza" as the locals called it. The yellow brick courthouse sat in the middle of the square, surrounded by beautiful old oaks. Aesop Bellamy, one of Marianna's first African American business owners, gave these trees to the town in 1873.[74] Perhaps the gift was a sign of his hope for a prosperous future for African Americans as full citizens of Jackson County. Sixty years later, it was from one of Aesop's trees that the mob suspended Neal's mutilated body.

In the days before his scheduled rendezvous at the church, Kester was busy while trying to appear as though he was not doing anything at all. With his southern accent, Virginian manners, and white skin, he was an ideal investigator for the NAACP. He went to burger joints and filling stations—anywhere people hung out—and chatted to everyone he met. He heard how local people wanted souvenirs of the lynching. Someone had one of Neal's toes preserved in a jar of alcohol. He heard of the photographer who made postcards of a picture of the mutilated body strung up in the Plaza, selling hundreds of them for fifty cents each. A pump attendant at the Gulf filling station sold Kester one.[75] He heard from some who had been out at the Cannidy's farm and seen children poking the body with sticks. And on Tuesday night he sat and listened for an hour and forty minutes to a man called Red, who claimed he had been there when Neal was begging for his life.[76]

"After taking the nigger to the woods, they cut off his penis. They cut off his testicles and made him eat them and say he liked it."

Kester concentrated on searing every word into his memory while trying to keep the horror and revulsion from his face.

"Then they sliced his sides and stomach with knives," Red bragged, "and every now and then somebody would cut off a finger or toe. Red hot irons were used on the nigger to burn him from top to bottom." A rope was "tied around Neal's neck and he was pulled up over a limb and held there until he almost choked to death." Then they let him down and the torture started all over again. The man boasted that this went on for hours until "they decided just to kill him."[77]

Kester rushed straight back to the hotel to write down the man's words; these were the details that Walter White requested. And the next day Kester mailed White a preliminary report.[78]

That week, Kester gathered additional details: of the rioting, of the terrorizing of the black residents in town, of how some whites had hidden their maids in closets to keep them from the mob. He also learned as much as he could about the town's economy. Jackson County was in the grips of the Great Depression, and employment was scarce for whites and blacks. Racial tensions rose even before Lola Cannidy's uncle discovered her body under the pile of brush. One store clerk told Kester, "A nigger hasn't got no right to have a job when there are white men who can do the work and are out of work."[79]

Kester also learned that two weeks before the lynching, the Federal Emergency Relief Administration (FERA) had stopped paying relief. And the Saturday before the riot, an organization known as the FERA Purification League demonstrated on the streets of Marianna, demanding that the county take African Americans off the relief rolls. Kester likely spoke with the founder of the league—a local newspaperman with the unfortunate name of Wankard Pooser—who held some of Huey Long's ideas of "share the wealth" alongside a "deep seated and violent race prejudice."[80] Everything Kester discovered in Marianna confirmed his socialist understanding that economics lay behind the phenomenon of spectacle lynching. Barney Graham and Claude Neal were both casualties of the class war: victims of capitalist exploitation and oppression.[81]

To complete his report, he needed to hear from the African American community—a hard task without raising suspicion. He hoped his meeting with the pastor and elders at the church would yield some useful information, but in the meantime, he befriended the staff at the seventy-five-room Chipola Hotel. He decided to trust one of the porters and told him he was working for the NAACP. Through him and others he learned that it was "common knowledge in the Negro community" that Neal and Cannidy had been having "intimate relations," perhaps for years. Some believed Neal had been framed, while others reported that Lola Cannidy had threatened to report their affair, and Neal killed her to protect himself.

The longer Kester stayed in town, the greater the chance that his curiosity would arouse suspicion, but he wanted to stay long enough to keep his Sunday evening appointment at the church.

Perhaps it was intuition, as Kester later claimed, or perhaps it was because it was only a half mile from the hotel, but Kester decided to walk to the church.[82] Dressed in his suit he looked like he was taking an innocent Sunday evening stroll past the Plaza, down Jackson Street into the black side of town and up the hill toward the red brick towers of Saint Luke Baptist Church.[83] There was nobody there. Feeling conspicuous on the front steps, he decided to wait around the side of the church among some trees. As the light was failing, cars started arriving in the church parking lot and men got out—he could tell by their voices that they were white—and started searching the grounds with flashlights.[84] Kester had no idea how they knew he was there, but he knew that he did not want them to find him. He dropped to the ground and crawled on his stomach back into the brush. The land fell steeply away from the church into a ravine, and Kester crawled for his life, briars and bushes tearing at his woolen suit. He followed the ravine five hundred yards down to the highway, and then he walked briskly, head down, keeping to the shadows, back into town.[85]

Kester didn't dare risk being seen entering the hotel in his muddied and disheveled state. He went around to the back of the building and found the porter, the man he had trusted with the secret of his mission. The porter let him in through the kitchen and up to his room. Hurriedly, Kester washed and changed his clothes. With his appearance restored, he went down to the lobby "just as if nothing had ever happened." After all the conversations that week, Kester was under no illusion as to what would have happened if those men had caught him at the church. "If they had laid hands on me that night, it would have been the last of me. I am sure of that."[86]

The next morning, Kester realized his secret was out. The filling station operator who had sold him the postcard of the lynching took him aside. "You better get out of town. They are looking for you." [87] He packed, checked out of the hotel, and thirty minutes later was driving north as fast as he could heading for the state line. Fearing he was being followed, he didn't stop for 130 miles, until he reached Eldorado, Georgia, and the safety of the home of its Episcopal priest.

Alice was relieved at Howard's safe return to Nashville, but she was alarmed by the state of his nerves. "I came from Marianna on Friday absolutely exhausted," he wrote to a friend. "I was physically tired to death and my spirits were never at a lower ebb."[88] "When I did get home I was so damned shot to pieces that I could scarcely take nourishment. Then too I had to get my report in to the NAACP by the middle of the week."[89] Traumatized by his experiences, Kester could not rest until he delivered the manuscript along with the horrific postcard. On Tuesday, November 20, just eight days after his escape from Marianna, Walter White sent a mimeographed copy of the finished report to Eleanor Roosevelt.[90] The first lady wrote to Walter White: "I talked to the president . . . and he said he hoped very much to get the Costigan-Wagner [anti-lynching] Bill passed in this coming session. The Marianna lynching was a horrible thing."[91]

The NAACP launched a public assault with Kester's powerful document. The five thousand copies of the first print run ran out after only six days; a second run of ten thousand copies followed.[92] Kester's name did not appear on the NAACP's eight-page report "because to do so," as Walter White explained, "might jeopardize his life and would almost certainly lessen his future usefulness in similar cases."[93] White, however, did not keep Kester in the shadows. On Wednesday, December 12, just a month after crawling on his stomach down a dark ravine in Marianna, Kester presented his findings in person to John D. Rockefeller III, Reinhold Niebuhr, and around 150 other notable guests of the NAACP at a luncheon in New York.[94]

Kester's report and White's campaign did not succeed in getting anti-lynching legislation passed; that didn't happen until 1968. However, the national media attention the report brought to the case—it had the most extensive newspaper coverage of any lynching in US history—made a decisive contribution to the end of festival lynching in the South.[95]

The experience in Marianna changed Kester. Just days after his return from Florida, he wrote to his friend and fellow radical preacher Claude Williams, "The lynching and subsequent developments are among the most ghastly things in all the long history of lynching. My nerves were frayed. . . . I have not yet shaken the horror of the thing off my mind." The horror fueled his righteous anger and forged an even stronger link in his mind between the current class struggle and his increasingly Niebuhrian prophetic religion. "These cockeyed people who go about talking of love and good-will in the midst of all this oppression and hell make me pretty tired," he told Williams. "We won't love people into the Kingdom, we've got to bust this damn society to hell before love can find a place in it."[96]

The opportunity to join the fray was not long in coming. Only the day after the NAACP had released the report on Claude Neal's lynching, H. L. Mitchell, one of the leaders of the STFU, wrote to Kester, "I hope it will be possible for you to come over and spend a few days right away—we are going to face some more of the terror." Mitchell warned him of the danger. "Hell may pop at anytime now. If you decide to come over bring your artillery."[97] Both Norman Thomas, the leader of the Socialist Party, and Reinhold Niebuhr, the chair of CERJ, thought Kester should lend his support to the band of black and white sharecroppers and preachers facing down oppression and hell in the Delta.

In January 1935, an unarmed Kester said goodbye to Alice and baby Nancy and set off for Arkansas.[98]

*   *   *

Late Friday evening, January 17, 1936, the phone rang at 1700 Edgehill Avenue in Nashville. Alice Kester was tired. Nancy's nurse Eva Martin had left for the night, and she was on her own in the house with the two-year-old.[99] Howard had been gone since Monday, and she struggled when he wasn't there.[100] Since Wilder, Alice knew the danger her husband faced in his work. She admired her husband for his courage and convictions, but she worried about him.[101] She worried not only about the harm he might come to at the hands of his enemies but also over his health: the emotional strain of bearing witness to the horrors of lynching, beatings, evictions, sickness, and starvation brought on suffocating spells of asthma. He tried to write her a letter every day—if he mailed his letter in Memphis in the afternoon it arrived in Nashville the next day—and there were the occasional short, expensive phone calls.[102] He had been gone most of the last year working almost exclusively with STFU in the Arkansas Delta and traveling to the Northeast and Midwest as an ambassador and promoter for the fledgling union. She waited for those letters: the sign that Howard was safe. They were both sure that it was this "loneliness and nerve wracking strain" that brought on the debilitating pain in her shoulders.[103]

Alice had known, almost from the moment that she met him, that life with Howard would not be straightforward. That must have been part of the attraction. When she agreed to marry him—just three weeks after they met—Kester was on his way to spend a month at Tuskegee with his friend and mentor, the famous African American scientist George Washington Carver.[104] Howard's father had exploded when he heard the news: "If you go, don't ever come back."[105] Her own father had hardly reacted any better to his prospective son-in-law's radical views on religion, politics, and race. He had refused to come to their wedding, and over the years, both of their families struggled to understand the couple's ardent beliefs, socialist politics, and outlandish behavior.[106]

"I understand Mother and Sister perfectly and I love them just as much as ever and wish so much that I could convince them of the rightness of our position," Howard had tried to reassure Alice back in 1933. "Maybe after the denouement of capitalistic civilization they will understand and appreciate some of the things we have been talking about."[107] Sometimes Howard put it more bluntly: "our neighbors and our families . . . could not seem to understand why we associated with 'niggers and poor white trash.'"[108]

Before Nancy's birth, Alice had often traveled with Howard, organizing relief for miners' families and attending interracial conferences. Now she worked from home. Their house, just four blocks down the hill from Vanderbilt University, served as the office for CERJ as well as for the Friends of the Soil and the Fellowship of Southern Churchmen. Alice brought order to the chaos by serving as stenographer, secretary, bookkeeper, and editor. That week she had been getting their accounts for 1935 in order to send to CERJ's treasurer.[109]

When Alice answered the phone, it wasn't Howard as she hoped. It was a long-distance call from one of their friends in New York.

"Alice, how is Buck? Is there anything we can do to help?"

Alice had no idea what they were talking about.

"Norman Thomas read us the telegram at dinner. . . . We heard they almost lynched him. . . . No, we don't know any more than that."[110]

When she replaced the receiver, Alice was beside herself with concern.

It was around 10:30 p.m. when the operator placed her call to the STFU's office in Memphis.[111] Howard was there with Mitchell working feverishly in a haze of cigarette smoke on a press release.[112] Earlier that evening they had sent this telegram to Norman Thomas in New York:[113]

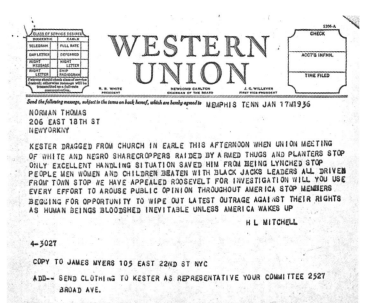

WESTERN UNION

MEMPHIS TENN JAN 17 M1936

NORMAN THOMAS
206 EAST 18TH ST
NEWYORKNY

KESTER DRAGGED FROM CHURCH IN EARLE THIS AFTERNOON WHEN UNION MEETING
OF WHITE AND NEGRO SHARECROPPERS RAIDED BY ARMED THUGS AND PLANTERS STOP
ONLY EXCELLENT HANDLING SITUATION SAVED HIM FROM BEING LYNCHED STOP
PEOPLE MEN WOMEN AND CHILDREN BEATEN WITH BLACK JACKS LEADERS ALL DRIVEN
FROM TOWN STOP WE HAVE APPEALED ROOSEVELT FOR INVESTIGATION WILL YOU USE
EVERY EFFORT TO AROUSE PUBLIC OPINION THROUGHOUT AMERICA STOP MEMBERS
BEGGING FOR OPPORTUNITY TO WIPE OUT LATEST OUTRAGE AGAINST THEIR RIGHTS
AS HUMAN BEINGS BLOODSHED INEVITABLE UNLESS AMERICA WAKES UP
                                    H L MITCHELL

4-3027

   COPY TO JAMES MYERS 105 EAST 22ND ST NYC

   ADD-- SEND CLOTHING TO KESTER AS REPRESENTATIVE YOUR COMMITTEE 2527
   BROAD AVE.

THE QUICKEST, SUREST AND SAFEST WAY TO SEND MONEY IS BY TELEGRAPH OR CABLE.

Relieved to hear Howard's voice, Alice was at the same time dismayed that she was the last person to find out what had happened; he had even thought to contact the president of the United States, but not her! Thirty-eight years later, Kester explained this failure. "My nerves were in tatters, and as [Mitchell and I] talked about the events of the afternoon, I forgot to call Alice."[114] Only a few hours earlier he had talked his way free from an angry group of planters armed with guns and a noose, but there was no calming Alice on the telephone.[115] Kester drove the two hundred miles to Nashville that night in his battered '32 Chevrolet, arriving home at four in the morning. They lit the fire, and in the early dawn, before their daughter awoke, Howard tried to reassure his wife. While he talked, Alice wept.[116]

*   *   *

Howard stayed with Alice and Nancy only a few days; after the weekend, he caught the train for a three-week tour of Washington, Baltimore, New York, and Philadelphia. He took with him the completed manuscript of *Revolt among the Sharecroppers* and was delighted when New York publishers Covici-Friede gave him a contract and promised to have it printed by March.[117] The *New York Post* issued him a press card in the hopes "that from time to time you'll be able to grab a spare moment to write a story for us."[118] Back in Nashville, Alice opened the flood of letters inviting Howard to speak about the plight of the sharecroppers. There were also the daily letters from her husband:

> I dream of you—really—every night. I do love you darling with all my heart and I will be glad when I can get back to you. . . .
>
> Give my darling Nancy a giant big hug for me and get her to hug you for daddy.[119]

Nineteen thirty-six marked the high-water mark of Kester's Christian socialist hopes that he was witnessing the birth pangs of a new society. He believed that he had found in the interracial, grassroots, faith-based activism of the STFU the "unalloyed faith" he sought in the lives of common men and women. "The Southern Tenant Farmers Union is a decisive answer to history and to segregationalists. Black men and white men *have* joined together in common cause against a common oppressor," he wrote in *Revolt among the Sharecroppers*.[120] "They know that the Galilean carpenter talked about the Kingdom of God on earth and they know that they alone can make his vision of brotherhood and justice a reality in this world."[121]

His was an agrarian vision, and he and Mitchell both believed in replacing the massive plantations and their armies of exploited tenants with smaller cooperative farms where those who tilled the soil truly shared in the profits.[122] He was excited when that summer, evangelist and social activist Sherwood Eddy came to Memphis and bought a cotton plantation in the Mississippi Delta for just such a purpose.[123] It was also the year that he was finally ordained, not by the Presbyterians—they had rejected him twice—but in the Congregational church. Far more than the union or Socialist Party, it was the community of ministers with which he primarily identified and into which he longed to be accepted. "The ordination was a sacred thing to me and my wife, and even our little girl seemed to understand what it meant to us," he wrote four years later.[124]

Now, as he believed capitalism was collapsing in ruins in the South, Kester imagined his growing network of like-minded clergy in the Fellowship of Southern Churchmen acting as spiritual first responders; they could be "a 'Preacher's Flying Squad' to go into mill villages and mining camps etc. and give . . . assistance to labor organizers and strikers."[125]

Meanwhile, Alice struggled to make ends meet on their "modest salary of $150 per month." They were paying Nancy's nurse one dollar per day (far above the going rate of $2.50 per week), and along with the rent and the cost of the car, there were the mounting medical bills.[126] There seemed to be no cure for the crippling pain in her shoulders.[127] The worry and pain stopped her sleeping. It was clear little Nancy was growing up not knowing her father, and Alice couldn't help her resentment building toward Howard, who had exciting and meaningful work while she was stuck in Nashville, her contribution to Howard's success unseen.[128]

Alice made Howard aware of her struggles, often through tearful exchanges over long-distance phone calls. "I cannot tell you how broken hearted I was to hear your sad voice over the phone," he typed from Memphis ten days before Christmas.[129] He could not, however, see any alternative arrangement for his work or their family.

> I cannot forever go this way. Trying to do a job, trying to do the best I can by you and Nancy and being forever torn, frustrated. . . . I want to come home now but to do so will simply cause me to love you less. . . . By trying to help others—by trying to make a better social order I feel that I am doing most for Nancy and for all those who are to follow. I believe that she would live to despise me if I failed to go out and work for them as I work for her and you.[130]

Alice's duty was clear to Howard: "Nancy must have a home, a mother to care for her. These are indispensable. She has some rights. If I cannot give them to her then you must."[131]

As the year turned, Kester's hopes started unraveling. The Delta Cooperative farm, already a business failure, threatened to fall apart as an experiment in interracial cooperation; he watched in dismay as the well-meaning white pillars of Christian socialism—lacking his own remarkable empathy and experience—were unaware of their own racist paternalism. Despite their talk of a cooperative, the farm's trustees imposed a top-down decision making process, appointed whites to the management positions, and treated the cooperative's members little differently than the sharecroppers on neighboring plantations. The black families threatened to walk off the farm.[132] Depression cloyed to Kester like the farm's buckshot clay. After another tearful phone conversation with Alice, Howard confessed, "I wish that I could write joyous letters to you but it doesn't seem to be in me any more. . . . I don't seem to have the inspiration and courage I once had and everything seems to be in a whirling mess."[133] Even as he was "tired," "restless," "uncertain," and "distant and out of tune," he kept working.

In April, Walter White asked Kester to investigate a double lynching in Duck Hill, Mississippi.[134] He produced a devastating report for the NAACP, but the stress of the investigation and the horror he uncovered literally and figuratively took his breath away.[135] What Kester encountered in the piney woods of Mississippi—"The mob's insatiable appetite for brutality and blood"—he could no longer simply explain as the violent outworking of a class struggle.[136] This was evil, pure and personal, and rooted in the human heart. Kester was suffering from asthma and mental and physical exhaustion, and the doctor ordered him to take a break.[137]

In May, the family, with the support of CERJ's committee, took a long vacation. Howard went fishing.[138] Then he went back to work. But the fall brought more disappointment. In September the STFU, against Kester's advice, voted to join the United Cannery, Agricultural, Packing, and Allied Workers of America and the Congress of Industrial Organizations (CIO). Kester feared the vote opened the union to communist infiltration and saw it as threatening the interracial and religious foundations of the STFU that he loved and fought so hard to maintain.[139]

*   *   *

It was in the company of the Fellowship of Southern Churchmen (FSC) that Kester found his work and renewed his strength. The members saw themselves as God's prophets: isolated Protestant

Elijahs (mostly white, mostly men) scattered from Texas to Virginia—a region with churches that had "bowed the knee to Baal." Rolling off the mimeograph machine at 1700 Edgehill Avenue—its handle cranked by Alice—came these words of encouragement: "Carmel days are gone; the fire is spent; victory has turned into ashes; inspiration has given way to inertia. Then it is that a prophet needs the double assurance of God's grace and the knowledge that other fellow mortals are still loyal to Him and His cause."[140]

The work with the Fellowship seemed to Kester to be going somewhere—the membership rolls grew slowly and it offered him a spiritual home and identity in a way that the ever-shifting politics and fratricidal infighting of the labor unions and the Socialist Party did not.

Years later, in conversation with the journalist John Egerton, Kester talked about his work with the FSC. "This to me was really the only thing I ever wanted to do. I had lost faith in the promises of politics, unionism, and the organized church. The kind of healing the nation needed wouldn't come through politics or economic organization—basically, there had to be an ethical orientation, a moral confrontation, based on the teachings of Jesus and the principles of democracy."[141]

In 1939, Kester wrote this poetic manifesto to explain the hope of the Fellowship and to inspire others to join their cause:

> We believe that Jesus was the greatest realist of all times. In his life we find that way of life for which man in his moments of sanity and in his evening of dreams longs and yearns. In his life we find the only certain answer for the injustice and brutality, the sham and hypocrisy, the evil and sin about us.
>
> We believe that the will of God will be done on earth and that his Kingdom will be established among men. Toward the realization of this goal—even in the midst of chaos and confusion, moral disintegration and spiritual blindness—we set our hands and our hearts.[142]

Kester in his writing, preaching, and organizing consistently tried to inspire and then maintain this connection between hands and hearts, sanity and dreams, action and faith. Christians, he preached, must be "dreamers and doers." He no longer agreed with Reinhold Niebuhr (if he ever had) that you could not apply Jesus's "law of love" directly to political situations. "If our faith has not gone out we shall make operational now in material and spiritual terms the life-giving forces of our Faith. The Word must again become flesh in an age of machines and power."[143]

But the Word becoming flesh is a tricky business. Back in his days at Princeton, Kester briefly considered the celibate life and serving the poor as a modern-day disciple of St. Francis. He soon gave up that idea, deciding "it was more natural and difficult for a man to marry and have a family with the home as the center of his life and still do what St. Francis demanded of his disciples."[144] But he had failed to maintain his home and family at the center of his life: he spent most of his time away from his wife and daughter. Back in December 1936, Howard had written to Alice, "What am I to do in the light of all the forces tearing at me? I think sometimes that I will go mad trying to resolve my two loves."[145]

In the fall of 1938, Howard, Alice, and four-year-old Nancy packed up their house in Nashville and moved three hundred miles west into the Blue Ridge Mountains of North Carolina. They had bought five acres in High Top Colony, just a short hike from the YMCA's Blue Ridge conference center, where they had first met twelve years before. The land had a house on it, though it was not much more than a shack and there was no source of water. It was good enough for camping out in the summer but no place to raise a family year-round, so they moved into rented accommodations in Black Mountain to see out the winter. The chamber of commerce boasted that at 2,400 feet, their "mountain paradise" of a town was "mosquito free" with "mountain pure water."[146] Kester hoped that getting away from the smoke and the summer heat of Nashville—not to mention the high rent—would be much better for

Alice's tenuous health. He also had plans to build a new house on the property, where they would live permanently and could host students and members of the Fellowship.[147] Most significantly, Howard and Alice agreed that the long periods of separation were over; whenever possible, they would travel and work together.[148]

*   *   *

In 1983, in her fiftieth year, Nancy Kester Neale sat down with sociologist Dallas Blanchard and his tape recorder. Every other weekend, Nancy, a professor of social work at Appalachian State University, drove with her husband, Russell, up to "Piney Moors," the house in the mountains with its stone fireplace and wide front porch that had taken her father twenty years to finish. The house stood empty the rest of the time: it was thirteen years since her mother's death and six since her father's.

As Blanchard listened and the tape rolled, Nancy shared one of her earliest memories. It was from January 1939. She was riding in an old-fashioned car, her parents sitting in the front. She was "all bunched up by myself in the backseat with cartons of Vicks Vapor-Rubs. We had all of these little cartons and my feet were all up." The drive seemed interminable to the young girl; "We rode for hours and hours." She remembered looking out of the window at the children living by the side of the road. "I would want to get out and play with the children. My mother wouldn't let me because they had terrible colds, and running sores. And I would cry because I wanted to play with the children and I was lonesome." The children she longed to play with were among the seventeen hundred Missouri sharecroppers who were camping out in a roadside protest along Highway 61 south of Sikeston in southeast Missouri. Given the stark choice by the landlords to either work as wage laborers or get off the plantations, they had followed the call of their charismatic black preacher, Rev. Owen H. Whitfield: "If we're gonna starve, let's starve right out on the highway so the whole world can see!"[149] The Kesters had no intention of letting anyone starve; representing the Fellowship of Southern Churchmen, they became a conduit for aid that came pouring in from all over the country.[150] Setting up union relief headquarters in Blytheville, Arkansas, they coordinated the transportation of food and clothing to the protestors.[151] Recalling that cold Missouri winter, Nancy said: "I learned a lot about poverty. About what it looked like and what it felt like, and what my parents were doing— what we as a family were doing. I felt a part of that."[152]

Here, in the memories of his daughter, Kester's restless quest for the true essence of Christianity—"that way of life for which man in his moments of sanity and in his evening of dreams longs and yearns"—finds its grail.

ELLA BAKER

(1903–1986)

Miss Ella Baker, September 18, 1941. Afro Newspaper / Gado / Getty Images.

WE WHO BELIEVE IN FREEDOM

Ella Baker's Creed

Nichole M. Flores

Five women sit in a semicircle on a stage in a crowded auditorium, wearing brilliant, rainbow-colored garments. The crowd falls silent as the cantor's voice fills the air, summoning the other women to prayer. One by one, each woman joins the chorus, and they plait their voices into a complex tapestry. The women clap and sway; the crowd joins in. Their voices weave a prophet's mantle, lush and lavender. They crescendo and converge, enfolding the room in a cloak of sound: "We who believe in freedom cannot rest until it comes!"[1]

This is "Ella's Song," inspired by the words and witness of Miss Ella Josephine Baker (1903–1986), a magisterial authority of the civil rights movement and a witness to true human freedom. The song's writer, Bernice Johnson Reagon said, "When we sing, we announce our existence." "Ella's Song" announces the existence of those who are often made invisible in our society: black people, poor people, young people, and women. More than announcing existence, says Reagon, the act of singing embodies a new way of being. "You cannot sing a song and not change your condition."[2] "Ella's Song" shines a light on Baker's belief in freedom and justice, but it also changes the condition of those who sing this song. It changes their hearts. It changes their actions. It becomes their creed.

119

"Ella's Song" became my own social justice creed in the summer of 2007. I spent three months working as an intern with the University of the Poor, one of several organizational inheritors of the Poor People's Campaign inaugurated during the civil rights movement.[3] I had one main assignment for this internship: get to know the organizers by listening to their stories. In New York, I listened to the experiences of housing justice organizers working under conditions of extreme inequality. In Ohio, I heard stories from deaf community organizers working to build coalitions for economic justice. In Florida, I attended to farmworker narratives of harrowing migration experiences and economic exploitation in agricultural fields. These stories revealed the extent to which human freedom, dignity, and just community are violated in our society. But they also demonstrated the power of ordinary people to defend these values by building relationships and working for justice. This was my first encounter with Miss Baker's mission: weaving together a tapestry of freedom and community through encounter with people's lives.

A creed is a statement of firmly held belief. Creeds are often recited and memorized. But they only become real when we live them out, when we put them into practice. "Ella's Song" is Miss Baker's creed: it's a statement of her firmly held belief in freedom. Her creed is at once deeply democratic and profoundly Christian, leading her to insist that special concern for "the least of these" (Matthew 25) and "lifting up the lowly" (Luke 1) are spiritual priorities as well as social and political ones.

Baker's creed resonates today, when many people are frustrated with the state of both US democracy and Christianity. Many suspect our democratic institutions are rigged against us, run by financial behemoths, and entrenched in special interests and in hierarchical power structures rather than guided by the will of the people. Many have also lost faith in the church to stand up against rigged institutions and powerful interests, suspecting that the church fears losing its own social position and political power.

For those tempted to lose hope in these institutions, Baker's life and witness offer a way forward. In a time of democratic doubt, she shows us a path of shared leadership and genuine human equality. In a time when the church so often fails to live up to its own best teaching, she reminds us of the power of our baptism to change our hearts and orient our actions. Baker's witness revives our hope in ordinary people to light the path toward authentic freedom.

*   *   *

Symbols point beyond themselves to deeper and more complex realities. They can highlight that which is most prominent or significant about an idea, a person, or a movement. Shaping imagination through imagery, symbols are capable of uniting people around a shared cause or idea.

While several leaders of the civil rights movements have become symbolic of the struggle, none is more iconic than Martin Luther King Jr. His image has become synonymous with strong leadership: a stern man of purpose in a crisp suit with a booming voice, admonishing the congregation from a high pulpit, a leader who marches at the front of the crowd. For many, King symbolized an ideal of leadership as being the work of a singular, authoritative man.

Baker has become a very different icon of leadership. To be sure, Baker was a skilled public speaker and often exerted her influence through captivating addresses. But she was more at home conversing in a circle of folding chairs than pontificating from a dais. She was wary of putting on a show for the cameras, and she saw the pursuit of personal attention as a hindrance to the movement. "You didn't see me on television," she once said. "You didn't see news stories about me. The kind of role that I tried to play was to pick up pieces or put pieces together out of which I hoped organization might come. My theory is, strong people don't need strong leaders." Where King became a symbol of strong, centralized moral direction, Baker's radically democratic style of leadership fostered a community where everyone was a leader. Stokely Carmichael, a community organizer in the Student Nonviolent Coordinating Committee (SNCC), once declared that Baker, not King, was "the most powerful person in the struggle for justice."[4]

*   *   *

Born December 13, 1903, in Norfolk, Virginia, Baker was raised in Littleton, North Carolina. The granddaughter of former slaves, she was raised amid communal memories of the atrocity of slavery. "I grew up with grandparents who talked to me a lot," she recalled, passing on their stories of resisting slavery for the sake of authentic freedom.[5] Baker heard the story of her grandmother, Betsy Ross, who refused to go along with the master and mistress's plan to have her marry for the sole purpose of breeding light skinned slaves. She refused to be handled like livestock. As punishment for her disobedience, Ross was banished from the house to toil in the fields. This punishment did not devastate her: "As the story goes, she plowed all day, and when there were social occasions, she danced all night to demonstrate her unbroken spirit."[6] Ross was determined not just to survive slavery's attempt to dominate her body and spirit, but to thrive in ways that could not be undone by this cruel system.

Baker's grandfather, Mitchell Ross, became a pastor after emancipation. Yet his deepest joy was in cultivating fresh food for his family and friends. He had vivid memories of the meager diet he consumed during bondage, a life of constant emptiness. He possessed a visceral aversion to the foods associated with captivity. "He could not eat corn bread as such," Baker once said. "He wouldn't let his wife even force the children to eat the corn bread."[7] After slavery, he was determined to give his family a sense of fullness that was denied to him for so long. He purchased a portion of the land on which he had been enslaved and planted a garden on it. Baker remembered tending the garden as a child:

"We had a big garden, much too big for the size of the family. I'd pick a bushel or more [of green peas], and we didn't need them, so you'd give them to the neighbors who didn't have them. That's the way you did. It was no hassle about it. I don't think it ever occurred to our immediate family to indoctrinate children against sharing. Because they had the privilege of growing up where they'd raised a lot of food. They were never hungry. They could share their food with people. And so you shared your lives with people."[8]

Mitchell Ross's love for sharing in community had a profound effect on his family. Anna Baker, Ella Baker's mother, engaged in mission work in service of those in need. "Miss Anna" was renowned for her generosity. "She shared from the family's relative prosperity, giving milk, fruit, eggs, and vegetables generously for the community's sick; and she gave special attention to poor women giving birth."[9] When they weren't tending the garden, Ella Baker and her siblings worked alongside their mother helping those in need.

Her grandparents' stories of slavery and her mother's devoted mission work developed in Baker a keen understanding of the gifts of freedom, dignity, and community. She appreciated that it was an ongoing challenge to secure and sustain them.

*   *   *

At the age of nine, Baker attended a revival at which two of her cousins confessed their sins in preparation for baptism. Not wanting to be left out, she and her brother, Curtis, decided that they should get baptized, too. "We weren't very dramatic about it," she once reflected, "but we were ready for baptism, and all four of us were baptized at the same time in the old mill pond."[10] While she didn't offer an intensely emotional account of the experience, she did see it as personally transformative: "I took the position that you were supposed to change after baptism."[11] This change meant owning her faults and always striving to be more like Jesus. "I was very quick-tempered. . . . And so this was my way of demonstrating my change, by trying to control my temper."[12]

In Baker's view, baptism called the baptized not only into personal change but also into the work of eradicating sin from society. She did not enter the ministry like her grandparents or do missionary work like her mother. Instead, her faith pulled her toward the work of social justice: "I was young when I became active in things and I became active in things largely because my mother was very active in the field of religion."[13] Her activism was imbued with biblical awareness: respecting the image of God in all people, lifting up the lowly, and caring for the least of these.

An exceptional student with a sharp intellect and a gift for rhetoric, Baker was a member of her high school debate team and earned the honor of valedictorian in both her high school and college classes. Instructed by her family's ministerial practice and her own experience serving those in great need, Baker aspired to serve as a medical missionary. While medicine was not to be her vocation, she would find that social activism was another high calling that required her righteous mind and rhetorical power in the endless work of lifting up the lowly (Luke 1:52).

She loved ideas and believed in their power to persuade others. Good ideas change minds. Good ideas break chains. The best response to a bad idea is a good one. Miss Baker didn't fear different ideas; she embraced them. She sought to empower ordinary people to share their best ideas with each other. "The problem in the South is not radical thought," she once said. "The problem is not even conservative thought. The problem in the South is not enough thought."[14] Racism is a bad idea that can only be brought down by a better one. Freedom will win because it is a great idea.

Christianity is often viewed as a conservative intellectual force. For Miss Baker, however, it catalyzed her exploration of radical social ideas. She had been disenchanted by her experience at Shaw University, which she found intellectually old-fashioned and committed to preserving the social status quo. Moving to Harlem after college, Baker found herself entangled in a "hot bed of radical thinking." The ideas she encountered there intrigued her even if she needed time "to hear and evaluate whether or not this was the kind of thing you wanted to get into."[15] Her membership at Friendship Baptist Church allowed her to remain grounded in Christian community even as she explored new ideas and revised previous positions.

Beyond the realm of ideas and debate, however, Baker felt deeply moved by the pervasive poverty she witnessed in the city. For the first time, she saw people "actually waiting on the breadline, for coffee and handouts."[16] The masses of hungry people were a stark contrast to her own experiences of abundance on her grandfather's farm. It was this encounter with poverty that precipitated her involvement with the Young Negroes' Cooperative League. This organization promoted cooperative buying and community development to alleviate suffering caused by the Great Depression. In this sense, her radical social ideas were consistent with the vision of Christian community that she had formed in her youth while working in her grandfather's garden.

It was also at this time that Baker began to use her considerable intellectual gifts to campaign for freedom. Working as a journalist in the late 1920s and 1930s, she advocated against the exploitation of black domestic workers in New York City. Baker teamed up with fellow journalist and socialist labor activist Marvel Cooke to expose the horrendous conditions facing domestic workers at the Bronx Slave Market: "Rain or shine, cold or hot, you will find them there—Negro women, old and young—sometimes bedraggled, sometimes neatly dressed—but with the invariable paper bundle, waiting expectantly for Bronx housewives to buy their strength and energy for an hour, two hours, or even for a day at the munificent rate of fifteen, twenty, twenty-five, or, if luck be with them, thirty cents an hour. If not the wives themselves, maybe their husbands, their sons, or their brothers, under the subterfuge of work, offer worldly-wise girls higher bids for their time."[17] At the market, white housewives scrutinized black women domestics for rent, inspecting their knees for calluses as evidence that they scrubbed floors.[18] Like Baker's grandmother Betsy during ante-bellum slavery, these women were handled like livestock valued only for their physical capacities. This abuse reinscribed the logic of domination that governed the institution of slavery.

To see slavery's resurgence must have infuriated Baker. Along with Cooke, Baker poured her righteous anger into writing their article on the slave market. They produced a searing journalistic classic that shed light on this atrocious abuse of human dignity. But at one moment of their article, anger veers toward an ethnic and religious resentment uncharacteristic of Baker. The authors refer to one of the women buyers as a "squatty Jewish housewife," employing demeaning language to describe a woman who had shown them great disrespect during their investigation of the market. Christian ethicist Traci West highlights the disturbing nature of this comment: "when Baker and Cooke describe 'a squatty Jewish housewife' who examines them and then questions them about work, their reference to the Jewishness of the housewife seems unnecessary except as a way of invoking a derogatory stereotype."[19]

How might we interpret this kind of remark coming from the pen of a woman devoted to human dignity and equality? The story should be understood in light of Baker's baptism, which inaugurated for her a constant pursuit of a disposition toward freedom. Baker had a "lifelong concern to overcome 'contradictions' between professed belief and practice."[20] This disposition required Baker to examine her conscience and confess her sins, renewing her commitment to the ongoing pursuit of freedom. Indeed, speaking truth to herself was necessary preparation for learning to speak truth to power. Change doesn't happen in an instant. Freedom is a habit, one requiring constant practice.

*   *   *

A petite woman with a sonorous voice, Baker had a distinctive sartorial style, donning neat suits and pillbox hats. Julian Bond of the SNCC described her as "pleasingly prim and benignly schoolmarmish, formal but not rigid, proper and proud but not arrogant."[21] She matched elocution with diction; she could strike up a conversation with a politician, a pastor, a factory worker, or a farmworker without ever seeming out of place. It was common in Baker's time for white people in the South to refer to all black people by their first names, regardless of their age or status. White people, of course, were to be referred to by their formal title. But no one who knew Baker called her Ella. Reflecting on her earliest encounters with the civil rights movement, Mary King observed this pattern of addressing Ella Baker: "I was soon to realize that everyone called Ella Baker, whether present or not, 'Miss Baker.' It was an expression of respect for this mature woman of stature. . . . Even though many in the movement knew her well, the acute sensitivity in the black community to this universal offense was reflected in the way she was addressed. I don't remember anyone familiarly calling her 'Ella.'"[22]

People stood up taller when Miss Baker entered a room. Her presence was commanding but understated, a force of nature in sensible shoes. Her no-nonsense style permitted her to focus on what mattered to her the most: the cultivation of a freedom movement fueled by the collective power of people.

Baker's concern for propriety permitted her to assert well-defined boundaries around her private life. Naturally reserved, she was reticent to volunteer information about her home life even to close friends who were deeply involved in the movement. Some members of the movement didn't know that she was married. Others knew better than to ask her too many questions about it.[23] Interviewing Baker in 1977, Sue Thrasher and Casey Hayden breached this boundary when they asked a question about her marriage. Baker laughed, replying, "Don't ask too many personal questions now."[24] They knew better than to press further.

While not often interested in talking about herself, she did value building authentic, charitable relationships with others. Her upbringing imbued her with an appreciation of the power of personal relationships, and she was wholeheartedly invested in nurturing them. She enjoyed meeting new people and heeding their stories: "Hello brother, and where do you hail from?"[25] Baker met people on their own terms, seeking partnerships with potential allies rather than enemies or even personal disciples. This ability positioned her to be an empowering force in the lives of those who would drive the civil rights movement: young people with the courage to stand up both to their oppressors and to hierarchical forces within the movement that sought to constrain their best ideas from becoming reality.

*   *   *

Baker's most significant work, both in terms of her historical legacy and personal fulfillment, was with young people. While Baker was a serious young person with an innate maturity—her grandfather called her "Grand Lady" because she was a great conversationalist even as a child—she had a natural sympathy for young people and their causes.[26] As an undergraduate student at Shaw University, Baker led protests for the right of female and male students to walk across campus together and for women to be able to wear silk stockings. She took on these causes despite not dating frequently or wearing silk stockings herself because she saw them as important expression of young people learning to secure and defend their liberty and autonomy.[27]

Her value for the perspectives and energy of young people reflects the foundational concern of Christian liberation theology: the preferential option for the poor and young. This principle highlights God's special concern for the least of these and desire to lift up the lowly. The preferential option does not mean that poor people and young people are more moral than other people, nor does it mean that God loves the poor and the young more than other people. Rather, this theology emphasizes the unique vulnerability of children and those suffering from material poverty who typically lack influence in social, economic, and political structures. It also acknowledges the special social, economic, and political power of these groups. Since they do not benefit from the unjust status quo, they have crucial insight into how to change it. These are the people who move freedom forward.

Baker exercised her preference for the poor and young in the face of tremendous pressure to mute her advocacy. Baker's conflict with the rest of the movement leadership came to a head in the debate over the organizational relationship between the SNCC and the Southern Christian Leadership Conference (SCLC). Whereas the SNCC represented the interests of students in the movement, the SCLC was led by the ministerial establishment. The student-led sit-ins resulted in hundreds of student arrests, raising questions among the SCLC's leadership about what role students ought to play in the movement. The leadership wished to capitalize on student energies while minimizing risks. They thought they could provide more supervision and stability by incorporating them as the youth arm of their own organization. But Baker saw the situation differently. She believed that the students needed space to develop their own voices, their own relationships, and their own agenda.

In 1960, Baker organized a caucus in Raleigh, North Carolina, to bring together the student leaders of the sit-ins with other movement leaders. A savvy politician, she knew she would have to promote and defend independent student leadership at this meeting. She suggested that James Lawson, who had been expelled from Vanderbilt University for his participation in the sit-ins, should serve as the caucus presider. While the SCLC leadership accepted Lawson's appointment, it became clear to Baker that the established leaders wanted to incorporate the SNCC into the SCLC's own structure. She resisted this move, resolutely stating her opposition to this hierarchical model of leadership. "She was furious at the temper of the discussion and outraged by the ministers' plans to manipulate the students. The sit-ins were, to her, the beginning of a new approach to the fight for equality. She did not want to see it co-opted, corrupted, or changed. She felt that the students had something new to offer and to make the students movement the youth arm of an adult organization was a mistake."[28] She refused to permit the student's efforts, including their leadership during the sit-ins, to become window dressing to the work of the ministerial establishment. When SCLC leaders persisted in their attempt, Baker walked out of the caucus.

Her action shook the caucus and the entire movement. "Baker's departure [from the caucus] signaled the beginning of a new phase for the civil rights movement. It was no longer controlled by a stodgy ministerial or bureaucratic presence. It was to be led by a new force."[29]

Despite Baker's anger over the SCLC's plan, she acted in good faith; she refused to twist arms to make the vote fall her way. Certainly, the SCLC possessed indispensable resources and political access that offered foundation and structure to the movement as a whole. Yet Baker maintained a position that became a hallmark of her Christian witness: there would be no movement without empowering and prioritizing the young people. The relationship between the SCLC and the SNCC remained tense, but the SNCC did continue as a student-led organization.

While Baker supported the students in their efforts, she insisted that the movement was about larger issues than lunch counters; it was about "more than a hamburger and a Coke."[30] True freedom required learning to treat others with dignity and equality outside of the realms of economics and politics. It was about teaching others to love freedom and to do the work required to sustain it. Baker considered human equality to be a divine calling, a state that was good for its own sake. And she offered the students another perspective on their organizing without dousing the flames of the passionate pursuit of their own most important issues and campaigns.

Baker didn't just teach the content of freedom to the students; she modeled what was required to live an authentically free life. This authenticity was key to her advocacy. "What was nice about Miss Baker," according to one SNCC worker, "is you never felt that she had a personal agenda that she was trying to put on. It was always about what is good for the organization, for black people, for whatever the larger issue was. [With] other adults you never really knew what was hidden."[31]

*   *   *

Despite her preference for a quiet life, Baker often found herself on the frontlines of intense public conflicts, putting to use the rhetorical prowess she demonstrated as a student. The story of her advocacy for racial justice at the 1964 Mississippi Freedom Democratic Party (MFDP) state convention reveals her unique capacity to speak truth to power.

Formed in opposition to the Mississippi Democratic Party (which only allowed for participation by whites), the MFDP opposed polling taxes, literacy tests, and other unjust barriers to black enfranchisement. Yet while the MFDP aimed to challenge the Democratic establishment, their convention was not free from racial conflict. Baker observed that black lives were still valued less than white ones, as evidenced by scant attention given to the slaughter of black people relative to the deaths of white civil rights workers. According to Bernice Johnson Reagon, Baker was dismayed by this blatant disrespect for God-given dignity: "She was talking about the Civil Rights movement workers who had been murdered in Mississippi in 1964. And as they searched for the bodies of the three missing workers, they turned up bodies of black men in the rivers of Mississippi that nobody had searched for because they were black and they did not get killed with white men. She was angry about that."[32]

Speaking immediately before Baker at the convention, the party's lawyer had belittled the black conference attendees by referring to them as "you people." This common but insulting phrase impelled Baker to rebuke his language. With the bodies of black men lying on the bottom of a river on her mind, Baker proclaimed to the delegates what was at stake in their struggle: "Until the killing of black mothers' sons becomes as important to the rest of the country as the killing of white mothers' sons, we who believe in freedom cannot rest."[33] Those gathered at the convention responded to her words with shouts of "Freedom! Freedom!"[34]

Baker understood the connection between grassroots advocacy and electoral politics. Full black enfranchisement, as Baker saw it, was necessary for passing laws and building institutions that valued black lives. She viewed black politics as a crucial step in balancing the scales of justice. Although the SNCC had initially pursued political ends away from the ballot box, the MFDP convention signaled a growing awareness of the potential to link political action to changing power dynamics:

> Yes, they could break down the barriers of segregated water fountains and lunch counters—so why not win the right to vote, to have a voice in who became the sheriff or mayor or town council member? ... All along the way Baker kept them focused on the need for education—they must have knowledge of how to use the system—but primarily she emphasized the need to develop local leaders and local movements. Perhaps she was personally responsible for the birth of the MFDP, because she had stressed so heavily the need to nurture local leadership.[35]

This was one of Baker's most valuable contributions to the civil rights movement—that education must always look beyond personal advancement to the cultivation of citizenship and democratic participation. Baker's affirmation of black dignity and political empowerment is the cornerstone of her legacy in democratic life in the United States. This legacy is especially evident in Black Lives Matter, the contemporary inheritor of Baker's democratic advocacy for the dignity of black lives.

*   *   *

Social justice activists of many causes have taken up "Ella's Song" as their creed, announcing their firmly held belief in women's rights, empowerment of young people, and a democratic culture characterized by equality and shared power. Yet it is important to remember that the animating content of the speech that inspired the song was the violation of black dignity. If singing songs has the power to change our condition, then singing "Ella's Song" can help us to learn the inherent value of black life.

"Ella's Song" became a renewed rallying cry for justice in February 2012 when Trayvon Martin was shot to death by George Zimmerman while walking home from a convenience store. Zimmerman's acquittal uncovered festering legacies of racism and antiblackness in a society that many thought to be "color blind."

Zimmerman's trial was a grotesque spectacle. The burden of proof fell to Martin, lying silently in his grave, to demonstrate that an unarmed teenager carrying a bag of Skittles and an Arizona Iced Tea did not present a threat to an adult man armed with a gun. That Martin was treated as the defendant rather than Zimmerman accentuated blatant antiblackness in a justice system purportedly intended to serve and protect all members of society.

Attention to the issue did not fade when the news cycle ended. This was the beginning of Black Lives Matter and, more broadly, the Movement for Black Lives. Activists formed in Baker's tradition started connecting the dots between all of the young, unarmed, black people killed at the hands of law enforcement officials in the United States. Protests erupted in Ferguson, Missouri, when Michael Brown was shot to death by Darren Wilson. Like Martin, Brown was required to demonstrate his innocence after being compared to a "demon"[36] by the white police officer who shot and killed him and declared to have been "no angel"[37] by the media. This pattern is repeated with each new death, a fresh reminder that black lives matter less in our society than white lives.

These movements have been criticized for their fundamental claim that black lives matter. "Don't all lives matter?" some ask. "What about police officers; don't their lives matter?" These questions miss the movement's guiding thesis: proclaiming that black lives matter is necessary because black lives have been treated as worthless. That black lives matter is a simple theological truth. That some in society cannot affirm this truth is why it still needs to be said.

Baker's voice echoes in the advocacy for black life in the twenty-first century. We can hear her song in the cries for mercy and justice coming from young people who fear losing their own lives at the hands of law enforcement or vigilantes simply for being black. We can feel her grief in the cries of mothers and fathers who have lost their children to this violence.

Baker also shows the way forward for those who want to eradicate racism from American society. She shows us that sharing our bounty with our neighbors builds a strong community. She teaches us to love good ideas even when they are new or unfamiliar. She demonstrates that loving our neighbors requires that we listen to their stories. She reveals that humility and self-critique are the friends of courage and power. She reminds us that believing in freedom means committing oneself to a lifetime of struggle to make it a reality.

In loving memory of Ella Jo Baker, witness to authentic freedom.

Dorothy Day

(1897–1980)

Young Dorothy Day reading at home. Courtesy of the Department of Special Collections and University Archives, Marquette University Libraries.

The Conflict
of Flesh and Spirit

A Reading of Dorothy Day

Carlene Bauer

There is a photograph of a teenaged Dorothy Day reading at home. She is stretched out on a couch in a white dress, holding a book whose title is unclear, while light coming in from a window shrouds the room in a kind of Sunday or summer haze. Her face, with lowered eyelids, suggests that the book has cast a spell, and her mind seems to be acquiescing to whatever is on the page.

At this moment, the girl in the picture, taken in a house on Webster Avenue in Chicago,[1] appears content, but in fact she was host to a clash of yearnings. What should the content of her dreams be, and how best to make them a reality? Is it God she wants? Or the masses? Or a grand undying romance?

Day's life before she entered the Catholic Church was defined by this struggle to reconcile flesh with spirit—to reconcile reality with dreams, and earthly happiness with spiritual happiness. The struggle took many forms. Should she demonstrate or write novels? Should she be content with personal happiness or join a larger movement for change? Love one man in particular or love God?

Before she could answer these questions, Day would experience three major conflicts between flesh and spirit: one as an adolescent, the second in her early twenties, and the last just as she was turning thirty. These were decisive moments in which she set aside previously held ideals in order to gain a surer foothold on some sort of stabilizing truth. As a teenager, she felt torn between the spiritual yearning she'd felt in her heart since childhood and the radical movement she'd started to read about. In her very early twenties, she felt torn between her radical commitments and her increasing sense that the idealizing of those commitments had led her to a tormenting "disorderly life," as she would later call it.[2] And as she approached thirty, newly a mother, moving closer to feeling at peace, she longed as she did in her youth for God, but the man she loved did not believe in him.

Only when she finally converted to Catholicism did these struggles settle just enough to allow her to see a road leading away from them, and the girl lost in a book grew up to become one of the twentieth century's most celebrated activists. In New York City in 1933, Day founded the *Catholic Worker* newspaper and its houses of hospitality, where volunteers lived side by side with the men and women they fed and gave shelter to, and began a movement that fought for workers' rights and civil rights, for an end to nuclear disarmament and to the Vietnam War.[3] It was through Catholicism and through the *Worker* that Day was able to lessen the tensions that had held her captive. The *Worker* provided a way to articulate both her political commitments and her spiritual beliefs, and the church provided her with a vocabulary that allowed her to speak of the ways the material world served as a witness to the divine.

This version of Day's story begins with the girl lost in a book and her desire to find a house to worship in. She had always known religious feeling, but since her parents did not have much use for organized religion, she'd never had a formal outlet for what had stirred within her, so she made do by conscripting her younger sister, Della, to play at being saints with her.[4] At twelve, however, a more regular home for her infant faith appeared when an Episcopal minister canvassing her Chicago neighborhood convinced her mother, who had been raised Episcopalian, to send her and her siblings to church.[5] So Dorothy, along with some of her siblings, went every Sunday, and was eventually baptized and confirmed there.[6]

But her true church at this time might have been reading. "I have always been a journalist and a diarist pure and simple, but as long as I could remember, I dreamed in terms of novels," Day wrote in *The Long Loneliness*.[7] In that house on Webster Avenue, she read novel after novel, and poems, and anything she could get her hands on. She read Thomas DeQuincey, Victor Hugo, and Charles Dickens—the latter would remain a companion all her life.[8] She read Edgar Allan Poe, James Fenimore Cooper, and Robert Louis Stevenson.[9] She read John Wesley's sermons after she read George Eliot's *Adam Bede* and *The Mill on the Floss*,[10] and it was the heroine of *The Mill on the Floss* who introduced her to another book she would return to over and over. Day first picked up *The Imitation of Christ*, she once wrote, because Maggie Tulliver did.[11]

She plowed through romance novels and her brothers' dime store novels, both of which she had to hide from her father, who disapproved of his children reading what he called "trash."[12] And yet he needn't have worried about the effects of that trash. Day, ever the populist, read everything, even the children's literature of the day, for a trace of what she called "spiritual adventure."[13] Looking back in her diaries at the age of seventy-two, Day wrote, "I think I have always read looking for the serious themes that draw men to noble deeds, to self-sacrifice, to a greater love of others. Even the most frivolous literature. I began to realize the seriousness implied in the word 'duty' for instance in a love story I read when I was 14." That love story? It concerned a nurse in the Klondike torn between two of her patients.[14]

Her reading at this time confirmed her in her religious tendencies, but it also set her on the path that would lead to her radical reporting and activism. She had become aware of the labor movement through her brother Don's job at a leftist newspaper,[15] and this led her away from love stories and toward writings by the anarchist Peter Kropotkin, whose book *Mutual Aid* argued that cooperation and not competition drove evolution.[16] She learned about Eugene Debs. She read Jack London's fiction, along with his essays on the class struggle, and Upton Sinclair's *The Jungle*.[17]

The girl who read also walked, and on those walks she became, as she would write in her diaries, converted to the poor.[18] In 1912, when she was fourteen, the last Day child, her baby brother John, was born, and she would take him on long walks in his carriage over to Chicago's West Side.[19] Those walks woke her up to a possible vocation. The desire to take part in some high endeavor—some spiritual adventure—now found a focus in a desire to change the world. "When what I read made me particularly class-conscious," she writes in *From Union Square to Rome*, "I used to turn from the park with all its beauty and peacefulness and walk down . . . through slum districts . . . and ponder over the poverty of the homes as contrasted with the wealth along the shore drive. I wanted even then to play my part. I wanted to write such books that thousands upon thousands of readers would be convinced of the injustice of things as they were."[20]

So much of what Day read remained unreal to her, whether because it took place in the realm of fantasy or transpired in a far-flung place. But she could walk through the Chicago neighborhoods of *The Jungle*.[21] And while the poverty pierced her heart, she was fascinated too by the immigrants' gardens blooming among what she called those "gray streets," struck by the wild and colorful vegetation in the yards and with the mix of scents emanating from these blocks: the tomato plants, flowers, geranium leaves, lumber, tar, coffee, and bread. There was poverty, but there was also life and industry. "Here was enough beauty to satisfy me," she wrote in *The Long Loneliness*.[22]

The beauty of the possibility of revolution led her to turn her back on religion: it seemed to her now that religion had turned its back on the poor. Day stopped going to church. When the Episcopal priest tried to persuade her to come back, there was no conflict now between flesh and spirit: her answer was a definitive no.[23]

Soon there was college, at the University of Illinois-Urbana. But college didn't exactly suit her, so she dropped out,[24] and in 1916, she moved to New York City, where her family had taken up residence.[25] In New York she threw herself into a search for experience and meaning that would culminate in a second major conflict between dreams and reality, until one night, in a jail cell in Chicago in the summer of 1922, all of her searching for earthly satisfaction would come to feel utterly meaningless.[26] But for those six years, from 1916 to 1922, religion faded further and further into the background as Day immersed herself wholly in reporting on and participating in an increasingly significant progressive movement. In New York she became a reporter for *The Call*, a socialist newspaper, where she was intoxicated by the rightness of her cause and by the round-the-clock camaraderie of newspaper life, talking all night with other staffers after they'd put an issue to bed.[27] Eventually she took up with a less radical, more bohemian crowd of writers—the playwright Eugene O'Neill being one of them—and spent her nights drinking and talking at a Village bar called the Hell Hole.[28] For a little while, she let herself play at being a saint again, drinking all night at the Hell Hole and then drifting toward early morning Mass at St. Joseph's on Sixth Avenue, perhaps imagining herself as the heroine in a novel that dramatized the theme that had interested her most in adolescence: the conflict of flesh and spirit.[29] When the United States entered World War I, she was struck by the need to do more with her life than just write, and she and her sister, Della, signed up to be nurses in Brooklyn at Kings County Hospital.[30]

In her novel *The Eleventh Virgin*, the protagonist (unmistakably Day's alter ego) has an affair with an orderly—a character based on a man named Lionel Moise, whom Day did indeed become involved with.[31] Moise would be the reason for a string of dark nights of the soul that forced Day to reckon with life as she'd been living it. Before landing in New York, Moise had been a reporter at the *Kansas City Star*, where his skill and swagger made an impression on a young man who'd go on to become a much more famous brute of a wordsmith: Ernest Hemingway, who was a young reporter on the paper at the time.[32] Moise made an impression on Day, too.

She fell deeply in love with him and moved herself into his apartment.[33] Although he did not believe in being tied down, he nursed a very unemancipated jealous streak and could be violent.[34] According to Day's letters, her relationship with Moise tormented her to the point of attempted suicide.[35] Eventually she discovered she was pregnant, and when she finally did tell him, her pregnancy made no difference to him.[36] Caught between her confusion and his lack of compassion, she then had an abortion that left her in great pain.[37]

Moise once told her that she should marry a rich man.[38] And soon after the abortion, she did just that: she married Berkeley Tobey, a publishing executive, who took her on a yearlong trip to Europe soon after.[39] As she later told a Catholic Worker, she might have married this man because she needed a rest.[40] But once back in New York, she broke it off with Tobey—perhaps because she was ashamed at having used a man to escape her troubles[41]—and then headed back to Chicago, Moise still on her mind.[42]

It was the summer of 1922, and she was twenty-four.[43] One day, while reading one of the Chicago papers, she found out that a friend of hers, in a moment of despondency, had taken bichloride of mercury and was in the city hospital. In *From Union Square to Rome*, Day writes that this woman was "unhappily in love with a newspaper man," but does not mention what she will confess years later in *The Long Loneliness*: that she and this woman were both unhappily in love with the same man:[44] Lionel Moise, who goes unnamed in Day's accounts.[45] Both were poisoned by the same unhealthy attachment. But if they were both in love with the same man, jealousy did not keep Day from rushing to this woman's side when help was needed.[46]

After being released from the hospital, the friend, still unwell, headed to a house maintained by the Industrial Workers of the World.[47] Later that night, Day brought her food and some clothes, and she paid for her selflessness: during a raid on the house, the two of them were arrested on suspicion of being prostitutes.[48] Because the house was run by suspected communists, it had become a target of the Palmer Red Raids, which Attorney General A. Mitchell Palmer was using to prevent a Bolshevik revolution on American soil.[49]

Day and her friend spent a handful of days in jail.[50] It was Day's second time. A few years before, in 1917, she was arrested alongside other women picketing for the vote outside the White House.[51] But this time was different, Day wrote in *The Long Loneliness*, because she was suffering shame at her own recklessness. "I was a victim, yes, of the red hysteria at the time, but I was also a victim of my own carelessness of convention." She continues: "It was as ugly an experience as I ever wish to pass through, and a useful one. I do not think that ever again, no matter of what I am accused, can I suffer more than I did then of shame and regret, and self-contempt. Not only because I had been caught, found out, branded, publicly humiliated, but because of my own consciousness that I deserved it."[52]

Her suffering might have come from reasons other than this arrest: the shame, regret, and self-contempt she felt in the wake of the love affair that led her to abortion and attempted suicide. Her romance with Moise may have been in accordance with Greenwich Village mores, but it did not conform to the deepest desires of her heart.

In that jail in Chicago, she'd been put into a cell next to a drug addict suffering withdrawal, and the woman's ceaseless howling undid Day. She writes: "It was most harrowing to think that this pain . . . was in a way self-inflicted with full knowledge of the torture involved. The madness, the perverseness of this seeking for pleasure that was bound to be accompanied by such mortal agony was hard to understand. To see human beings racked, by their own will, made one feel the depth of the disorder of the world."[53] The disorder in her own heart at that time might have been as tormenting as those sounds—more tormenting than she felt free to say in a nonfiction account.

In that jail cell, Day's carelessness of convention—and that of her friends—might have started to seem to her like a callow act of bravado. "I must always remember to pray for those in whose sins I shared in the early 20s," she wrote in her diaries at the age of eighty, and by the time Day had arrived in that cell, she might have been wondering at the value of the rebellion she and others of her generation had worshiped.[54] "I thought I was a free and emancipated woman and found out I wasn't at all, really," says the narrator of *The Eleventh Virgin*, adding that "freedom is just a modernity gown, a new trapping that we women affect to capture the man we want. There are exceptions to the rule, of course, but they only prove it."[55] Perhaps she felt she was paying the consequences for a self-dramatization that she might have, understandably, been demanding of herself partly because of the books she'd read as a girl and partly because of a desire to perform the role of fire-breathing member of her generation. She had lived as she thought her times asked her to—but no more. "Rebellion, too, I find exhausting," Day wrote in a 1962 issue of the *Catholic Worker*, forty years after this episode.[56]

In the howling of the woman in the cell next to her, it is possible that Day heard not just her own grief but the grief of those she'd traveled with in the 1920s. Day was in that jail because she'd gone to comfort someone who could not bear up under the loss of love. Before then, there'd been a night at the Hell Hole when a playwright friend, also driven to despair over romantic rejection, drank a drug and then died in front of Day.[57] Perhaps she was thinking, too, of the sorrow suffered by Eugene O'Neill, who she knew longed for God but never could submit to religion.[58] All that walking she did around New York City at night with her fellow young radicals and bohemians, talking and dreaming—it might have felt like walking in circles.

In that jail cell, Day, for the first time it seems, was willing and able to stop looking outward, to stop the ceaseless activity of journalism and activism, and start looking at her own behavior. She might have been coming to realize that her radical commitments could only go so far in changing her heart, as revolutionary as they had been in changing the world. They had not been able to stop the yearning for God that she had harbored as a girl. That yearning had no place in the radical movement, which all but required that one be an atheist in order to realize a more equal heaven on earth for all. She might have been tired of privileging the flesh—whether her own or that of the masses—at the expense of the spirit. Day did not want to suffer for a cause or stand in solidarity with the other prisoners. She just wanted to be freed. Luckily, a friend managed to find the two women a lawyer, and their case was dismissed.[59]

Moise, perhaps feeling guilty, got her a job at the paper where he worked.[60] His assistant loaned Day some novels by the French writer Joris-Karl Huysmans, and those books, she wrote in her diaries, were "the only good that came of that life" because they turned her thoughts again toward religion.[61] Huysmans' *The Return*, which follows a decadent Parisian aesthete from cathedral haunting to a ten-day monastery stay, made a particular impression.[62] She probably saw her own apprehension in that book's protagonist, who at the end of that monastery stay was no better off than when he started. "I am still too much a man of letters to become a monk," he says, "and yet I am already too much a monk to remain among men of letters."[63] The parallels were obvious; the path to her own permanent cathedral less so. But she was again dreaming of faith—and doing that dreaming through novels.

However much that time in her life pained her, it informed *The Eleventh Virgin*, which she published in 1924 at the age of twenty-six.[64] The book, which revised some of the darkest moments of her life into cheerful, sentimental comedy, helped pave the way for her entrance into the church. The year it was published, a movie studio bought the film rights to the book, and with the money she received, Day bought a tiny house on a beach in Staten Island.[65] A friend encouraged her to buy it, saying that she should get herself a place that would give her peace and quiet to write.[66] The seclusion resulted not in another published book—her editors rejected the novel she wrote there[67]—but in her conversion.

On Staten Island her conflict between flesh and spirit saw an abatement. She was no longer marching, protesting, or reporting. She was no longer staying out until the sun rose. Instead, most nights she took to bed with a book, the wind howling around her.[68] She was still reading, as she had always done, but also giving herself over to digging and planting, fishing and swimming. Her imagination was not feeding on stories as much as it was feeding on the world in front of her. She was in love and so did not need stories. The world as it was—and not as it could be—kept bringing her joy. By the sea, rooted and content, a mysticism was taking hold again.

Day wrote that her conversion came about over the years through her senses,[69] and here, in a borough of New York City as miraculously sedate as a New England fishing village, she returned to the state of receptivity that she had known as a child. For Day, Staten Island was full of what Augustine called visible signs that honor the invisible.[70] Horseshoe crab shells. Clams steamed in a bucket right from the sea. Dandelion wine. The talk of her neighbors.[71] The body of the man she loved, Forster Batterham, and one day, outdoors together, overwhelmed by the beauty of her surroundings, she asked him this question: "How can there be no God, when there are all these beautiful things?"[72] Her childhood's soul, which had been filled with a sense of wonder while playing in the grasses at the water's edge in Fort Hamilton, Brooklyn, echoed in that question.[73]

The concept of the sacramentality of things recurs throughout Day's writings.[74] She heard it in a 1951 talk given at one of

Day at her typewriter, circa 1925. Courtesy of the Department of Special Collections and University Archives, Marquette University Libraries.

the Worker farms by Fritz Eichenberg, the artist whose woodcuts were often featured in the paper.[75] It could be said that Day had been seeing things sacramentally all her life. From childhood she had an almost instinctive appreciation of the small instances of beauty that break through the dullness of daily life, and her writings are full of such details. She repeatedly emphasizes small joys like eating apples by a fire as she read, or the smell of clover, or the jukeboxes pulled out on to Mott Street for feast days, or those gardens on the South Side of Chicago.[76] Even the making of curtains could bear a signifying radiance. As she writes on a page of her 1960 diary: "Certainly it is tranquilizing to see beautiful curtains and drapes and blankets in one's home, the front of the house. What it does too is restore the sacramental aspect of things. One gets a feeling and a knowledge of materials, of God's creation, and becomes co-creator, in fashioning wool from a fleece and towels from hemp and flax and to plant a bed of flax is to see a most heavenly blue mass of flowers."[77]

On Staten Island, her sense of the sacramentality of things deepened as her natural happiness led to a spiritual happiness. "One cannot be properly said to understand the love of God without understanding the deepest fleshly as well as spiritual love between man and woman," she wrote in her diary nearly ten years after she had converted, expressing a belief recorded often in her writings. "The two should go hand in hand. You cannot separate the soul from the body."[78] But the man she was in love with, whom she'd met through friends, was, according to Day, an atheist.[79] He did not want to engage in alienated labor, preferring to work at jobs that allowed him to spend time as he wished, and he preferred the sea to most human society.[80] Like Lionel Moise, he did not believe in marriage.[81] There were conflicts other than her tendency to recognize the metaphysical where he saw no traces at all, but still, Day felt that Batterham had given her life stability.

Without this stability, she might not have ever come to possess the settled heart that allowed her to renew her search for God. This happiness with Batterham, and her gratitude for it, moved Day to pray and to begin attending Mass on Sundays.[82] In the summer of 1925, she discovered that she was pregnant.[83] She was overjoyed, but Batterham was fearful. He did not want to bring a child into this world.[84] Neither was he pleased with Day's increasing religiosity, and Day's joy was clouded by the intensification of her double life. When their daughter, Tamar, was born in March of 1926, Day, hoping to protect this child from the disorder that had marked her own youth, decided to have the baby baptized.[85] The iron-souled nun helping to arrange that sacrament told Day that it made no sense for Tamar to have an unbaptized mother, but Day could not submit.[86] Converting would mean a final break from Batterham and from many of her friends. Motherhood was indeed more happiness than she had ever known, but her ambivalence toward the church sowed additional conflict with Batterham. For months, he visited a storm of silences and departures on her.[87]

And then some headlines tore away at her seaside cocoon. In August 1927, Sacco and Vanzetti, the Italian immigrant anarchists wrongly accused of murder during a robbery of a shoe factory, were executed in Boston.[88] This grieved both Day and Batterham, and Day was struck by the fact that they shared this sorrow with radicals and workers all over the world. It called her back to herself—the self that had longed since adolescence to live with and serve the masses. The solidarity occasioned by this grief, seen in the light of her growing love of the church, seen in the light of a faith that would allow her to speak freely of the relationship between body, mind, and soul, sent her not into the streets this time but into a sanctuary.

Here, two years of intense struggle came to an end; flesh and spirit were no longer entirely at war. "My whole experience as a radical, my whole makeup, led me to want to associate with others, with the masses, in loving and praising God," she wrote in *The Long Loneliness*. "Without even looking into the claims of the Catholic church, I was willing to admit that for me she was the one true Church. She had come down through the centuries since the time of Peter, and far from being dead, she claimed and held the allegiance of the masses of people in all the cities where I had lived. They poured in and out of her doors on Sundays and holy days, for novenas and missions."[89]

Day's sacramental understanding made it possible for her to see this outpouring of sorrow for these radical heroes as an illustration of the unity experienced by members of the Catholic Church. She writes in *The Long Loneliness* that the widespread mourning of Sacco and Vanzetti was something that "made me gradually understand the doctrine of the Mystical Body of Christ whereby we are members of one another."[90] In *From Union Square to Rome*, her 1938 book written in order to explain to her brother why she converted, she writes: "Often there is a mystical element in the love of a radical worker for his brother, for his fellow worker. It extends to the scene of his sufferings, and those spots where he has suffered and died are hallowed."[91]

By the end of the year, Day resolved to put an end to the storms raging within and without. That winter, after yet another fight sent Batterham from the cottage, she did not let him back in.[92] On December 29, 1927, having just turned thirty, she knelt at the altar of Our Lady Help of Christians in Tottenville and received her First Communion.[93] She had entered the house of the Lord, but it would not feel like home to her for a long while.

Six years would pass before she knew with any certainty what her place in the church would be—and even then, to truly feel that she was a part of the institution that had been passed down for centuries, she had to build a structure that stood alongside it. In doing so she created not just a home for the homeless but a home for those puzzled by the same questions and inner conflicts that had troubled her. "The truth about Dorothy is that she is a great poet," her friend the Catholic publisher Maisie Ward once remarked.[94] Day's writings, at their best, bear it out. But perhaps Ward also meant that Day's capacity for seeing further than the facts—which is what both poets and novelists do—was not just a spiritual gift but an artistic one. And perhaps, given her practical streak, Day was finally more artist than mystic. Could we define an artist as a creative force who cannot help but see further than the dualities we insist on—further than the dualities of flesh and spirit, of right and wrong, of left and right? If so, then Day certainly seems to have been one, and perhaps it was Day's artist imagination that made it possible for her to fashion a Catholic movement so catholic that its works and her writings go on compelling even those who are not religious.

"To the saints," she once wrote, "everyone is child and lover," and to Day, every good thing of this world could awaken our souls and bring us closer to God.[95] She did not tell us to choose between the things of this world and God; she knew that what was not overtly spiritual could still be enlarging of the soul. "We have so much, we are so rich in interests, books, music, friends, ideas. God gives us such lights that it is a temptation to rest in them," she wrote in her diaries.[96] She quoted from books by Dickens, Dostoevsky, and Ignazio Silone as if they were ancillary gospels.[97] The smallest bit of nature, whether in city or country—her special loves were sweet clover and ailanthus trees[98]—made her voice ring as joyfully as a psalmist. "But how wonderful it is to be out here in this Christian community," reads another diary entry, "set up in the midst of fields, atop a hill, and to have samples of Heaven all about, not hell. I truly love sweet clover in God and thank Him."[99]

Day's willingness to stand, literally, in the streets with those who sought justice is more pertinent than ever. The tyranny that she and decades of Catholic Workers fought against has resurrected itself in the United States in a newly terrifying way; the darker forces that dwell in our American psyche are everywhere erupting. Reading again about the fears and fights faced by Day and other early twentieth-century progressives, one can see numerous parallels between then and now—from the demonizing of immigrants like Sacco and Vanzetti and their implied links to communism, to the current demonization of immigrants who, it's imagined, take jobs and threaten economic and personal security—which has led the Trump administration to enact horrific policies that separate migrant children from their parents at our borders, and to issue an executive order refusing visas to applicants from seven countries. In 1913, an estimated five thousand women seeking the vote marched on Washington. In January of 2017, an estimated one hundred thousand women marched on the Capitol to demonstrate, once again, resistance to challenges against their freedom.

But what makes Day relevant and radical isn't just her courage and her admirably consistent, admirably composed rebuke of the institutions that conspire against our freedom, whether they be war, racism, or capitalism, and it isn't just her tireless fight against the world's injustices. It's her insistence on seeing the world as more than just a welter of irredeemably ugly truths. It may be that, riven as she was by conflicts and contradictions, it would have been impossible for her to think like a Manichean. It would have been impossible for her to see only death and destruction and never glimpse hope. It would have been impossible to see the flesh as always damned and the spirit as always elect. If one way to see sacramentally is to always be alert to the presence of beauty in a fallen world, then her helpless love of it may really be what makes Day radical.

Many hesitate several times before saying the word *beauty*, steeped as we are in a culture that views the word as hyperbolical, even vacuous. But Day never shied away from it. She loved this line from Dostoevsky: "The world will be saved by beauty."[100] Her delight in beauty in the face of the world's suspicion is perhaps as brave as her pacifism in the face of her leftist peers' support of the Spanish Civil War and her fellow Catholics' support of World War II.[101] It's hard to believe in beauty, and to say so unequivocally, joyfully, and consistently, without losing spiritual and political authority. Even artists, ostensibly loosed from dogma, have trouble doing it. Day faced down the ugliness of the world without letting it make her blind to what she saw as its wonders—trees, flowers, people, conversation, opera, literature of all kinds. Light needs to be as stubborn, as ferocious, as tenacious as darkness. She knew this. We may never learn it.

JOHN A. RYAN

(1869–1945)

Fr. John A. Ryan portrait. Photo by Harris & Ewing, Library of Congress, Prints & Photographs Division, LC-DIG-hec-20251.

BEFITTING THE DIGNITY
OF A HUMAN BEING

John A. Ryan, Father of the Living Wage

Heather A. Warren

A few years ago, a crowd of college students, staff, and faculty gathered on the red brick terracing in front of Thomas Jefferson's Rotunda, the historic landmark of the University of Virginia. The blue skies and slight breeze on the early spring day belied the turmoil that had captured public attention when students launched a campaign for the university to pay its full-time wage laborers an hourly rate that would almost double the minimum wage. They called it a living wage.

The people had gathered for a teach-in that featured faculty members who would talk about the history of labor exploitation in the United States, business ethics, and the poverty that the university's wage earners suffered because of their small, minimum-wage paychecks. The first speaker, a female professor of twentieth-century Southern history, talked about the history of unjust labor practices beginning with slavery and carrying up through Virginia's contemporary, wage-depressing anti-unionism. The second faculty member, a man in his late fifties and a social justice advocate since his college days, taught about present-day poverty and the large numbers of full-time working poor even in the university. Both faculty members seemed likely experts for the rally. When I took the microphone as the third speaker, a puzzled quiet moved among the people. I imagined that I, as a religious studies professor and an ordained minister, seemed an unlikely "expert" to the gathered protestors. I imagined that they were asking themselves, how could such a person have anything to say about workers and wage-labor?

Two days earlier, when I agreed to speak, I had puzzled over the same question in anticipation of that moment. In the forty-eight hours that I had to prepare, I combed my heart and mind and prayed that the Holy Spirit would give me words to say. I summoned the memories of the pastors, priests, and laypeople of the late nineteenth- and early twentieth centuries who criticized so-called Christian industrialists for living by "the law of supply and demand" rather than "the law of love."[1] And I considered the witness of Fr. John Ryan, the Catholic priest who likely coined the phrase "a living wage" and who pressed tirelessly over thirty years for wage legislation and other measures that would lift workers out of their hardscrabble, subsistence-pay lives.

When the day came, once the first two speakers had finished, I stepped up, took the microphone, and began: "The idea and effort to pay workers a living wage is not new. It is particularly not new to American Christians, though many have forgotten their recent past." I took a deep breath. "In 1906, a Catholic priest named Father John Ryan wrote an influential book with the title *A Living Wage*." I heard a murmur of surprise from the crowd. "Fr. John Ryan defined a living wage as 'a wage that befits the dignity of a human being.'" Shouts of "Yes! Go on! Go on!" accompanied loud applause. Who knew that Christian teaching lay at the heart of the living wage campaign? Who would have thought that a Catholic priest's witness would have been so welcomed at this event?

Fr. John Ryan was no stranger to secular settings when it came to promoting measures for working people's well-being. In 1913, dressed in unmistakable priestly garb, Ryan walked the halls of power in the capitol building of his home state. Ryan, a professor of moral theology at St. Paul's Seminary, had asked one of his seminarians, who had been a lawyer, to help him write a wage law specifically for Minnesota. As chairman of a small, informal group calling themselves the Minnesota Committee on Social Legislation, Ryan had the bill introduced in the Minnesota legislature; it failed to get out of committee.

Not one to quit, Ryan drew up a revised version and then kept pressure on the politicians as the bill made its way through the legislative process. In contrast with laws adopted in a few other states, Ryan's explicitly stated that a minimum wage for women and children should be high enough to afford them the "necessary comforts and conditions of reasonable life"—"a living wage."[2] Aware that the unionist Minnesota Federation of Labor opposed the bill, he met with its members to allay their underlying fears that a minimum wage would discourage union membership and make a minimum wage the maximum wage in practice.[3] The legislation passed.[4]

More surprising than the passage of the bill was the direct role that a Catholic priest had played in securing the victory. What was a Catholic priest doing writing a bill and promoting it in the halls of a state capitol? But he might have responded, What is a priest good for if not witnessing to the inescapable connection of physical thriving and spiritual thriving, if not working to honor the God-given dignity of *all* by seeking something more sustaining than starvation and subsistence-level existence?

*   *   *

John A. Ryan (1869-1945), the oldest of ten children born to Irish Catholic immigrants, grew up on a farm in Vermillion, Minnesota, twenty miles southeast of Minneapolis. Raised in a pious Catholic household, he heard about the devastating effects of economic depressions—the milder but prolonged depression from 1873 to 1879 and the more devastating depression from 1882 to 1885. As a teen, he witnessed the power that persuasive oratory and the legislative process could have on improving or frustrating relief for hardworking people crushed by economic calamity. Such perceptions, along with Ryan's deep Catholic formation, made him into a new kind of priest: one committed to advocating national legislative reform on behalf of industrial laborers—men, women, and children.

The economic depressions of Ryan's childhood were disasters brought on quickly, blindsiding the wealthy and workers alike, but were far more damaging to farmers and the swelling ranks of urban, industrial laborers. The railroads and other businesses that had boomed in the immediate aftermath of the Civil War fell into deep financial holes, even bankruptcy. To offset their losses and repay loans, railroad owners decided to charge farmers significantly higher rates for conveying their goods to markets. With far less net gain, farmers, who typically carried large debt in advance of harvests, found themselves squeezed even more tightly, many to the point of foreclosure.

Monopolies, also known as "trusts" and "holding companies," formed for the first time and allowed robber barons such as John D. Rockefeller, J. P. Morgan, and Andrew Carnegie to combine their several businesses into multitentacled enterprises—simultaneously owning banks, freight carriers, ore lands, factories, and the like—thus reducing competition and driving down workers' pay.[5] Between 1870 and 1880 real wages declined by 25 percent from the subsistence level of $400 per year to $300 per year. Greater numbers of children had to work in factories to contribute to their families' survival. In cities, housing costs soared, often forcing two or three families to share a windowless tenement apartment. For many, their largest room was only ten feet wide; coal-burning stoves provided heat and spread soot throughout the rooms; few places had indoor plumbing. Depressed wages meant that families had difficulty affording food, causing children to suffer the crippling effects of rickets and even death from malnutrition.

*   *   *

Ryan's interest in economic justice stirred when he was about eleven. He read one of the few periodicals that came regularly into his home, *The Irish World and American Industrial Liberator*, and saw that the newspaper daringly called on priests to promote the economic rights of the Church's many laborers.[6] Ryan credited the *Irish World* for giving him "an interest in and love of economic justice, as well as political justice."[7] The young Ryan also learned about populist organizations that worked politically to change the economic system so that farmers would not be so vulnerable to such upheavals. The Farmers' Alliance, one of the most widespread populist groups, had such a presence in Ryan's town that it grabbed his attention. When neighbors stopped at the Ryan house to talk over Alliance matters with his father, John's siblings noticed that he soaked up every word. After Mass on Sundays, when the Vermillion town radical ranted about the railroad monopoly, John listened intently, perhaps trying to understand the reasons that monopolies grew and hoping to hear ways of constraining them.[8]

In the same years that Ryan was losing his naïveté about American economics, his parents saw to it that he and his siblings grew up as devout Catholics. On Sundays when they could not attend any church because of foul weather, they gathered to recite the Rosary in the common room of their house. Every Sunday, his parents made each child read a chapter of *The Life of Jesus Christ*, a devotional book the Ryan parents read, too. Ultimately, two of the Ryans' sons were ordained to the priesthood and two daughters became nuns.[9]

To ensure Catholic influence, Ryan's parents sent him to high school at the Christian Brothers' School in St. Paul. In the city, Ryan experienced what turned out to be the most significant event in his school years—the election of Ignatius Donnelly, the widely known leader of the Farmers' Alliance, to the Minnesota House of Representatives. Donnelly epitomized the Midwestern populist politician who championed farmers and urban laborers against large corporations. So fascinated was Ryan with Donnelly that he went to the capitol almost daily to hear Donnelly speak. His classmates dubbed him "Senator."[10]

Ryan stayed in St. Paul to prepare for the priesthood by first attending St. Thomas College and then St. Paul Seminary. There, he learned about new steps that some in the Catholic hierarchy were taking to promote the welfare of industrial workers. Ryan fell under the direction and influence of Archbishop John Ireland, the Diocese of St. Paul's progressive, energetic leader and founder of the seminary.[11] As important as Ireland's patronage was for Ryan, so was Ireland's outspokenness on the evils of the industrial economy and support for reform. Perhaps no speech of Ireland's made as deep an impression on Ryan as the one he gave in 1889 at the centennial celebration of John Carroll's appointment as the first Catholic bishop in the United States. Ireland chastised Catholics for their passivity in the face of widespread social ills. "It is deplorable," he declared, "that Catholics grow timid, take refuge in sanctuary and cloister, and leave the bustling, throbbing world with its miseries and sins to the wiles of false friends and cunning practitioners. . . . These are days of action. . . . Into the arena, priest and layman! Seek out social evils, and lead in movements that tend to rectify them. . . . Strive, by word and example, by the enactment and enforcement of good laws, to correct them."[12] Already inspired by Donnelly and the populists, Ryan now heard the call to action in a Catholic register.

In the second year of Ryan's "clerical" course, a professor of English made his students write an essay on *Rerum Novarum*, Pope Leo XIII's landmark encyclical on industrial labor. Ryan found the pope's statements about the regulatory role of the state over industry "new and, indeed, startling," challenging basic assumptions held by Catholics and non-Catholics alike about the relation between society and economics. With papal backing, priests could promote workers' rights, including the right to form unions, and they could call nation-states to protect those rights—all previously considered "socialist."[13] While *Rerum Novarum* was personally "pleasing and reassuring" to Ryan, it also became increasingly important to him as he delved into the ethics of industrial economics and sought to right its wrongs.

The seminary's daily life and curriculum formed Ryan as he matured into the priesthood. As dictated by Archbishop Ireland, Ryan lived the monastic schedule that interspersed prayer and work.[14] At 5:25 a.m. every day, a designated student knocked on his door, shouting, "Benedicamus Domino!" (Let us bless the Lord!), to which Ryan replied, "Deo Gratias" (Thanks be to God), indicating that he was awake. Dress was a cassock—the long-sleeved, ankle-length robe that buttoned all the way down the front from collar to hem (most often with thirty-two buttons, representing the years of Christ's earthly life)—a literal reminder of having taken on holiness of life. The day ended with prayer, a personal inventory of conscience, and bed at 10:00 p.m. For Ryan, seminary was not a rigid exercise in dour living and reading moldy tomes. To the contrary, Ryan found himself periodically overwhelmed by the task of freely probing Catholic doctrine for deeper understanding. Nevertheless, he enjoyed the liberty to question and explore, and particularly to pursue practical solutions for the multitudes suffering economic hardship.

The theological foundations of Ryan's life work coalesced during his years at the seminary. Though little mentioned in his many publications, God's love—"God's unutterable and mysterious solicitude and love"—lay at the heart of his conviction about the infinite worth of every person created in this incomprehensible movement of God's love.[15] Likewise for Ryan, human dignity and equality had their basis in the doctrine that all people were made in the image of God, the *imago Dei*. Underscoring his belief in social equality as well as the innate equality of being in all people, he noted in his seminary journal that "every man should be . . .

accessible and affable alike to the pauper and the millionaire, since both are men and the images of God."[16]

*   *   *

As he had seen in Donnelly and Archbishop Ireland, Ryan grew to believe that action necessarily went with thought, not as a by-product of faith but intimately connected with it. "The true language of the heart," he wrote, "comes *not* through the channel of the mouth as through the commonplace actions."[17] Consistent with this belief, he wrote passionately that the priest's call was to correct exploitative social systems. "Where should the priest be," he asked rhetorically,

> if not in the midst of this movement, restraining the destructionist, encouraging the true reformer, and applying the ethics of the Gospel everywhere? This is his paramount duty, to apply Christ's teaching, to the practical aspects of the problems that confront men. The priest must be able and anxious to point [out] what in the present system is wrong and to what extent the Brotherhood of Man means social equality. He must instill the Gospel doctrines of justice between man and man, of love for the poor and unfortunate, of denunciations for the plunderers of the people whether these plunderers be the lords of commerce or the rulers of nations. . . . This may be called the technical reason of the priest's participation in the social movement.[18]

According to Ryan, witness of this nature also served evangelistic purpose. "This should be the watchword of those who would win multitudes to Christ," he wrote. "Christian doctrine applied to the social needs of the age."[19] Intentional or not, Ryan had drafted the blueprint of his vocation.

*   *   *

On June 4, 1898, in the presence of his parents and nine siblings, John Augustine Ryan stood before Archbishop Ireland to be ordained a priest. He wore the traditional vestments of an ordinand: a long white robe known as an alb, encircled with a belt; a stole draped across his left shoulder and hanging to the right; and a short stole-like vestment, a maniple, draped over his left arm.[20] As stipulated by the liturgy, Ireland commended the "long lasting observance of justice" to Ryan and prayed that the "form of all justice [or righteousness]" would "shine forth" in him.[21] Three months later, in obedience to Ireland, Fr. Ryan gladly moved to Washington, DC, for advanced study in moral theology at the Catholic University of America.

For four years Ryan received his doctoral education from some of the sharpest Catholic minds of the time, chief among them Thomas J. Bouquillon, DD, the noted Belgian scholar of moral theology to whom Archbishop Ireland had sent Ryan.[22] Bouquillon instilled in Ryan a rigorous method of study in which theory and principles were not to be divorced from social conditions and individual lives. Moreover, under Bouquillon, Ryan gained his understanding of why economic depressions and devastating unemployment recurred with such frequency in liberal, laissez-faire economies: underconsumption. When wage earners' paychecks did not increase in proportion to the rising price of the industrial goods they made, then an underconsumption of goods occurred, with the effect that the wealthy clung to their money. In the face of reduced sales, an economy's cash flow froze, plunging society into an economic depression. The small number of magnates who had vast fortunes could weather such a storm, but middle-class and working-class people could not. This drew Ryan's attention to wages and the role of the state in securing just wages for laborers.

In the fall of 1902, at Archbishop Ireland's behest, Ryan returned to St. Paul as a professor of moral theology and to complete his dissertation.[23] Four years later when he finished the dissertation, Macmillan published it as *A Living Wage: Its Ethical and Eco-*

nomic Aspects.[24] The book drew high praise and called attention to Ryan as a Catholic voice who spoke to Protestants as well as Catholics.[25]

Ryan argued that a living wage was an hourly rate that accorded with the dignity of a human being. It was also a *right*. At the heart of this understanding lay Ryan's emphasis on the worker's God-given "intrinsic worth as a person"—"human dignity" or "personal dignity" as he called it.[26] According to Ryan, a living wage was a moral right that, if denied, violated God's will for human existence. A living wage provided a laborer the way to meet the basic, "essential needs" necessary for his or her "personal development."[27] He identified these essential needs as "food, clothing and shelter," and "within reasonable limits" the development of a person's "faculties," "physical, intellectual, moral and spiritual." Only a "decent livelihood" that provided "a certain amount of material goods" could meet the standard of human dignity. Anything "less than this minimum," he said, means that a person "is treated as somewhat less than a man."[28]

But why did Ryan call specifically for a living wage? The answer was simple: "in the present industrial organization of society, there is no other way in which the right [of personal development] can be realized."[29] Human flourishing was God's will.

*　　　*　　　*

Ryan thought that employers bore the biggest responsibility for the living wage. Although "landowners" and "capitalists" were also "obliged to refrain from . . . hindering the gaining of a decent livelihood by their fellow man," employers stood as the unique contracting contact with laborers in factories, mines, and the like. "The employer," Ryan wrote, "is bound to compensate human exertion that he buys at its *ethical* value. He should deal with it as the attribute, the output, of a *person* . . . endowed with the indestructible right to live a decent human life."[30] The employer's objection that he could not pay a living wage based on his own circumstances held no water for Ryan. Distinguishing between the "essential needs" of all people and the socially "conventional necessaries" of the employer, Ryan castigated employers who prioritized their far-less-vital needs over their laborers' primary ones.[31] Unsparingly he declared: "Until he [the employer] has paid all his employees a Living Wage he ought to refrain from all costly expenditure for . . . lavish feasting, all extravagant forms of amusement, and all ostentation in dress, equipage, and household appointments."[32]

In Ryan's view, the state, too, had a significant role in ensuring a living wage for workers. The state had to implement measures to ameliorate the conditions that a living wage would otherwise correct. Drawing on Pope Leo XIII's *Rerum Novarum*, Ryan pointed out that the state's function was to protect people's natural rights by promoting social welfare and prosperity.[33] The state could take a big step in this direction by legislating a living wage. Not only would it benefit workers, it would also be an act in favor of justice and life. "To compel a man to work for less than a Living Wage," he wrote, "is as truly an act of injustice as to pick his pocket. . . . An ordinance prohibiting this species of oppression would, therefore, be a measure for the protection of life and property."[34] Ryan prescribed four additional measures: the eight-hour workday, restriction of child labor to those sixteen years or older, a program of public housing that would lead to home ownership, and an old-age pension.[35] The eight-hour workday and a minimum child labor age would create more demand for labor and an increase in wages; housing and a pension would compensate workers for wages that did not afford them the ability to buy a house and save for the day when old age made work impossible. Ryan also identified a way for the state to fund this: a progressive federal income tax and a progressive tax on inherited wealth.

Against the argument that a progressive income tax amounted to robbing from the rich and giving to the poor, Ryan charged that such rationalization arose from "a false notion of the morality of the proposal." Moral reasoning, he said, dictated that the state make up for the ways in which the affluent had benefited from the denial of laborers' natural right to a decent livelihood. Thus, a progressive tax that had a less severe effect on "the man of modest means" than "the richer man" provided justice for the unjustly paid laborer.[36]

By appealing to natural law—the God-given awareness of right and wrong in a person's conscience—and using the language of rights in *A Living Wage*, Ryan had cast his call for more than subsistence pay in words that associated Catholic thought with America's Founding Fathers. Consequently, he had set forth theological principles as well as a program for social reform that Protestants could and did share. To anti-Catholic, Protestant-dominated America, he demonstrated that Catholics held the same basic Christian values as Protestants and did not threaten American democracy.

Now able to take up his priestly vocation more fully, Ryan stepped into public action even as he worked full-time at the seminary. He vigorously generated support for the living wage by delivering speeches around the nation, serving as an active member of national labor reform organizations, writing prolifically, and steering living wage legislation through his own Minnesota General Assembly. With the success of *A Living Wage* Ryan adopted a busy speaking schedule. Invited to speak to Catholic and workers' assemblies, he traveled across the United States. He made such an impression that non-Catholic national labor bodies asked him to join them and promote not only a living wage but also the other reforms he urged in his book. He accepted the National Consumers' League's membership invitation because it aimed to wield consumers' purchasing power in ways that punished industrialists who did not pay a living wage. He worked with the National Child Labor Committee to limit the age at which children could enter the industrial labor force. Ryan wound up serving on so many national

Catholic and civic organizations, or was consulted by them, that his sphere of his ministerial influence expanded in both religious and secular directions.

To push reform that accorded with Catholic teaching and make it accessible so that church members would take action, he published two ten-page pamphlets presenting his entire plan.[37] His first pamphlet featured a summary of his program in two lists. List number one pertained to legislated labor reform: a minimum wage; an eight-hour workday; protections for women and children; provisions for peaceful picketing and boycotts; unemployment insurance and employment bureaus; and provisions for sickness, old age, and accidental injury. The second list had to do with antitrust and the redistribution of wealth: public ownership of utilities, mines, and forests; breaking up monopolies or placing price controls on them; progressive income and inheritance taxes; taxation of the future increase of land values; and prohibition of speculation on stocks and commodity exchanges. Two years later, he published his second pamphlet, *A Minimum Wage by Legislation.*[38] The title spoke for itself.

Ryan's social reform program—especially his antitrust, public ownership, and taxation policies—aligned him with populists, the Progressive Party, and socialists, though the basis of his proposals arose from principles rooted in Catholic theology rather than politics. Nevertheless he ruffled conservative Catholics' feathers, and they labeled him "socialistic," a "radical," and a "dangerous agitator."[39]

Ryan was having nothing of it. Frustrated by Catholics' ignorance of socialism and their failure to participate in local reform groups, he saw it as his task—as an aspect of his priesthood—to educate his coreligionists about socialism and the reasons it was incompatible with Catholic social justice. Between 1908 and 1915 he spoke "more frequently and more fundamentally" on socialism.[40] To defend himself and inform his coreligionists, he dealt with socialism in three ways: as "a social philosophy" that he laid out and then demonstrated was "historically false and ethically wrong" because of its emphasis on materialism as the driving force in human existence; as "a social movement" that he proved was indeed "anti-religious," felicitously in concert with his detractors; and as "an economic program" that was "impracticable and unjust." This did not mean that he shied away from the subject of social reform. Rather, as he later quipped, "I had a good deal to say about social reform."[41]

Such controversy only enhanced Ryan's public visibility and distinguished him as an expert on socialism and the Catholic critique of it. By the summer of 1913, Ryan had agreed to be the Catholic representative in a debate that pitted Catholic social principles against socialist ones in a series of articles in *Everybody's Magazine*, a popular monthly.[42] His counterpart was Morris Hillquit, the founder and leader of the Socialist Party in America. As the debate unfolded in print between October 1913 and April 1914 the demand for additional copies of the feature grew so large that within a year both men consented to having it published as *Socialism: Promise or Menace?*—Ryan clearly coming down on the menace side.[43]

*   *   *

Eager to make more of his social reform proposals become reality, Ryan wanted to leave St. Paul for a city putting him closer to the center of politics and the publishing world. In June 1915 Ireland assented to the move, and Ryan moved to Washington, DC, to take up a post at Catholic University. Although Ryan was a successful public speaker, he had a reputation for dull lectures. Students recalled that Ryan droned on "dry as a stick."[44]

In 1919, three months after the Great War ended, Ryan authored a landmark statement issued by the American bishops as the American Church's call for social reform in rebuilding postwar America. As labor violence turned into armed conflict between workers and factory owners, the bishops had begun to consider the need for issuing a pronouncement about reforms for postwar America like other religious groups and civic organizations were doing. By December 1918, Fr. John O'Grady, secretary of the National Catholic War Council's Committee on Reconstruction, had solicited such a statement from Ryan.[45] Ryan initially refused, but in the meantime had agreed to deliver a speech on postwar reconstruction in Louisville. O'Grady happened to see the social reconstruction text in Ryan's typewriter and asked to look at it. Recognizing gold when he saw it, he "begged and pleaded" with Ryan to expand the text and let him give it to the bishops. Ryan agreed reluctantly and quickly prepared the text.[46]

On February 12, 1919, the National Catholic War Council issued Ryan's statement as their own "Bishops' Program of Social Reconstruction."[47] The reason for publishing the document lay in the bishops' desire to address the "deep unrest so emphatically and so widely voiced throughout the world" that threatened "the future peace of every nation and the entire world." While the program mainly presented practical remedies for economic trouble that had already caused clashes between workers and employers, Ryan placed its origin in moral theology: "all [of the program's] essential declarations are based upon the principles of charity and justice that have always been held and taught by the Catholic Church."[48] Ryan and the bishops called their fellow Catholics to put their belief into action, "translating our faith into works."[49]

Ryan identified twelve actions the nation could and should take to build a more just, happy, and peaceful nation. Among them were continuation of government-funded employment services and the worker-employer mediating War Labor Board, the building of public housing, the passing of child labor laws, creation of cooperative industrial enterprises, regulation of monopolies, and a social insurance program for the unemployed, disabled, and aged. Unsurprisingly, action pertaining to "Wage Rates" received lengthy comment and included advocacy for the living wage.[50]

Ethics and economics mandated that the higher hourly rate paid during the war not return to its lower, prewar level. Ryan was quick to point out that the average wage hike had "not increased faster than the cost of living" and that "the majority of wage earners . . . were not receiving living wages when prices began to rise in 1915."[51] While he (and the bishops) promoted the living wage, he noted that in terms of justice it was only a beginning. "All the Catholic authorities on the subject," he wrote, "explicitly declare that this is only the minimum of justice. In a country as rich as ours, there are few cases in which it is possible to prove that the worker would be getting more than that to which he has a right."[52] Ryan (and the bishops) called for a "new spirit" and reinforcement of the "Christian view of work and wealth" among the wealthy, particularly the commitment to "cultivate and strengthen . . . the truth . . . that the laborer is a human being, not merely an instrument of production."[53]

Closing the document with a ringing indictment of corporate practice, Ryan (and the bishops) declared that their program was "human and Christian, in contrast to the purely commercial and *pagan* ethics, of industry."[54] Ryan had crafted the most socially progressive statement the American Catholic Church had seen, and he aligned the Church with the political forces marshalling for social reform.[55]

Before the year ended, the bishops decided that for the Church to implement their program, they needed an agency. They reconfigured their National Catholic War Council for this purpose and created the National Catholic Welfare Council, three years later renamed the National Catholic Welfare Conference.[56] The agency consisted of four departments, one of which was the Social Action Department, headed by Bishop Muldoon of Rockford, Illinois. Among Muldoon's first acts was to appoint John Ryan director of the department. From this post and his faculty position at Catholic University, he worked tirelessly over the next twenty-five years to bring his (and the bishops') reforms to fruition.

Ryan continued to promote reform by writing prolifically. His articles found homes in a variety of Catholic publications, some aimed at scholars and priests, others at middle-brow laity, all making him a recognizable name.

His efforts to pass labor reform legislation continued, too. Among his biggest efforts in the 1920s was to press for a child labor amendment to the Constitution that would prohibit the employment of children under sixteen. Ryan's involvement in the required state-by-state ratification process caused a nasty conflict between him and Archbishop O'Connell of Boston, who targeted Ryan for his "queer crooked views." O'Connell protested furiously to Archbishop Michael Curley of Baltimore, Ryan's superior: "Yesterday this city was flooded with the nefarious and false views on the amendment supposed falsely to be in the interest of the Child, sent out from Washington by sly methods in which he seems to be an expert, by Rev. J. A. Ryan Professor in the [Catholic] University."[57] O'Connell urged Curley to rein in his man Ryan or dismiss him from the university and the NCWC staff. Curley did no such thing, nor did Ryan stop promoting the child labor amendment. O'Connell, however, prohibited Ryan from setting foot in his diocese ever again.

In 1933, in the early months of the new Roosevelt administration, Ryan received a letter from Secretary of Labor Frances Perkins inviting him to a labor conference in March. From June through December 1933, the administration sought his help frequently,[58] and before the year ended, Secretary Perkins asked him to draw up a complete program of labor legislation.[59] Whether he did or not, no record exists. Most likely the task fell to Ryan's assistant, Fr. Raymond McGowan, who had been taking up the assignments Ryan fumbled while Ryan put himself, and arguably the Church, more in the public eye.[60]

In 1934, Ryan served on Roosevelt's Industrial Appeals Board, a three-man committee established to hear and address the burdens that National Recovery codes put on small manufacturers.

Ryan was dismayed when the Supreme Court struck down the National Recovery Administration in May 1935, but his support for the Roosevelt administration did not flag. He had confidence that the social security legislation, which he had a small hand in creating, would pass.[61] That summer his optimism grew when Congress adopted major pieces of legislation supporting workers' rights. Against those who decried the New Deal measures for inhibiting freedom and being "socialist," he declared: "Every one of them is in accordance with humanity, Christianity, and social justice. The only liberty that they interfere with is the liberty of the economically strong to oppress the economically weak."[62] Liberty did not simply mean a social arrangement with a lack of restraints in which people could do whatever they wanted to do in their own self-interest simply because they had the political, social, or economic power to do so. Liberty meant being free to act on behalf of others' welfare for the good of all, not only a favored segment of the population. For such progress to continue and to keep the United States from going down the immoral fascist paths that Italy and Germany had taken, Ryan thought it vital for FDR to win reelection in 1936.

In the United States, one fascist threat reared its ugly head in the person of Fr. Charles E. Coughlin, a popular Catholic priest in Detroit whose charismatic radio broadcasts spellbound countless listeners and turned them toward a third political party that he helped create, the Union Party.[63] As the "radio priest" expressed disenchantment with the New Deal, he became bolder and bolder in his denunciations of Roosevelt, going so far as to call him a "liar" and "double-crosser." Ryan tried his best to stay out of the fray. As a public Catholic figure, Ryan had already received complaints about Coughlin. In correspondence, Arthur Meyerowitz of New York City had written Ryan that the "vulgar and violent language which this . . . priest of the Catholic Church uses would be a discredit even to a member of the underworld."[64] Coughlin's slander of Roosevelt, however, provoked Ryan. When the Democratic National Committee grew anxious that Coughlin's presidential candidate would siphon votes from FDR and open the door to a Republican victory, they called on Ryan to speak.[65] He took to the airwaves.

On October 8, 1936, Ryan positioned himself behind a large radio microphone for a national broadcast. Ostensibly intending to defend FDR from alleged charges of communism, he sounded the critical Catholic voice against Coughlin. Positioning himself as priest who knew moral theology, he said that he was going to provide mainly "a discussion of certain political events in the light of moral law."[66] Nevertheless he delivered a carefully crafted speech that championed Roosevelt. With a touch of humor he appealed to the eighth of the Ten Commandments—"Thou shalt not lie"—to rebut Coughlin's charge that FDR was a communist. Ryan argued that FDR was not an atheist (as communists were), pointing out that before FDR went to the Capitol for his inauguration in 1933, he and his family went to worship at the church across Lafayette Park from the White House.[67] Ryan defended New Deal legislation from the charge of "communistic tendencies" by arguing that it accorded with papal teaching. "The Labor Disputes Act," he explained, "simply makes effective the right of labor to organize, a right which was strongly proclaimed by both Pope Leo XIII and Pope Pius XI."[68] Ryan asserted that far from opening America to communist influence, FDR's presidency had prevented its spread.

Ryan explicitly addressed the last part of his speech to Catholic laborers and criticized Coughlin's policies on economic and Catholic moral grounds. On the basis of his own expertise he argued, "Father Coughlin's explanation of our economic maladies is at least 50 percent wrong.... Moreover, Father Coughlin's monetary theories and proposals find no support in the encyclicals." Ryan concluded the speech in an unambiguously partisan way: "I urge you to use every effort at your command among your relatives, friends and acquaintances in support of Franklin D. Roosevelt."[69]

The broadcast met with wide press coverage. Democratic-leaning secular newspapers and liberal Catholic publications applauded Ryan, while the conservative press—secular and Catholic—attacked him for so openly endorsing FDR and criticizing a fellow priest. Coughlin himself responded by snidely calling Ryan the "Right Reverend New Dealer," a name that stuck, but not pejoratively.[70] Ryan claimed nationwide attention because he was a priest speaking politically in such a public way. One manual worker heard the speech as a priest's pastoral concern for laborers, and a touching response came to Ryan as a small handwritten note from a quarryman. He addressed Ryan directly, apparently responding to Ryan's periodic pastoral tone, and asked for Ryan to send him copies of the speech so that he could distribute it among workers at a nearby WPA–New Deal project. He closed the short note with the humble statement, "I am a laborer on Project 169, Hammerville Quarry."[71]

Although FDR won the election convincingly, Ryan's speech played a role in keeping the Catholic vote with Roosevelt and helping swing at least one bloc of Catholic voters behind a Democratic congressman whose incumbency was threatened.[72] Perhaps as a reward for the radio speech, FDR invited Ryan to deliver the benediction at his second inauguration. Ryan accepted, marking the first time in historically anti-Catholic America that a Catholic priest had such a role in the national ritual.[73] Eight years later, Ryan delivered the benediction again at Roosevelt's fourth inauguration.

Throughout the rest of the New Deal years, Ryan continued his witness by pressing for passage of laws that guaranteed a minimum wage, created the forty-hour work week, regulated child labor, secured antitrust relief, regulated public utilities, established public ownership of forests, protected organized labor, and launched unemployment insurance. Before 1940 ended, Ryan saw Congress enact reforms that he had advocated for over thirty years as a priest. The lives of laborers and the most vulnerable in American society had taken a turn for the better, though Ryan believed that more work lay ahead before all Americans enjoyed "the dignity that befits a human being."

The campaign for a living wage continues to this day. Wage laborers across the United States are still not guaranteed an income that affords housing, food, medical care, and disability or retirement savings. As in Ryan's day, industry executives accrue tremendous profits from wage laborers at the expense of such workers' dignity and well-being. In all of his thinking, writing, networking, public speaking, and legislative efforts, Ryan endeavored to spread the gospel through the social reform that grew out of Catholic moral theology. He lived out his vocation, following the call he had heard as a young seminarian: "He [the priest] must instill the Gospel doctrines of justice between man and man, of love for the poor and unfortunate, of denunciations for the plunderers of the people whether these plunderers be the lords of commerce or the rulers of nations. . . . This should be the watchword of those who would win multitudes to Christ: Christian doctrine applied to the social needs of the age."[74]

FRANK WILLIAM STRINGFELLOW

(1928–1985)

William Stringfellow. William Stringfellow papers, 1940–1985, Division of Rare and Manuscript Collections, Cornell University Library.

LIVING INTO THE PROPHETIC VOICE

Frank William Stringfellow's Greatest Witness

Becca Stevens

Three times since my father was killed by a drunk driver, when I was just five and before my memories could take root, I have dreamed of him: once in college, once in 2003, and most recently on a trip as I slept in the hills of Alabama. My father was an Episcopal priest, and I have loved carrying on his legacy since my ordination in 1995. In my most recent dream, we were together in the sacristy behind a chapel, where vestments, candlesticks, and incense are kept.

In the dream, I picked up two candlesticks given to me by my father's old mission church. He showed me how to open a secret compartment underneath the candlestick base, where I found wads of lamb's wool that he had hidden long ago (lamb's wool is the traditional fiber that priests use to anoint parishioners with healing oil while administering the sacraments). When I took out the wool, another older man appeared in the sacristy with us. He had tears welling up in his eyes, and my father gave me permission to take the wool to dry his tears. I wasn't sure at first who this other man was, but I was sure of his heart and that he too had sacrificed a great deal to be a witness to the church. As I walked toward him, I suddenly knew that the man in my dream, whose eyes I was anointing with my father's lamb's wool, was William Stringfellow.

In the dream and in the hours after waking, I felt compassion and awe and a profound gratitude for his life and legacy within and beyond the Episcopal Church.

William Stringfellow's witness draws you into the wilderness of your own dreams. And his is the voice that compels me to live into my convictions as I try to reconcile the gospel to the political, economic, and social realities I live within. His is also a hard gospel to read: he challenges his readers to see the world with ever more compassionate eyes and to speak to that world with a clearer voice for justice.

Born in Rhode Island in 1928, William Stringfellow grew up to excel academically, graduating high school at the age of fifteen to then attend Bates College. He waded into the waters of activism in his junior year, and he stepped out further into those troubling waters in his early twenties as he became part of student organizations and international ecumenical movements where he tried to reconcile the faith he was taught with the injustices he met.

After his graduation from Harvard Law School, Stringfellow dove head first into the deep waters of a life of justice: he moved to the slums of East Harlem to work and live among the disenfranchised, whom he described as being neglected by the law and systematically oppressed by powers and principalities. Stringfellow, who died in 1985, spent most of his life in New York, exploring the vast sea of an activist life, defending people who knew the short side of justice, and working as a theologian committed to helping the church find its way.

As a lifelong critic of the social, military, and economic policies of the United States, he was perceived as a radical and marginalized by mainstream movements of his day. Stringfellow wrote extensively about racial and social justice rooted in the teachings of Jesus. When I met him in my dream, in my father's company, I realized their similarity: They both spent their lives serving the hungry, naked, thirsty, imprisoned, sick, and dying. And they both died too soon.

* * *

While Stringfellow offered many gifts to the world, his greatest witness as a twentieth-century prophetic voice can be found in his writing. By profession he was an activist lawyer with a penchant for theology, but he also wrote seventeen books and contributed to many more through interviews and forewords. His writings are prolific and prophetic, and his voice maintains a clarity throughout his work. Filled with personal and biographical information, his books offer a theological and political perspective, with significant writings on his acts of dissidence. He believed that biography is "good rudimentary data for theology, and every biography is significant for the knowledge it yields of the Word of God incarnate in common life."[1]

A masterful storyteller, Stringfellow believed that storytelling was a means by which to exercise the prophetic hope of conversion of the heart. He wove stories into longer tapestries that proclaimed room at the table for everyone. His passion, like the prophets in Hebrew Scripture, was unrelenting as he shared small events and personal stories that reflected larger biblical themes about justice and truth. Unafraid of judgment, and challenging others to step out, he called readers into the bold work of looking at old injustices with new eyes.

William Stringfellow humbly went about his own work as a dissident, inspiring his readers to find their own dissident voices on behalf of brothers and sisters suffering under oppressive systems. He effortlessly employed seemingly small events and anecdotes to exemplify powerful theological lessons. We are all parables, he believed, and all the events in our lives expound on gospel truths.

Each of Stringfellow's books uses stories as the through-lines that expose the radical nature of love in the gospel, witnessing to justice and allowing the reader to glimpse the ways love can thrive. These stories reveal a truth greater than the narrative of just one life.

Stringfellow's witness wasn't limited to his writings. He never hesitated to help those in need—whether in the slums of Harlem or in ecclesiastic court—often at great personal cost. At times, he disregarded his own health in order to speak to various groups; he gave money to families struggling to make their rent, even when he himself had financial difficulties; and he dined with those others considered outcasts. Over the course of his life and work, Stringfellow's prophetic voice grew, as his own work convinced him that all of us can share the burden of justice through daily activism and dissent. Justice work, he believed, is rooted in the ability to see the values of the kingdom in small acts like selling a tapestry, welcoming a fugitive, or mourning a friend.

*   *   *

Stringfellow was running late one day, rushing to leave his apartment and reach the airport in time for a flight to Boston, where he was lecturing at the Harvard Business School, when his phone rang. "I had not the willpower not to answer it, in spite of my rush," he recalled.[2] The priest on the other end of the line said there was a woman in his office who was going to be evicted the next day, and he needed guidance about what to do. After asking him a few questions about the situation, Stringfellow ascertained that the woman had no legal recourse and needed to pay the rent to stay in her apartment. "By this time," Stringfellow wrote, "I was even more anxious about catching the airplane and said to the minister, 'Well, sell one of your tapestries and pay the rent.'"[3] Hanging up the phone, he rushed to catch the plane.

During his flight, Stringfellow reflected on the conversation. He thought perhaps he had been rude in his rush to get off the phone and wondered if he owed the priest an apology. But by the time he landed in Boston, he "had rejected that idea." Only when the church and its members have the freedom to let it go, Stringfellow concluded, does the tapestry take on religious significance.

William Stringfellow. William Stringfellow papers, 1940–1985, Division of Rare and Manuscript Collections, Cornell University Library.

"The tapestry hanging in a church becomes and is a wholesome and holy thing, an appropriate and decent part of the scene of worship, only if the congregation which has the tapestry is free to take it down and sell it in order to feed the hungry or care for the sick or pay the rent or in any other way serve the world."[4]

To Stringfellow and to his audiences, this story demonstrated how often churches "are engaged in serving themselves instead of the world, that is, how far they have withdrawn from the ministry of the body of Christ."[5] We can only hold onto beautiful things with integrity if we are free to give them up for the sake of the world, he would insist. It is this freedom to use something in the work of loving the world that transforms everyday objects into sacramental signs.

What could have been the story of a woman becoming homeless while a woven cloth hung in the church collecting dust became a poignant summons to serve love's higher calling and a reminder to use our sacred objects for the love of others. Stringfellow's insights have led many to examine the objects we think of as sacred and determine how love and justice can speak clearly through them when they are put in service of another. In this way, our treasured objects become truly sacramental and their value directly proportional to how we offer them in love.

"The mission of the church," wrote Stringfellow, "depends not upon social reformation in these neighborhoods [Harlem] as desperately as that is needed, but upon the presence of the Word of God in the society of the poor as it is right now. . . . Mission does not follow charity. . . . On the contrary, mission is itself the only charity which Christians have to offer the poor. . . . The church must be free to be poor in order to minister among the poor." The sale of the tapestry creates a radical alchemy in communities of faith, transforming seemingly worthless objects into limitless wealth. "The Church must trust the Gospel enough to come among the poor with nothing to offer the poor but the Gospel, except the power to discern and the courage to expose the Gospel as it is already mediated in the life of the poor."[6]

*　　　*　　　*

In 1968, a Jesuit priest named Daniel Berrigan and eight other antiwar activists burned draft files in protest of the Vietnam War.[7] In an introduction to Stringfellow's book *Suspect Tenderness,* Berrigan wrote about his motivations for protest: "Dear Friends, I would not have any child born into this world, into this nation, into this church, in order to bear arms, in order to obey the Pentagon, in order to ravage the poor in distant lands, to die there, to kill there, in any sense, in any case, to perish, there as man. . . . In the kingdom of Death we could not but resist Death with all our means and might."[8]

The Catonsville Nine, as the activists came to be known, were arrested, tried, convicted, and sentenced. In November of 1968, Berrigan was sentenced to three years in prison, but with the help of friends, he managed to avoid incarceration for almost two years. In 1970, fully aware that the Catonsville Nine were engaging in criminal activity, Stringfellow and his longtime companion, Anthony Towne, offered the priest asylum. This single act became a cornerstone of Stringfellow's witness as he worked to change the minds and hearts of mainline Christians, calling them to be dissenters and advocates for the oppressed.

In August, Berrigan was arrested in their home on Block Island, New York. Following his arrest, Stringfellow and Towne, unwavering in their commitment to justice, released the following statement:

Grave charges have been made against us by the public authorities and we have pleaded innocent to those charges because we *are* innocent. . . .

Daniel Berrigan is our friend. We rejoice in that fact and strive to be worthy of it. Our hospitality to Daniel Berrigan is no crime. At a certain time and in a certain place we did "relieve, receive, comfort and assist" him and we did "offer and give sustenance and lodging" to him. We did not "harbor" or "conceal" him. We did not "hinder" the authorities.

Father Berrigan has and had no need to be concealed. By his own extraordinary vocation, and by the grace of God, he has become one of the conspicuous Christians of these wretched times. We have done what we could do to affirm him in this regard. We categorically deny that we have done anything to conceal him.

We are not disposed to hide what light there is under a bushel.[9]

For Stringfellow, the moment of Berrigan's arrest became a symbol of all the ways that government can act unjustly against people living out their beliefs. He understood that moment to be symbolic of all the issues that Christians need to address with full understanding and in direct opposition to governing authority.

In the Christian tradition, this movement began the moment Jesus said, "Love your enemies." Lines are blurred by the light and power of this command. Through his own act of dissidence, Stringfellow called the faithful into the question, Who are these enemies of whom Jesus is speaking? To be a person of faith means standing against unjust acts, not out of hatred for the evil committed, but out of a love held for all people. By standing, we act out of love. Stringfellow and Towne dared to house an activist and a wanted criminal, believing as they did that love should be the guiding law, and they opened their hearts and home to love's leading.

When Stringfellow joined in the choir of dissenters against the Vietnam War, he said there was a whole generation of Americans of "voting age who [had] never experienced the vigor of free public debate"[10] and didn't know how to question the prevailing policies of the ruling regime. If war couldn't be debated, it would be propagated without regard for destruction. Even churches, he wrote, had vested interests "in the preservation of incumbent political regimes, military establishments, and the economic status quo."[11] When large corporations, like pharmaceutical companies, benefit from the ongoing institution of war over time, they dehumanize others and idolatrize death. He believed acts of war deluded people's minds and that the powerful antidote was protest.

Throughout his books, Stringfellow returned to this theme: Jesus should be integral to the conversation about the state of injustices before us. Jesus's life and witness should change how we act and what we believe. Jesus's witness should radicalize our beliefs. With this core belief, faith, politics, and the economy became woven together for Stringfellow. "Nothing seems more bewildering," he wrote, "to a person outside the Church about those inside the Church than the contrast between how Christians behave in society and what Christians do in the sanctuary."[12] Not one of his books contains the tightly closed theological systems that were removed from his practice of faith and experience of injustice. He rejected the Marxist-infused ideology that pits the oppressed against the oppressor, and he eschewed championing the experience of the poor over that of the rich. Whether defending a bishop in a heresy trial or representing a Puerto Rican woman in Harlem, his faith had others describing him, as the newspaper *The Nation* did, as a "radically relevant Christian."[13] Rooted in his actions were gleanings from his work and life in Harlem during the civil rights movement. Stringfellow believed "the ministry of Christ is the ministry of the servant in the world and for the world."[14] And he did this work in the name of God and for the sake of the world that God loved.

Stringfellow spent many years of his life, in Harlem and beyond, trying to challenge and remove entrenched systems of injustice. Still, fifty years later there are more than seven million people in the industrial prison complex in the United States and more than sixteen million children living in poverty.[15] There are more than one hundred thousand minors at risk for trafficking in the United States this year.[16] There are more than twenty million refugees risking their lives to find peace. While those numbers are staggering, it is impossible to count the even more numerous injustices that lead to those figures.

Though William Stringfellow's work took place in the wider theological context of the revolutionary 1960s, his search for truth was timeless. He didn't fit neatly into liberation and identity theologies coming into fashion. A fierce critic of the Vietnam War, capitalism, and white supremacy, Stringfellow undoubtedly influenced many dissenters, and his voice remains relevant still as the church seeks to speak to the same injustices that plagued his time.

*　　　*　　　*

More than twenty years ago, just a few years after my ordination but long before I met William Stringfellow in my dream, I founded a community called Thistle Farms, which works with survivors of trafficking, addiction, and prostitution. There, I have witnessed the power of homegrown love to transform politics and economics. This power is limitless because direct intervention in people's lives ripples through society. It is impossible to think about loving the whole world unless you love the individuals on your path. When those individuals are oppressed by forces greater than you, and you find a way to love, those forces are diminished.

When Thistle Farms began, we simply offered sanctuary to five women survivors. Those survivors helped bring hundreds more women into our community. They also worked to change laws in several states, started the largest justice enterprise run by survivors in the United States, and showed the world that we don't have to leave people behind. In the tradition of William Stringfellow, we embody the conviction that an act of love toward a single individual, in defiance of unjust laws, can have exponential effects. That powerful love is a practice of the faithful dissident.

At Thistle Farms, we proclaim that "Love Heals." It is easy to let this phrase become a mere slogan or a distant ideal, subject to the limitations of our resources and the magnitude of need. On the contrary, William Stringfellow was equipped to fight against the mightiest forces—the powers and principalities— precisely because he believed in the ethic of love. He struggled against the restraints of oppression with a sense of calling and purpose. Stringfellow urged us to stop fearing what will happen when we step out of a place of comfort, and to do so with great confidence, carrying that cross as long as necessary. This type of Christianity is, without a doubt, political. Love is political and demands more of us than the complacency constructed by our fears. That Stringfellow's writing and theology speak so powerfully into the injustices of today reminds us we need his passion and voice still.

*   *   *

Stringfellow's dissidence, legal work, and theology were rooted in love, but his was a tough love, often characterized by criticism. No Christian institution was exempt from his direct critique. "Masses of solid, respectable, moderate folk who are members and leaders and clergy," he claimed, "cling to the doctrine which severs religion from life."[17] When theology is conformed to the needs of academic categories and divinity schools, it is training people not for the priesthood but simply as historians, social workers, and ecclesiastical bureaucrats. "Even among those eventually ordained from such seminaries, the danger is that they will come to regard the ordained ministry as a profession pertaining to a certain commodity—religion—which they have been trained in their particular trade school to manufacture or procure and market."[18] Leaders who come out of institutional training lead in such a way that congregations retreat into themselves, becoming "so inverted, so caught up in internal maintenance and procedure, so entrapped in reserving and proliferating a cumbersome, costly, self-serving, officious, indulgent, soft ecclesiastical apparatus that it becomes easy to think they don't have to care about the world."[19] For Stringfellow, theology, unlike religion or philosophy, can never be aloof, as its major concern is the "celebration of the presence of the Word of God in the common life of the world."[20] It takes a servant of the gospel to be a faithful preacher, just as it has always taken sinners to commend the Word of God in the public sphere.

Stringfellow was unabashedly devoted to Scripture, frequently quoting it even as he pointed out the lack of scriptural engagement of fundamentalists and biblical literalists: "If [they] actually took the Bible seriously," he wrote, "they would *inevitably* love the world more readily."[21] Stringfellow believed religion should spark new thoughts in the faithful, changing people's everyday lives. And his writing evidences a weariness in confronting the ecclesiastical structures whose endless arguments focused on political identification or complacency. Only when we remove ourselves from the lonely practices of religion in America, he claimed, can we begin to live into our baptismal covenant as the people of God.

Not only did he target the church, but no political party or international corporation was too powerful for Stringfellow to tackle. He believed that America was a fallen nation because of the way it enslaved human beings, dehumanized people, and intimidated its citizens. Racism, he believed, was woven into the fabric of America, and he was bold in his opposition to the violence and injustices it created. In his writings, he emphasized with italic font, *"white supremacy has been the dominant ethic in virtually every realm of society in America for the past three hundred years and remains entrenched even today."*[22] He lamented "the numberless men of integrity, talent, and enterprise, who suffer emasculation because they were born black, who are wasted because they have been educationally deprived, who are restricted to marginal and menial jobs and now face the prospect that even these become obsolete and eliminated. . . . As far as poverty is concerned, the choice is between nihilists and nominalists. Meanwhile, millions of people are born, endure for a while, and then die, all the while prisoners of the urban ghettos or the rural wastelands."[23]

He also criticized the justice system in the United States. In the East Harlem slums and in the church courts, he encountered systems that imprisoned and discriminated against people and laws that valued property rights over human rights. For Stringfellow, the evil began in seminaries, which normalized the law's neglect and abuse of the dispossessed in the slums. He decried "the scandal of illegal, unconstitutional, and often criminal offenses accomplished by military, police, security, and the intelligence officials within the federal regime."[24] For Stringfellow, Christians in

America—whether lawyers or activists—are called to fight against the powers of death and to work toward freedom.

These uncompromising stances and harsh criticisms made Stringfellow vulnerable to harsh retaliation and marginalization by the church. He suspected some people who referred to him as a "lay theologian" of attempting to discredit and undermine his teachings. Considering the backlash he faced, his critical writings bear a fierce tenderness, as he quotes psalms of lament, such as Psalms 137 and 42. Stringfellow had many tears to wipe with the suffering he encountered, with the failings of the church he loved, and with the losses in his personal life. A life of faithful dissent comes at a cost and doesn't secure power. Even so, Stringfellow believed it allowed him something better: the radical freedom of prophetic witness and the true integrity of the gospel.

*   *   *

In 1962, at a party for the World Council of Churches, Stringfellow met Anthony Towne. Some months later, they reconnected when Towne came to Stringfellow's law office because he was being evicted. Within five months, they had moved in together. Five years later, when Stringfellow was battling a lingering illness, they migrated to Block Island, where they composed books and poetry and defended immigrants, criminals, and the economic poor.

Stringfellow and Towne spoke of the death in Christ "that emancipates a human being from bondage to death."[25] They shared a theology of liberation from death and idolatry, and their collaborations arose from deep discussion and research. Towne was a poet, and in a description of his work, Stringfellow wrote, "I consider that Anthony regarded the use of the language as the distinguishing feature between that which is civil and human and that which is brutal and dehumanized."[26] Towne believed that America had chosen the latter use of the language and spent his life trying to write with language that would cause people to re-think entrenched notions through the power of poetic justice.

For years Stringfellow and Towne lived on the island, fighting together for peace and human rights. Then suddenly and inexplicably, Towne died in 1980. Stringfellow, who died five years later, recounted his first year of mourning in his tribute to Towne, *A Simplicity of Faith*, a book that combines a profound look at grief with intense theological reflection about living in the present.

Stringfellow described being in love as a metaphor for the dual nature of being a person of faith. There are days when love is a very human endeavor and days when one is caught in the lover's sight, seen with God's eyes. The story of Stringfellow and his partner, Anthony Towne, was not celebrated for the height, depth, and breadth of their relationship. What mysteries passed between them are mysteries for the ages, but their seventeen years together inspired Stringfellow to walk through theological imaginings in ways beautiful and haunting. Their relationship was grounding for much of Stringfellow's writing, and it was Towne who participated in Stringfellow's dissent work, stayed by his side when they were arrested, nursed him back to health during his year of convalescence, and inspired in him a deeper and simpler faith during his period of mourning. Through Towne's death, Stringfellow began to distinguish the grief of loss from the mourning he endured for his own life as a means to come to a simpler faith.

Stringfellow's unsentimental theology was an exercise in direct, honest engagement with the human realities of aging, illness, and loss—but also with the relevance of faith to his political and social realities. In his writing, death was not an abstraction: "death names a moral power claiming sovereignty over all men and all things in history. Apart from God, death is the living power."[27] "Theologically speaking, what I am talking about is the meaning of death in Christ that emancipates a human being from bondage to death. Anthony had, long since, suffered whatever the power of death and the fear or thrall of the power of death could do to him,

William Stringfellow and Anthony Towne. William Stringfellow papers, 1940–1985, Division of Rare and Manuscript Collections, Cornell University Library.

and in that suffering, he had encountered the grace of the Word of God enabling him to transcend that suffering. So the threat of death no longer held sway over his life."[28]

For Stringfellow, the hope of the resurrection was not some future dream but the freedom to be dynamic and active in the world through faith—whether speaking to the needs of those on Block Island or tenants treated unjustly in Harlem. Stringfellow was not satisfied to merely *feel* his Christian faith; he wanted to act and write on it. His was a faith that was lived out, even when it meant living fully into pain and loss. Stringfellow's treatise on mourning ends with a eucharistic celebration a year after Towne's death with, as he said, tears done, because the ending isn't death; it is God.

*   *   *

To this day, William Stringfellow remains a profound guide and mentor to those struggling with institutions—particularly the institution of the church. There remains a debate over whether Stringfellow and Towne were lovers, but there is no debate on Stringfellow's denouncing homophobic practices in the church as a sin the institution needed to lay to rest. The cause of full inclusion is still a struggle. There are so many saints in the church of the twenty-first century who have lived quietly in closets, fearing judgment within the body of Christ. In my twenty years at Thistle Farms, I've heard heartbreaking stories about the struggle of men and women trying to unite their sexuality and spirituality, trying to come back into community after being exiled in prisons, and trying to find security when doors are barred on housing and jobs.

For them and for all of us, Stringfellow is a clear and persistent witness to the gospel call to love all creation and to serve the most vulnerable. He never wavered in that call, even when he was frustrated, sick, or grieving. He never shied away from an argument about the policies and practices that cause systematic injustices, and he lived out his call rooted in Scripture. Injustice didn't end in death, he insisted. It ended in God. In the dedication of his book *Dissenter in a Great Society: A Christian View of America in Crisis*, he leads with a passage from 2 Corinthians 8:13-14: "I do not mean that others should be eased and you burdened, but that as a matter of equality your abundance at the present time should supply their want, so that their abundance may supply your want, that there might be equality" (RSV).

I would have been honored to know William Stringfellow outside of my dreams: a dissenter within the church, a witness to the radical nature of Jesus, but also a mentor and colleague whose eyes I could wipe when the work became too much. He said that in living out his vocation he sometimes felt indignation, sometimes grief, sometimes idealism and anguish.[29] When I imagine Stringfellow loving the world and the church so deeply, and yet never being able to be fully himself within the institution, I imagine that beyond the righteous indignation, there was grief.

Stringfellow was a teacher generous enough to make his way into my dream and fill me with hope that, even as the struggle continues, there is time to be loving and pastoral. His vision wasn't of mountaintops: it was of a world where people are honored and respected for their inherent value.

Stringfellow didn't befriend the church or seminaries; he didn't start not-for-profit organizations that outlived him; and because of that, his witness is easily hidden. But his words can change the lives of those who stop and read them. In his short fifty-six years, he impacted movements, articulated the central mission for the church, and influenced dissenters and priests in the decades that followed his life. "In the end, what distinguishes the Christian faith from mere religion . . . is the fear of God. The fear of God in the Christian faith is the unanimous and elementary knowledge of the Church that God is God."[30] For Stringfellow, this meant knowing that God was freed from humanity and in God's freedom chose to be wholly intimate with us so that we too can become free.

In my dream, Stringfellow showed me that those of us who want to be witnesses must love and heal in the midst of our own suffering as well as the suffering of the world. We are called to look beneath the glistening candles adorning altars to find healing for all that is broken. As I have read his work and dreamed of him,

I have wondered how communities of faith can begin to amass enough lamb's wool to wipe away the oceans of tears that we have created. In my dream, the healing balm in the lamb's wool, tucked beneath the golden candlesticks, is the compassion that comes from a fearless love for all people. It makes sense to me that the bearer of the healing wool was my father, whose only line of preaching I know is from a slip of paper that reads, "In the shadow of his cross may your soul find rest."

*   *   *

Once, on a Sunday night flight, I was sitting with a young woman who had been in the Thistle Farms community for a little over a year. She had been in the juvenile system since she dropped out of school in the sixth grade and then graduated into the prison system at her eighteenth birthday. We were traveling to another state to start another community for women survivors, and the trip was her first experience with flying. As we reached cruising altitude, she leaned over me to look out the small window at the full moon and said, "I didn't ever know there was a whole sky above the clouds."

The parables found in the life and writing of William Stringfellow preach the truth of the gospel's call that past the suffering of the world and our own grief there is a greater vista than any of us can imagine. I want to stand with him as he witnesses to that vista where there is space for all of us.

* The author is grateful to Jean Callahan who helped obtain photos and permissions from the Cornell University Division of Rare and Manuscript Collections.

Mahalia Jackson

(1911–1972)

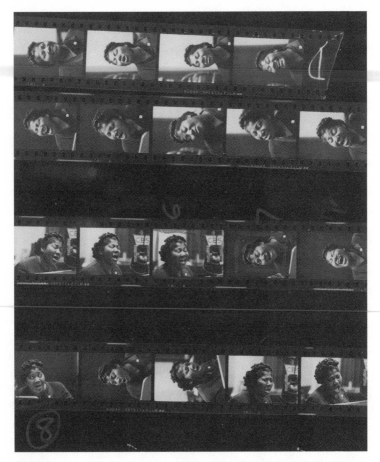

Mahalia Jackson in a CBS studio, recording her debut Columbia Records album, "The World's Greatest Gospel Singer," in November 1954. Photo by Bob Lerner / LOOK Magazine Photograph Collection, Library of Congress, Print & Photographs Division, LC-DIG-ds-10623.

I Will Move on Up
a Little Higher

Mahalia Jackson's Power to Witness through Music

W. Ralph Eubanks

On many a Sunday morning when I was growing up, my father, a slender man with smooth skin the color of warm caramel, would take a black and gray Sears Silvertone record player and roll it on its noisy wheeled stand down the hall into my parents' bedroom. Although he had a couple of Mahalia Jackson records, it seemed as if he played only one: an Apollo Records recording from 1957 called "In the Upper Room with Mahalia Jackson."

The cover featured a stained-glass window in an empty church—the black-and-white photograph had a green tint behind it—and the title song "In the Upper Room" was the first track. When he listened to "In the Upper Room," he was always dressed in a dark suit with a skinny tie. Even today, I can see him standing over the record and watching its incantatory spin as he listened to the music flowing from the scratchy speakers. His head was always bowed as Jackson quietly sang with the gentle accompaniment of her longtime pianist, Mildred Falls. Of course, as a child I found my father's ritual annoying, since he seemed to be obsessed with the lyrics, particularly in the slower part one of the song. The second part became much more up-tempo and had the "bounce" Jackson often said was an essential part of her music, but my father remained in a meditative state during the first part. It may

199

be the fog of memory, but I think he would even play the first part several times—lifting the phonograph needle with the greatest of care—before letting the record move to part two, since to him, part one included the words and message of Mahalia Jackson, spoken just for him. "In the Upper Room" is a traditional spiritual, one whose power comes from its slow, meditative call to prayer followed by a call-and-response affirmation of belief. The lyrics ask the listener to believe, but the singer must express belief for the song to get its message through. What captured my father each Sunday was that Mahalia Jackson sang "In the Upper Room" as if she was making a personal profession of faith and asking him to do the same.

The writer Nelson Algren once proclaimed to a friend, "The way Mahalia sings the Lord's Prayer, now that's the way the Lord intended for it to be sung."[1] As I listen now to my digitally remastered recording of "In the Upper Room," I realize one of Jackson's greatest gifts as a gospel singer was connecting listeners with her faith as well as their own. When she was singing, Jackson said, "I don't seem to be myself. I am transformed from Mahalia Jackson into something divine."[2] In turn, her listeners felt a connection to something sacred and spiritual. Mahalia Jackson truly believed that she talked with the Lord when she sang and asked listeners like my father to do the same, which is why he used the words of "In the Upper Room" to center himself in prayer before church.

Although I am now a Catholic, I was raised in the Christian Methodist Episcopal (CME) Church. In the 1940s and 1950s, CMEs were the Colored Methodist Episcopal Church, and by the sixties became the Christian Methodist Episcopal Church. But to our more refined African Methodist Episcopal (AME) brethren, we were just known as the Country Methodist Episcopal Church, given our sometimes raucous and less staid liturgical music.

When it came to liturgy and music, CMEs were unabashedly down-home and unpretentious. Rather than singing "Amazing Grace" like a traditional hymn, in the CME church we sang it as a call and response anthem. Like Mahalia—and unlike the AMEs—we would shout and clap a little, in a style the Mount Pleasant CME Church choir in Mount Olive, Mississippi, adopted from Jackson.

In an attempt to connect with my father's ritual and reconnect with my country Methodist roots, one Sunday before heading to Mass I stopped and listened to "In The Upper Room." It may simply be the power of suggestion, but that morning I felt ready to go to church thanks to the music of Mahalia Jackson. Her singing provided a tangible connection with the divine.

Then, during the consecration in Mass that morning, with "In the Upper Room" still playing on a loop in my head, it hit me that the expression that I saw on my father's face in front of that old Silvertone record player on Sunday mornings was mirrored in the faces I saw a few nights before in a scratchy YouTube video. The video was taken as Jackson performed at the Newport Jazz Festival in 1958, and the audience seemed truly moved, many of them dancing and clapping their hands. As festival organizer George Wein recalled in an interview with National Public Radio, Jackson's vocal style and performance moved an audience to forget jazz that evening and embrace the power and spirit of gospel.[3]

Mahalia Jackson always preached through her music, using the powerful delivery of the lyrics she sang to get her message across to an audience. That evening in Newport was no different. Many in the crowd that night unwittingly participated in a divine moment. Unlike the revelers at Newport, who connected with Jackson indirectly, my father was actually seeking to commune with the real presence of God through Mahalia's singing.

Through her testimonial style of singing, Jackson was preaching to my father, and that helped him keep some semblance of a connection with the divine as he took his four noisy children to Sunday school and church. Thinking about my father led to another epiphany: Jackson also preached to that crowd at Newport, and based on their raucous yet reverent response, she connected the secular and the spiritual that evening. And, like my father, and like the Newport audience, I was centered by Jackson's voice that morning. It stayed with me and connected me with the divine as I approached the altar to receive the Eucharist. That Sunday, I felt part of a spiritual continuum: I connected with the Lord, with my father, and with the music of Mahalia Jackson.

My father died more than forty years ago, but through him I found a line linking me with Jackson and her music not only in an academic way but also in a personal one, and it's with both the personal interest and the scholar's heart that this chapter looks at Jackson's work as a radical Christian witness, as she herself aligned her personal perspective with historical moments. Jackson left few personal papers behind, and her performances and recordings form the best way to connect with the historical. The songs Jackson chose to record and perform, as well as the performances themselves, reveal the ways that Jackson saw her performance as ministry.

Gospel music has always walked a fine line between ministry and entertainment, and during Jackson's time if you moved into the entertainment realm—as Aretha Franklin and Sam Cooke did—you performed popular music that came to be known as soul. In spite of her international appeal, Jackson's music never truly bridged the divide between the sacred and the secular. Yet when looking at Jackson's body of work, the question arises as to whether her work was performance, ministry, or both. Looking at Jackson's life on the national stage, it's clear Jackson's performance served as ministry.

My personal background as a black Southerner who grew up during the civil rights movement is linked with the way Jackson used her voice to create social change, and social change was part of her larger ministry. Jackson used her music to advance the goals of the civil rights movement, through the songs she chose to sing and through direct action. Yet her desire for social change was not limited to the lives of African Americans; it also included the lives of women. Through song and example, Mahalia Jackson was in-

Mahalia Jackson relaxing backstage at the Newport Jazz Festival in 1957, when she performed as part of the festival's first gospel music showcase. The next year the festival devoted an entire evening to gospel music, and Jackson was the headlining performer. Photo by Ted Williams / Iconic Images.

strumental in shining a light on the circumstances of poor working women, a world from which she was not far removed. She was also instrumental in getting Protestant laypeople to see that women could be preachers. I witnessed this as Mahalia Jackson preached to my father many a Sunday morning during his lifetime. Then, I could not hear her preaching, but today I can hear Mahalia and her message loud and clear.

*　　　*　　　*

Mahalia Jackson's booming contralto may have led her to renown as a gospel singer, but she believed her music had a very simple purpose: it served as a witness for the Lord. On the surface, her handclaps, facial expressions, and impressive vocal range may be viewed as just part of Jackson's onstage persona or the way she communicated with an audience. But Mahalia Jackson was no ordinary performer. In an interview with her friend and fellow Chicagoan Studs Terkel, she was emphatic that she saw her voice—as well as her presence and actions on the stage—as a means of bringing her listeners to God. She referred to her singing and the songs she chose to sing as "a testimony" and told Terkel that in order to sing gospel music a singer needed to be "spirit filled."[4] Whether you watch a scratchy old video of a Jackson performance or listen to a pristine digitally remastered recording of her music, through the very timbre of her voice she reveals a connection with the spirit. There is no doubt you are watching and listening to a woman witnessing through music.

Mahalia Jackson's radical witness seems simple: her singing was a testimony. But it was more than that. Even while Jackson witnessed to the glory of God, she witnessed to the state of life in America for black people and sought to end racial injustice in America through what she sang. Jackson knew that she held a unique position because of the gift of her voice, and she recognized the power of her gift early. Jackson's acts of musical witness began when she recorded her first song, "You Better Run, Run, Run," in 1931, just four years after arriving in Chicago. Yet it was not until the late 1940s that Jackson's power to witness through her music drew wide public recognition.

In 1948, Jackson had her first hit, a recording of composer William Brewster's "Move on Up a Little Higher." The record sold eight million copies nationally and catapulted her to stardom. This rousing gospel anthem also became one of the most requested songs on jukeboxes around Jackson's adopted hometown of Chicago and could sometimes be heard in harmony with the click of pool balls and the buzzing of neon beer signs. When asked by Terkel whether she was concerned about her songs being played in bars and pool halls—venues not thought of as the holiest of places—she responded, "Well, I really feel it is wonderful for people of the world to stop and listen to a sacred record. The Lord commanded us to go in the highways and hedges and compel men to come to God."[5]

By 1950, Jackson became the first gospel singer to perform at Carnegie Hall—she gave five concerts there during her lifetime—and achieved international fame. Jackson's concerts drew thousands worldwide, but she knew it was through recordings of her songs that her witness flowed through the highways and the hedges to ordinary people looking for a moment of uplift and spiritual connection. I know this because I grew up seeing the influence Jackson's voice had in my own household. The power of Mahalia Jackson's music as Christian witness is something I have experienced firsthand.

*   *   *

Born in 1911, Mahalia Jackson described herself as a "back of town girl" from New Orleans, since she was raised in a shotgun shack placed between Water and Audubon Streets facing the Mississippi River in a neighborhood people today call either Uptown Triangle or the Black Pearl.[6] In a conversation with filmmaker Jules Schwerin, this is the way she described her childhood:

> The houses were pretty shabby. . . . The rent was no more than six or eight dollars a month, and things were pretty lean. As a girl, it was nothing for me to go down by the levee on the waterfront and pick up wood that had drifted off the river onto the banks. I'd let it dry, and then carry it back on my head, for cooking, and to keep us warm in the winter. You could be in the house and you could see the sun outside, through the roof. If it rained, it rained inside. We'd rush about putting pots and pans around the floor to catch the run-off before we got flooded.[7]

Music and the church served as distractions from this intense physical poverty. From the age of eight, Jackson knew that her voice was a gift, since she was often praised for it. Of course, in New Orleans music was everywhere, whether it was when she attended Mount Moriah Baptist Church with her family, or when she heard strains of "Nearer My God to Thee" in a nearby funeral procession, or when she listened to the records of blues singers.

Jackson once said, "I was too poor to have any musical training. I just learned to sing from listening to other people, I learned from records, like Bessie Smith and Ma Rainey, and when I came north I had a chance to hear Marian Anderson and Paul Robeson."[8] Jackson lacked the formality of Marian Anderson, but the influence of the blues in her music is unmistakable, with phrasing Jackson uses when she sings "trouble" or "troubles"—rhythmically elongating both syllables—resulting in a sound remarkably similar to Bessie Smith. In some ways they were similar singers in different traditions. If Mahalia Jackson had ever sung the blues, she would sound like Bessie Smith, and if Bessie Smith had ever sung gospel, she would sound like Mahalia Jackson.

Although she was a lifelong Baptist, Jackson said she got a great deal of inspiration from the music of the holiness church. "They had a beat," Jackson once recalled, "a powerful beat, a rhythm we held on to from slavery days, and their music was so strong and expressive, it used to bring tears to my eyes."[9] So if Jackson learned some of her phrasing from Bessie Smith, the moans, groans, shouts, and clapping came from the holiness church. When Jackson left New Orleans for Chicago in 1927, she packed her Southern blues and sanctified rhythm along with what few material goods she owned and headed north.

Like many black Southerners, Mahalia Jackson left the South in the hope of a better job and a better life. The North was a promised land, an escape from the Jim Crow South. But even in the North, black migrants from the South realized they were still subject to the demands of white society. As Richard Wright noted in *12 Million Black Voices*, his reflection on the Great Migration in words and photographs, "Before we black folk can move, we must first look in to the white man's mind to see what is there, to see what he is thinking, and the white man's mind is a mind that is always changing."[10] What Jackson found when she moved north was not new opportunities but work that was similar to what she knew in New Orleans: domestic employment in rich white homes or work as a laundress. She found herself still subject to the ever-changing mind of whites.

Church served as a source of emotional security for many black migrants from the South, and it was no different for Mahalia Jackson. Shortly after moving to Chicago, Jackson became a part of the Johnson Singers, a group she described as "the first organized gospel group in the city."[11] The group included Jackson and three brothers, and they were known for performing black religious songs in a down-home manner. This style of singing was discouraged in old-line churches, which were trying to teach Southern migrants during the Great Migration to leave their unsophisticated ways behind. One pastor was so offended by the style of the Johnson Singers that he told them "Get this twisting and jazz out of the church." On the way out of the door, Jackson was said to reply, "This is the way we sing down South!"[12]

Many black Northern churches tried to emulate the formal hymns of white churches, using choirs to sing European classical songs and anthems. These same churches also served an emerging middle class who saw the black Southern style of worship as an impediment to upward mobility and respectability. Some Southern migrants remained in these mainline churches, while others migrated to storefront churches, where the style of worship was less constrained. But in time, black Baptist and Methodist churches began to embrace the musical style of the new arrivals from the South, since they came to be a majority in these churches and wanted a style of music that melded the South with their new urban way of life.[13]

In *The Souls of Black Folk*, W. E. B. DuBois noted that "the Negro folk-song—the rhythmic cry of the slave—stands today not simply as the sole American music, but as the most beautiful expression of human experience born this side the seas."[14] DuBois understood music as a way of shining a light on the idea of dual consciousness, his belief that black people have to learn to operate in two Americas, one that is black and one that is white. Dual consciousness is the awareness of the "two-ness" of being black and American and the largely unconscious, almost instinctive movement between these two identities. But as Northern blacks confronted DuBois's idea of dual consciousness—one could argue that this duality was brought about by the pressures of the dominant white culture to assimilate—as well as merged their dual consciousness into "a better and truer self," they sought to abandon or erase their pasts rather than embrace them. Instead of seeing beauty in their spiritual origins, they sought to blend their way of musical worship into the ways of the dominant culture. The gospel music movement embraced DuBois's idea that, in this merging of selves and dual consciousness, the older selves would not be lost. Dual consciousness did not mean cultural erasure.

And DuBois intended for the divided self to be a spiritually and socially evolving phenomenon, one that gradually attained "self-conscious manhood" through "strife."[15] The whole process was to come to concretion in a mighty people with a unique soul, since the divided self was destined to cohere and merge. As an intellectual idea, this was not part of Jackson's and the Johnson Singers' thinking, yet their gospel music embodies DuBois's philosophy, serving as a bridge not only between the duality of being black and American but also between the black culture of the North and the South.

*   *   *

Gospel music and the black church may have linked Northern and Southern cultures, but one figure played a dominant role in making gospel music a social force: Thomas Dorsey. When

Mahalia Jackson met Thomas Dorsey in 1928 at the age of seventeen, Dorsey was already well known in Chicago gospel circles. He was also the former accompanist and arranger for blues singer Ma Rainey—back in those days he was known as "Barrellhouse Tom"—and in Jackson he found the blend of blues and spirituality he had been looking for since he turned his work away from jazz and blues toward gospel music. In Jackson, historian Michael Harris notes, Dorsey found a singer who could connect with an audience and catch the communal spirit of performance.[16] From the beginning of their professional relationship, Dorsey seized on her talent and natural audience appeal. "She had it [talent] naturally," Dorsey noted. "But you have a lot of things naturally, but you don't know how to use it, to exhibit it. [I wanted her] to get them trills and the turns and the moans and the expressions."[17]

Jackson had a natural tendency to "start off shouting" and sing her songs faster than Dorsey wanted. Jackson was what was known as a "stretch out" singer, meaning that she chased the melody and meter of music as the spirit moved her. Her style was borrowed from the "Baptist lining style," which allowed the singer to reshape a melody into a form of personal testimony. Dorsey recognized these traits in Jackson and sought to help her find a way to temper her performances, to gradually build up to her trademark shouts, claps, and moans.

Technique was important in teaching Jackson to shape her style, but Dorsey was also relying on an evangelical spirituality rooted in the down-home expressiveness of the African American South. He found that spirituality in Mahalia Jackson, who became the "preacher" of his sermons, the songs he wrote. In Jackson, Dorsey found an ability to capture the communal spirit of a performance and a way to connect that personally and directly with whoever was listening.[18] Thomas Dorsey knew that people like my own father would feel as if she was speaking directly to them. "Fiery and exciting" is how Dorsey described Jackson's singing, even as he coached her to depend less on hymnals and other "books" and more on being filled with the Spirit.

Whether or not Dorsey can be definitively credited with creating the singer Mahalia Jackson became is under question. But what is clear is that Jackson's interpretation of the writing and lyrics of others became one of the ways she preached and gave witness. Jackson frequently performed "His Eye Is on the Sparrow," a song drawn from the Gospel of Matthew showing Jesus's care for the dispossessed. It is a simple song, one that relies on the performer to connect the audience with the core of its message. It is also a song that opens with a rhetorical question—"Why should I be discouraged?"—so the singer must make the answer feel real. When Jackson sings "I know he watches over me," listeners connect with the message of the song. Jackson's ability to make her faith real through music was her ministry.

Jackson also testified through song—whether it was "His Eye Is on the Sparrow," "In the Upper Room," or "Balm in Gilead"— not only with words but with rhythm, movement, and heartfelt expressiveness. The spirit was a call to action. It was through her unique, self-taught vocal style that she found a way to preach God's message, even though the lyrics were created by others. She may have relied on strong lyricists and drawn on the style of black preachers she heard, but the way she would "start off shouting" was uniquely her own.

*   *   *

Jackson believed in singing songs that testified to the glory of the Lord and she found such a song in her breakout "Move on Up a Little Higher." While this was not her first recording, what makes it exceptional is that through the recording she preached and witnessed through her spirit-filled voice to the widest audience she had ever reached. What gives the song the feeling of a Baptist sermon is the way Jackson sings it, with her signature moans, shouts, and pauses, as well as the repetition of the lyrics. Like a good preacher, Jackson starts off slow and tells her audience that she's going to "lay down her cross and get a crown" and when she gets that crown she's going to put on her robe. She then proceeds to tell us what happens once she gets that robe and "moves on up a little higher." When she begins to sing "will you be there?" you can practically hear a congregation responding "yes, we will." That is not a lyric in the song, but the response is implied, just as it is when she sings "meet me there, early one morning, meet me there, somewhere 'round the altar.'" You can hear the rousing and resounding sound of an everlasting "yes, I'll be there" even though it is nowhere on the recording.

"Move on Up a Little Higher," a song about the afterlife, also is a song about equality. Hidden in the message to Jackson's listeners is the preaching that they could overcome all of their "heavy burdens": poverty, segregation, and racism, as well as sexism. You can feel it when listening to her radio performances of many of her songs, including on Studs Terkel's "Hi-Fi Show" in 1957. Jackson performed a wide repertory of her songs and practically stole the show from Terkel when she led the audience to sing along to "Down by the Riverside." She made it clear the song had a message and implored the audience to "lay down their burdens," whatever they may be. In the decade of the 1950s, the cultural norm called for women to be submissive; the way Jackson took command—clearly not shy, not demure—pushes those cultural norms. This led Terkel to quip, "If any woman has a mind of her own, it is Mahalia."[19]

Today we live in an era filled with examples of female artistic empowerment, so it does not seem unusual for a singer like Mahalia Jackson to pack a message or sermon into a song. But in the conformity of 1950s America—the period when Jackson was at her peak—Jackson's message of empowerment had to be conveyed more subversively, since a woman openly pushing against social norms would have not been broadly accepted. Bear in mind that gospel holds its cultural antecedents in the spirituals that slaves sang, and both forms of music carry coded messages. Jackson's performances also include a measure of "signifying," or encoding ideas or perspectives into safe gospel songs.[20]

What Jackson was signifying in her songs was not just the gospel message but also a message that equality for African Americans was part of the gospel message. "Salvation and the Word of God can do things for you," Jackson recalled to Studs Terkel in 1963. "It can open doors for you. And I know it can, Studs. Look what it's done for me. And my people have—we're coming along, but my God, we've come along so slow till we chokin'."[21] Jackson believed if she could push against oppression in our society, then her listeners—both black and white—could do the same. But that message was wrapped inside a gospel message. As a woman performer in the mid-twentieth century, encoding her message in her music was the safe and perhaps only option Jackson had.

Because she had a mind of her own, Jackson interpreted the music she sang just as she wanted. Jackson's songs were for everyone, but they were also targeted toward women with an affirmative gospel message, that God supports them in their survival and liberation from whatever forces are keeping them from moving forward and higher, as with the message in "Jesus Steps Right in When I Need Him Most," which assured the listener of Jesus's provision even "when the meat is low and the money is gone."[22] Through her songs, Jackson let her audience know that even if you have to cook and clean for the white folks, one day in this life—not just in the afterlife—you can lay down your cross for a crown.

Jackson's music reflected the issues black people were facing at the time, yet interestingly her music also appealed to white audiences. With the media exposure Jackson received in the 1950s, many whites considered her a "safe" black figure, someone they felt did not challenge the status quo. Jackson used this unique position to issue a prophetic challenge to white audiences, making them aware of the way white America affected black lives. In

Studs Terkel and his radio show, Jackson found a willing partner in preaching and witnessing her message to white audiences. Jackson once explained to Terkel that when she sang "A City Called Heaven," the city was here on earth, not somewhere up in the clouds. "It was not a question of getting to heaven," Terkel noted. "It was about getting liberation here on earth."[23] So when Jackson sang her message to all her listeners, but white audiences in particular, her message was that love facilitates the working of the spirit, that hate kills hope and peace, and that we should all be working together to build a city called heaven here on earth. Jackson's underlying message was that we all should be working together to knock down the walls of segregation and Jim Crow.

Of course, it took a while for her message to get through to her white listeners. Still, Jackson felt she could change things through her music, and Terkel willingly helped her accomplish that goal through his radio show. At the opening of the 1957 show, he made it clear that Jackson was in charge artistically, although both acknowledge the contribution of accompanist Mildred Falls. Jackson chose all the songs, and many of them were songs she sang at civil rights gatherings, including "Joshua Fit the Battle of Jericho," which she once sang to introduce Martin Luther King Jr. at a civil rights rally.

*   *   *

Singing for Jackson was both salvation and spiritual commitment. That is why, despite many offers to sing jazz and the blues, Mahalia Jackson remained committed to being a gospel singer. Because of that promise to proclaim the gospel in song, Jackson sang in all of her performances as if it was the last thing she was going to do. And she followed the dictum of the holiness church that influenced her musical style: her music served as a witness to the Lord. Although some would argue that the power of her voice was the core of her musical genius, it was also her primary tool in being a strong witness. And in the male-dominated world of Chicago gospel music in the 1920s and 1930s, this was not a role that many women were willing to take. Yet Jackson willingly took a role as witness to her Christian faith and to the struggles of African Americans.

One song aptly demonstrates the duality of Jackson's witness: "Didn't It Rain" is rooted in the blues in its explanation of reality and change. When Jackson sang the words "Didn't it rain, children"—"children" rang out as a term of endearment—she was not talking just about the destruction brought by the rain that went "forty nights without stopping" but also about how a community is going to pull itself together again. This is a song about the reality of the black experience: the disintegration of the individual and the community that came through the experience of racism. Rather than singing the blues, Jackson used a metaphor derived from the blues as a witness for the reality of black life.

Jackson's performances of "Didn't It Rain" were always rooted in the ideas of survival and hope. When you realize that Jackson grew up in a house where "if it rained outside, it rained inside," the song speaks to how she survived a level of poverty that borders on hopelessness. The up-tempo swing of the song is the way Jackson conveyed hope for how African Americans would confront the situations they face in American culture, whether racism or poverty. It is also emblematic of the way Jackson used her art to bear witness for her life and her people, and her songs were her testimony.

Mahalia Jackson's music always reflected her religious faith and her belief in obeying the psalmist's command to "make a joyful noise to the Lord." Although millions experienced Jackson's music through her recordings, her performances brought the recordings alive and mirrored her origins in the black church. It was Jackson's 1950 concert in Carnegie Hall that served as her "coming-out party" for both popular music and the jazz cognoscenti. That performance led many to discover Jackson's voice and to compare it to the great blues singer Bessie Smith. Although Jackson had begun to perform in secular venues, she wanted to keep her music safely in the realm of religion. "Blues are the songs of despair," Jackson once declared, but "Gospel songs are the songs of hope. When you sing gospel you have the feeling there is a cure for what's wrong, but when you are through with the blues, you've got nothing to rest on."[24]

Jackson's concerts were always put on in a way to give both her and the audience something to rest on. The Carnegie Hall performance fit within that realm. Although it was an electrifying and memorable performance, Jackson felt somewhat intimidated by the venue and felt she had to hold back on her religious display. "I got carried away," Jackson acknowledged after the performance. "[I] found myself singing on my knees for them. I had to straighten up and say, 'Now we'd best remember we're in Carnegie Hall and if we cut up too much, they might put us out.'"[25] But it was her 1958 appearance at the Newport Jazz Festival that is known as a performance that felt like a religious event even though it was a secular one. Jackson appeared at Newport in 1957 but requested that the 1958 festival devote an entire evening to gospel music, and she was the headlining performer.

She was introduced to the audience that evening simply: "Ladies and gentlemen, it is Sunday, and it is time for the world's greatest gospel singer, Miss Mahalia Jackson." From that moment on, it was not just a concert but a moment of witness for her religious faith. With the 1950s folk revival in full swing, Jackson's appearance that evening was billed as a secular affair. But from the very moment she was introduced, Jackson shifted the tone and made her performance a sacred moment. In other words, she took her audience to church.

Jackson opened with "An Evening Prayer," and she performed it as if she were actually praying for the audience rather than singing for them. Something intensely personal became public in that moment, not for dramatic effect but as an actual spiritual offering. Jackson always read from the Bible before taking to the stage for inspiration. We will never know what verse or chapter she read from that evening, but you can't watch or listen to the performance without feeling that it comes from a place of deep religious conviction.

Following the pattern of preaching from the Baptist tradition in which she was raised, Jackson began her performance on a slow tempo and gradually built it up. Her singing style began with what gospel scholar Horace Clarence Boyer described as a slow, languorous way of singing "that allowed the singer to execute each syllable by adding several extra tones, bending these added tones in myriad directions, and reshaping the melody into a personal testimony."[26] The performance at Newport drew on this style and was one of personal testimony, which is clear in the way that she clapped along as she sang "Everybody Talkin' 'Bout Heaven" and got members of the audience to do the same. After she took the concert up-tempo by performing "Didn't It Rain?" the audience became raucous and several couples begin to swing dance as Jackson sang. "It started to rain when she sang that song," recalled festival producer George Wein in 2000. "It was unearthly. It was just beautiful." When most of us think of the music of Mahalia Jackson, we don't think crowds of people dancing, but that is exactly what happened in the rain that night at Newport. Jackson may have seen her ministry as bound in religion and social change, yet people were still inspired to dance to her music. Jackson communicated a moral moment through her music, but she also used a beat to permeate the secular sphere with her spiritual message.

After getting the crowd whipped up in the spirit of the song, she started to bring the audience back from secular pursuits to prayer when she sang "The Lord's Prayer." Several members of the audience even bowed their heads as she sang and appeared to be as engaged in a moment of prayer as Jackson.

"The Lord's Prayer" was to be Jackson's last song of the evening, but the audience got her to perform three more songs as an encore: "Joshua Fit the Battle of Jericho," "Jesus Met the Woman at the Well," and "His Eye Is on the Sparrow." Although this threw off the arc of her performance—Jackson intended to leave the audience in a reflective moment with "The Lord's Prayer"—she found the energy to keep her audience focused on the sacred by concluding with "His Eye Is on the Sparrow." As Jackson sang and clapped her hands, thousands of people that evening in Newport, Rhode Island, knowingly or unknowingly participated in a divine moment. Some in the integrated crowd of 1950s hipsters even began to adopt the cadence of Jackson's handclaps, as if they were in church and were moved by the Spirit—exactly what Jackson hoped would happen.

*   *   *

Jackson's Newport Jazz Festival performance signaled that her work was reaching a broader audience, and appearances on the stage led to approaches from film and television. Her performance on twenty episodes of her own television show on CBS led writer and filmmaker Jules Schwerin to make a deal with Jackson to develop a documentary on her life. As part of that, Schwerin wrote a check for $200 to reserve his option. Upon receiving the check, Jackson told Schwerin that he must have left a zero off the check. When he said he hadn't, Jackson responded by waving the check at him and saying, "What do you expect me to do with this? Wipe my ass with it?" Jackson had just signed an agreement with Universal Pictures to be paid $10,000 per week to appear in one scene of a remake of *Imitation of Life*. Jackson still described herself as a "back of town" girl from New Orleans, but she had become more sophisticated about money—although she only worked for cash—and was concerned about the status of her performance venues.

Director Douglas Sirk used Jackson's dirgelike performance of "Troubles of the World" in his 1959 version of *Imitation of Life* for dramatic impact—and perhaps box office appeal—but when the performance is viewed on its own, it is a moment of witness rather than melodrama. Although Jackson wanted to be well compensated for her work, she still had not left behind the idea that her performances served as a testimony to her faith. And her film performance had real power. For that reason, in popular memory, the 1959 version of *Imitation of Life* is known as "the version with Mahalia."

Some film historians have argued that, in *Imitation of Life*, Sirk sought to make Jackson seem grotesque. Before casting Jackson, Sirk went to a concert Jackson gave at the University of California at Los Angeles. Commenting on the concert, Sirk said he knew nothing about Jackson before "but here on this stage was this large, homely, ungainly woman—and all those beautiful young faces turned up to her, and absolutely smitten with her. I tried to get some of that experience in the picture."[27]

In drawing the camera close on Jackson and overexposing her mouth as she sang, Sirk used Jackson to amplify the dramatic climax of the movie. But Jackson's voice overrode anything Sirk could do with a camera. It is her rendering of "Troubles of the World," not the camera angle, that serves as the height of drama. When Jackson slowly and confidently sang "soon I will be done with the troubles of the world," those words became an expression of deep faith. To shift the viewer away from the display of faith and back to the film's narrative, Sirk had to pan the camera away from Jackson quickly. Jackson's moment of witness transcended the plot of the film and its director's attempts to manipulate the emotions of its viewers.

What Sirk probably did not realize is that "Troubles of the World" was a song usually performed with a faster tempo. In Jackson's role as the soloist at the funeral of the film's long-suffering maid, Annie—a black woman who could only enjoy the riches of the world as long as she was employed by a white woman—the slower, dirgelike arrangement makes the song take on a role of social commentary beyond Sirk's trademark melodrama. Jackson sings of Annie going home to God with true conviction, particularly when she stretches out "troubles," making it the focus of the lyrics. Black audiences understood the subtext of Jackson's performance in a way white audiences—and the film's director—could not. And that subtext was that Annie was leaving a world where she could not be treated as an equal, and that lack of equality was one of the great troubles of this world.

Toward the end of Jackson's life, she did "cross over" into performing some secular music, such as "You'll Never Walk Alone" from Lerner and Loewe's *Carousel*. Yet in her interpretation of popular songs, she infused her blues and holiness roots rather than Tin Pan Alley showmanship. When Jackson sings "You'll Never Walk Alone," she erases the way that song fits into the narrative of *Carousel* and makes it her own by merging her gospel inflections with the interpretation of that song. Lerner and Loewe's lyrics speak more of the real presence of God when Mahalia Jackson sings them, removing them from the narrative context of *Carousel*. When Jackson sings, "walk on, walk on with hope in your heart," the gospel inflection of her solo piano accompaniment sends a message to the listener that the word "hope" in this song actually means "faith," particularly faith in God.

Mahalia Jackson's witness didn't come through theological training but through her singing, as a tangible act as well as a feeling. Witness for Mahalia Jackson was about what you felt rather than what you understood intellectually. And once Jackson became nationally and internationally known, as well as financially independent, her acts of witness became more overt. But she began that process slowly and did so in the safety of the Berkshire mountains in western Massachusetts in the early 1950s.

*   *   *

In the summer of 1951, Mahalia Jackson traveled to Lenox, Massachusetts, with her longtime accompanist, Mildred Falls, to be a guest of the summer school of the Institute of Jazz Studies. Jackson and Falls were the guest of musicologist Marshall Stearns, a student of the West African origins of jazz, who asked Jackson to relate to an audience the origins of her music. But Jackson would not place her work in the jazz tradition. "Now I hear a lot of sound, like it's half jazz. Well gospel isn't! The way I see it, if you sing the gospel, you don't need artificial anything."[28]

Over the years, Falls learned to play to bring out every nuance of Jackson's voice, and that day in the Berkshires was no exception. In his diary, Stearns noted "She [Jackson] breaks every rule of concert singing, taking breaths in the middle of a word, and sometimes garbing the words together. But the full-throated feeling and expression are seraphic."[29] And Stearns noted that Falls anticipated all of the rules Jackson broke.

After discussing her music and her self-taught style, Jackson's remarks took a turn away from music toward civil rights. On a warm summer evening in 1951, Jackson warned her benign audience in the Berkshires that Jim Crow must go and that there would be consequences if there were not changes to the way black people were being treated. It was a rare moment of direct advocacy and witness for Jackson—one through her words rather than her music—to an audience of academics, and it foreshadowed Jackson's public association with the civil rights movement.

Years later, when asked about her pronouncement to the audience in the Berkshires, on both music and civil rights, Jackson said, "I just flatfooted told them what I knew, and what I didn't know. No use in trying to hide that. We ended up having us a time."[30] It fit with Jackson's persona: self-taught singer, self-taught activist. Both the words Jackson sang and those she spoke that day in the Berkshires came from her deep personal beliefs, not from an intensely analytical point of view, like the PhD musicologists Jackson thought were picking apart her music and words like "birds at a box of corn." As the decade progressed, and as the civil rights movement began, Jackson continued to use her public profile and celebrity to promote social change.

Five years after her public announcement of support for civil rights in the safety of the Berkshires, the Reverend Ralph D. Abernathy asked Jackson to perform in Montgomery, Alabama, at a symposium on the politics of social change. The event also honored those who had kept the Montgomery bus boycott going. When Abernathy asked Jackson what her fee would be, her response was "I ain't comin' to Montgomery to make no money off them walkin' folks!"[31]

On Thursday, December 6, 1956, Jackson performed at the St. John AME Church of Montgomery free of charge. The stately red-brick church with stained-glass windows was packed by noon, and she performed well into the night to sounds of joy from the audience, many of whom were ending a day of fasting and thanksgiving. She opened with what she called a "soft number": "I've Heard of a City Called Heaven" and slowly increased the tempo of the evening up to her trademark bounce, leading to her signature "Move on Up a Little Higher." By the end of the evening the church was raucous and emotional, with shouts from the well-dressed crowd gathered there of "Sing the song, girl!" and "Oh, yes, Jesus!" bouncing off the rafters. Then Jackson calmed the audience through a pre-Christmas performance of "Silent Night," which is how she sent the people of Montgomery out to continue their work in promoting nonviolent protest.

Although Jackson's trip to Montgomery marked the beginning of her association with Martin Luther King Jr., it was not long after her trip to Montgomery that the issue of civil rights and racial violence played a more personal role in her life. In 1957 Jackson bought a house in a white neighborhood on Chicago's South Side. Today the historic marker placed by the city of Chicago outside the house tells you that 8358 S. Indiana Avenue was once owned by a woman known as the world's greatest gospel singer, but it doesn't tell about the personal struggle Jackson endured to live there.

The news of Jackson's purchase of the red-brick ranch-style house was received with hostility and led to her receiving calls at all hours of the night, some threatening to blow her house up with dynamite. Rifle bullets were fired through her windows, and a police guard was posted at her house for an entire year. CBS journalist Edward R. Murrow, after a broadcast interview with Jackson, charged that the attack on Jackson's home was an incident in the rising tide of racism.[32]

Jackson's celebrity did not make her immune from racism. She often had to sleep in her lavender Cadillac when she traveled to the South since segregation prohibited even the world's greatest gospel singer from getting a hotel room. On those trips South she was often stopped by police, and she would tell them that she was a maid and was just driving the car for the white woman she claimed to work for. Once, in a particularly threating situation, she made up a name for the "madam" who owned the car: Mildred Dorsey. The name is a combination of her accompanist, Mildred Falls, and her great mentor, Thomas Dorsey.[33]

Rather than retreating from the public eye after her very public encounter with racism, Jackson began to be more vigorous in her support of civil rights and used her music as a means of promoting the idea of racial justice, just as she had in Montgomery. Jackson became a close confidant of Martin Luther King Jr.—so close that in times of trouble and distress King would call Jackson on the phone and ask her to sing Thomas Dorsey's "Precious Lord Take My Hand." At the urging of Dr. King, Jackson performed "I've Been 'Buked and I've Been Scorned" at the Lincoln Memorial at the March on Washington in August 1963. Given the expressive way she sang that day, it's hard not to see this song as a witness to all of the injustices she had experienced in her life. She also sang the song for those who had traveled to the March on Washington, since she knew they had been "'buked and scorned" as well. As she looked out from where she sat on the steps of the Lincoln Memorial, she saw the faces of "a nation of people marching together . . . like the vision of Moses, that the Children of Israel would march into Canaan."[34] "I've Been 'Buked and I've Been

Scorned" is a song that serves as witness to the pain and suffering of slavery, and Jackson's performance transformed the song into one about the pain and suffering of Jim Crow.

March on Washington organizer Bayard Rustin stood stately and composed at Jackson's side as she sang, holding a pad that probably held a minute-by-minute schedule of speakers. Once Jackson had been singing for three minutes, Rustin reached toward her, but she motioned to him—without taking her eyes off her audience—that she was not done and continued singing. Jackson shouted a heartfelt "hallelujah," extended her arms, and began to move as if she was in church. Halfway through her nearly seven-minute performance, Jackson put her hands on her hips and moved her shoulders as she shouted to the crowd, "I'm going to tell my Lord when I get home, that you've been mistreating me for so long."[35] It's almost as if she was exercising some emotional restraint, since Jackson certainly would have made her movements even more dramatic had the stage not been so crowded that day, given the way she often moved around a stage as she sang and used her hands, body, and feet. The movements Jackson usually made on stage were what she called "demonstrating," which had many meanings but in this case referred to showing her connection to the Holy Spirit. Instead of more demonstrative movements, Jackson twisted her head as she sang and used the crown-like hat she wore to frame the emotion in her face.

Later, seated near King as he took the stage, Jackson continued her witness. As King stood at the podium, she encouraged him to speak: "Tell them about the dream, Martin! Tell them about the dream!"[36] That's what those close to the podium heard the gospel great shout midway through the speech. King had urged Jackson to perform "I've Been 'Buked and I've Been Scorned," and now she was making her own request of Dr. King. Jackson's prompt had a startling effect: without pausing, King pushed his notes off to the side. He stopped looking down at the prepared text, and as he went extemporaneous, his voice took on a preacherly oratorical style. The historic section of the speech famously begins "And so even though we face the difficulties of today and tomorrow, I still have a dream. It is a dream deeply rooted in the American dream."

Some believe that without Jackson's urging that day, King would have delivered a different speech and would not have talked about his dream. And perhaps without Jackson's being moved by the spirit as she sang at the Lincoln Memorial, as well as her using her voice to "demonstrate" to the audience what it felt like to be "'buked and scorned," she may never have asked King to tell the audience about his dream.

*   *   *

Mahalia Jackson's political activism is often overlooked because it is hidden in the music. From a cultural perspective, gospel music and spirituals during the civil rights movement are often thought of as just a way to escape from the harsh realities of Jim Crow and the indignities of racism. However, an artist like Jackson saw her music as a means of drawing people to action rather than simply being "a balm in Gilead" or escape from the pain of discrimination.

Jackson's performance of gospel music, from the highways and hedges of America to Carnegie Hall, was indeed a ministry, just not in the traditional sense. She had no church, but through the songs she sang and the style in which she performed them, she changed the lives of the people who heard her voice and listened to the message of her songs. When you sing gospel, Jackson once noted, "you have a feeling there is a cure for what is wrong."[37] Jackson saw gospel music as a call to action, whether it was to follow the teaching of Jesus to love one another or to use her music to push others to action, much as she did with Martin Luther King Jr. at the March on Washington. Of course, many were drawn to Jackson because of the power of her voice, but her art also bore witness to her life and the life of African Americans. That witness holds the power of her art and the power of her ministry. Her music combined with her activism was a powerful way that Jackson embodied the lived theology of black Christianity, and wherever she performed became the pulpit for her message of love, hope, and social activism.

Mahalia Jackson understood and lived an important lesson taught to me in my country Methodist Sunday school: faith without works is useless. On those childhood Sunday mornings in my Mississippi household, my father may have seen the music of Mahalia Jackson as a call to prayer, but I have come to see it slightly differently. Jackson's music is a call to action through prayer, and it is a form of ministry. Whenever I hear Mahalia Jackson's "In the Upper Room" I may think of my father, but now I also think about the grace and power of Jackson's music and the influence that her radical ministry of music exerted around the world.

Lucy Randolph Mason

(1882–1959)

Lucy Randolph Mason, photographed here for an article in the *Winston-Salem Journal and Sentinel*. Lucy Randolph Mason Papers, David M. Rubenstein Rare Book & Manuscript Library, Duke University.

The Rest of Us

*Lucy Randolph Mason and the Search
for Dignity for American Workers*

Susan M. Glisson and Charles H. Tucker

The renegade Baptist preacher and civil rights activist Will Campbell once said that nice people are hard to write about because they're boring. But it was Campbell and his peers who led students to rediscover figures like Lucy Randolph Mason, a white woman of aristocratic-Virginia origins who broke with the white supremacist norms of her day and helped organize interracial unions in the American South in the 1930s.

It's difficult to uncover any scandals in Mason's life. There is no compelling morality play scenario, no Damascus Road conversion experience to lend a dramatic and gripping "before and after" narrative of how she lived her life. Her family, privileged in status through a prominent historical name but not in money, raised her in an Episcopalian home and taught her to care for others. Her parents demonstrated that lesson through their own examples. So when Mason began her own public life, there was no theatrical family rift whereby she was cast out on her own to follow her revolutionary cause. For part of her life, she was a mundane civil servant, working under a Democratic administration in the Great Depression environment that toyed with radically progressive ideas and that approved of her stances, so there was no whistleblowing, WikiLeaks-style upending of an oppressive regime.

Even as a union organizer, she wasn't on strike lines or part of boycotts of union-busting bosses.

What did Mason do instead? She wrote a lot of letters. She wrote press releases and media advisories about factory conditions. She identified officials, ministers, newspaper editors, and business leaders who opposed unions, and she met with them. She asked them, politely, to reconsider their positions. And sometimes, she changed their minds, or at least persuaded them to soften their public denouncements of union activity. Even when they disagreed with her, the men (and they were always men) remarked on how charming and polite "Miss Lucy" was, how respectful and engaging.

You will not find a Che Guevara–style revolutionary trope in any story about Lucy Mason. In our current climate of reality television and celebrity worship, the story of a nice, petite, white-haired woman writing letters and meeting with powerful elites doesn't have the soundbite-shaped, headline-grabbing drama that would earn attention. Even beyond the entertainment-driven approach of most media, what most draws our attention in efforts to protest social injustice are marches and public protests, not relationship building across enemy lines or educational brochures (the memes of their day) to subtly shift mind-sets.

But don't let her mildness fool you into missing how radical she was. Mason was not only a true iconoclast, she was also the most terrifying of change-agents: she was a member of the social elite who saw the system for what it was, its faults and fallacies, and actively worked to change it, not only for minorities but also for poor and working class whites. It was unheard of that a white woman, let alone a white woman of aristocratic-Virginia origins, would break with the white supremacist norms of her day and help organize interracial unions in the American South in the 1930s. But she did.

She was a woman who acted as go-between for union reps and business owners at a time when women in leadership roles in either rank were rare. Interestingly, Mason was a person who truly took her faith to heart and lived a quiet, consistent life based on its convictions. She loved her "enemies," in word and deed. Moreover, to those she encountered, Mason offered herself as a witness to that faith by using the talents and gifts bestowed on her by God (even though they were usually not recognized as such until much later) to make a difference not only in the perceptions of labor by management but also in how people of differing economic, ethnic, and religious strata viewed each other.

*   *   *

Tifton, Georgia, 1948. Tensions ran high in this small town. Like many rural towns, Tifton grew around a railroad stop. It had a cotton gin, a lumber mill, and other business that supported the local farm and timber industries, where cotton and raw lumber could be processed and loaded on railroad cars for shipment up North or back East. It was a sleepy town where nothing much happened. A town where, since the end of World War II, the weather was the chief topic of conversation.

But not that spring. That spring, conflict was in the air. The local chapter of the United Packing House Workers of America had called a strike. Not only that: the officials of the union had enlisted the aid of the Congress of Industrial Organizations (CIO), a federation of unions formed in 1935, to assist them in their strike against local packing companies. The CIO agreed to help and sent word that a representative would arrive shortly. In many ways, this was salt in the wounds of the business owners—not only was the CIO from "up North," but they accepted African American workers into their ranks. This was a challenge to the business owners' authority and, indeed, the social order as a whole.

Meanwhile, tensions continued to escalate between the strikers and the plant owners. The evening before the CIO representative was scheduled to arrive, company guards seized an African

American worker. The guards beat the man severely. They told him that they would burn his home if he did not go back to work and convince others to do the same.

The next morning the CIO intermediary arrived in Tifton.

There are no accounts of the reaction of the union reps who waited for the CIO organizer at the train depot when the "roving ambassador" for the CIO stepped down onto the platform. Most likely, they expected the fearless CIO organizer to be a man, tall and broad shouldered with big hands scarred by work and knuckles deformed from a dozen fights on docks and loading platforms. Most likely they were still looking for him when a slight, bespectacled, fifty-five-year-old white woman carefully made her way down the metal steps and stepped lightly onto the platform. The woman was physically small, with fine, white hair. Lucy Randolph Mason had arrived.

When she introduced herself, little did the union reps guess that, within this daughter of Southern aristocracy, fierce determination, radical ideals, and Southern manners and charm coexisted in equal measure, all of it held together by an iron faith. Those she met soon found themselves calling her "Miss Lucy," as befitting one of her social station.

After the initial shock faded, Mason asked to meet with the man who had been beaten. After speaking with him, Mason proceeded directly to the sheriff's office to register a complaint. The sheriff was unavailable. Undaunted, Mason paid a visit to the local judge and requested assistance.

That afternoon, the sheriff, his deputies, the local union organizers, and Mason met to discuss the strike. The meeting soon escalated into a shouting match and threats of violence. The sheriff and the union reps pushed back from the table, rising to their feet. When it seemed certain that an all-out brawl was imminent, Mason stepped between the men, calming them and ushering the labor leaders out of the building. Although the union reps were loath to turn tail and run, Mason promised that there would be a full investigation by the US District Attorney's office into violations of civil rights by the authorities and the factory owners.

The FBI began the promised investigation. Eventually, the packing companies and workers settled the strike successfully. The sheriff who had condoned the violence against the union workers lost his seat, replaced by a newly elected sheriff who proved to be more amenable to labor activity.[1]

*   *   *

The daughter of an Episcopal minister, Lucy Randolph Mason was born in northern Virginia on July 26, 1882, at a tumultuous time in the South. By the year of her birth, the Civil War had been over for almost twenty years. Reconstruction, too, having ended thirteen years before in Virginia, was becoming a memory; the North had traded its military presence in the rest of the South for a presidential victory in 1877 and returned governance of the region to its white citizens. Into this changing, often confusing, and sometimes even violent environment, the Masons gave birth to Lucy, who took her place among a family of famed lineage in a state that prized its esteemed names. To be born a Mason in the Commonwealth of Virginia was no minor matter. Ralph McGill, editor of the *Atlanta Constitution*, later noted of Mason's ancestry that it "entitled her to membership in both the Daughters of the American Revolution and the United Daughters of the Confederacy . . . 'When it came to ancestors she made all the others seem parvenus.'" The first Mason to arrive in the new colony in 1651 prospered, became a member of the House of Burgesses, and established a reputation as a protector of the rights of the underprivileged. Through both parents, Lucy Mason was related to George Mason, who authored the Virginia Bill of Rights, on which the Constitution's would be based. In 1775, he called for the new nation to abolish slavery, warning, "Providence punishes national sins by national calamities."[2] The practice of speaking for and of aiding those perceived as less fortunate became a hallmark of the Mason family, one repeated by Lucy Mason's parents.[3]

Despite her pedigree, Mason was not wealthy.[4] In her autobiography, she defended her "background for action," dispelling any notion of having a "silver spoon in [her] mouth." Mason's family relied on her father's small church salary, "paid mostly in black-eyed peas and bacon."[5] Mason attended the exclusive Powell's School for Girls in Richmond, but she did not finish high school because her parents could not afford it.[6] While Mason's parents did not leave her a legacy of wealth and comfort, they bestowed on her a commitment to community service, having, as Mason described, "a strong sense of social responsibility [growing] out of religious conviction."[7] Mason recalled later in life her insistence as a child on praying for the devil. When asked why she did so, young Lucy replied, "He is so bad he must be very unhappy, and I want to ask God to make him good."[8] Even in childhood, Mason had a growing social conscience. Her ability to empathize with a perceived "enemy" would become a hallmark of her life's work.

Mason's mother was concerned particularly with social improvement and committed herself to alleviating some of society's ills through prison reform. She conducted a Bible class in the state penitentiary, located near Richmond, and on learning of the horrible conditions there, distributed pamphlets throughout the state, calling for reform. Apparently, her efforts threatened the authorities of the penitentiary, which closed its doors to visitors for a year, citing a smallpox scare in Norfolk, one hundred miles away. Mason notes that her mother's activities led "to some immediate reforms and doubtless contributed to the sweeping changes that took place some years after her death."[9] Mason's mother did not content herself with letter writing or distributing pamphlets. She took many released convicts into her home until their situations improved, and they lived in the third-floor bedroom next to Mason's room. Mason's father shared his wife's social concerns, using his position as a minister to aid people in his community. Mason recalled one instance in which her father braved heavy snows to get coal for heat and cooking to a poor widow who was not even one of his parishioners.[10] Thus, Lucy Mason's parents raised her in an atmosphere of social awareness and, more importantly, exemplified committed social action. That association from childhood with marginalized people encouraged Mason to identify more easily with those who did not share her protected status or the privileges attendant to it.

Mason's faith in God and the teachings of her parents inspired her belief that as an evangelical Protestant she bore a responsibility to care for others.[11] Mason reported later in life that, "If I had been a man, I would have become a minister." She remembered that, at the age of fourteen, a visiting missionary's sermon so profoundly moved her that she determined to become a missionary herself. But then she "recognized that religion can be put to work right in one's own community."[12] Throughout her life, Mason continued to attribute the basis for her commitment to social activism to her religious beliefs; that religious framework is crucial to understanding her motivations as well as the character of her activism. She placed moral conviction over cultural expectation. And yet Mason's involvement in such issues resulted from a process developed over time. She grew from a concerned young woman so worried about embarrassing her father with her liberal causes that she wrote early pamphlets under a pen name, into a vehement supporter of interracial labor activity who faced down angry sheriffs and persuaded recalcitrant factory owners, politicians, and ministers to support the cause of organized labor.[13]

When she was eighteen, Mason taught a Sunday school class in a mission church in one of Richmond's working-class districts. The bleakness of her students' lives struck Mason and piqued her social conscience.[14] She began a period of self-education, including reading the work of Walter Rauschenbusch. The philosophy of the Social Gospel taught that human missteps were not merely the result of individual flaws; rather, they were compelled by inequitable social conditions. Her exposure to Social Gospel ideas led Mason to depart decisively from the religious understandings of her region; it advocated a systemic rather than an individual approach to helping others. As she said, "Church people ought to do something to bring about the Kingdom of God on earth."[15] In the Social Gospel, Mason saw the beginnings of an organized response to the ills around her. Thus, a person living in a tenement building or sharecropper's shack might suffer from alcoholism less because of some inherent personal weakness but more as a coping mechanism resulting from their lack of control over oppressive social conditions. Lucy Mason believed in the ultimate potential of that system to be redeemed and became a steadfast adherent, despite larger denominational resistance to the Social Gospel theology in the South.[16]

Mason worked most of her life, chiefly from necessity resulting from her family's lack of wealth.[17] At the age of twenty-two, Mason taught herself stenography and, through a family connection, found a job with a Richmond law firm that often handled large insurance casualty cases that stemmed from industrial injuries. It was there at her first occupation that she encountered the often-devastating effects of industrial capitalism. What she witnessed reinforced her understanding of the need for an organized response to inequities in the workplace. She began to encounter others whose lives differed drastically from her own.

As an employee at the law firm for eight years, Mason witnessed how little protection employers afforded workers injured on the job. She toured factories and saw firsthand the poor working conditions. She was particularly struck by the effects of these conditions on female workers. "I saw girls of 14 working 10 hours a day for less than a living wage as a matter of course," she said later. "I saw women who had worked under those conditions from 14 to 25. They looked like women of 50."[18]

One particular instance haunted Mason throughout her life. Mason, assigned to a young attorney, was asked one day to come to his office to record the conversation he was about to have with a factory worker on behalf of a client. Steno pad in hand, Mason knocked on the door and slipped inside, taking her seat next to the young attorney's desk.

Across from the attorney sat the worker. Although the worker was only seventeen years old, she looked much older, worn by years of fourteen-hour workdays. Her hair was lank and oily. Cradled protectively in her lap was her hand—or what was left of it.

"I'm sure you'll agree that what our client is offering you is more than generous," the attorney may have said. "After all, seventy-five dollars is a lot of money."

Eventually, the young woman, poor, uneducated, and without representation, accepted the offer.

Mason "was appalled. That is what I mean when I talk about the indifference of most of us to what happens to the rest of us," she recalled later. "How could that young lawyer have stood by and seen a girl of 17 get $75 for her right hand? The loss of her right hand meant that she was unfit for work in a factory and that was all she knew how to do," Mason remembered. "I can never forget her. All my life, she has followed me."[19]

Mason became convinced of the need for labor unions to assist working people. She would later say that she did not know when she became "union conscious." Rather, she seemed to express particular concern for those who suffered from industrial accidents and in the process noticed that "the best paid workers were union and [they] had an eight-hour day and a half a day off on Saturday."[20] Two years into her employment at the law firm, in 1906, she became a member of the Union Labor League of Richmond and began lobbying for an eight-hour working day for women, and also worked for the Equal Suffrage League and the League of Women Voters because, she said, "both were interested in labor and social legislation."[21]

Mason's growing interest in interracial activities led her to take a position in the YWCA. Even in the South, where state and local governments and factory owners largely condemned union activity, local YWCA officers held progressive positions on labor issues. Her work with the YWCA cemented her concern for the working class and her belief that labor unions were a way of alleviating some of the problems among working people. In addition, a growing interest in securing aid for all of Richmond's citizens, black and white, led in 1929 to Mason's public disavowal of segregation. A courageous stand in the former capital of the Confederacy, Mason's opposition to segregation and her public statements on matters of race indicate a growing commitment to working on behalf of and with blacks. She had begun to understand what a current social critic has articulated:

> If you are a white ally, but are not aware of the pain of whiteness, when push comes to shove you will crumble. Because racial equality isn't going to look like having a statistically acceptable number of black CEOs. Racial equality isn't your life now, except with more POC [people of color] friends. Racial equality will require a deep restructuring of a society that is *founded* on slavery. Gender equality will require a deep restructuring of a society that is founded on patriarchy. Society is currently set up to grant privilege to those who are able to do the tasks white men are good at; a more equitable society will *value different tasks.*[22]

During her tenure as an industrial secretary for the YWCA, Mason became a member of the Virginia Commission on Interracial Cooperation, and in 1928 she cochaired a subcommittee of the Richmond Council of Social Agencies, which examined the economic status of Richmond's black community. The conditions she found horrified her; the subcommittee concluded that the "inferior economic status" of Richmond's black community "constituted its most fundamental and pressing problem."[23] That problem caused Mason's outspoken support of improvements for Richmond's black citizens, including the reorganization of Richmond's Urban League.[24] Her support endeared her to Richmond's black community, which honored her just before she left Richmond a few years later.[25] One friend wrote of Mason in this period, "I admire her for her many splendid qualities, but most of all for the fact that she is not afraid of tomorrow."[26] Throughout this early activity, Mason confessed a keen interest "in better understanding and cooperation between the white and Negro races."[27]

She began supporting women's suffrage as a way to bring what she saw as the humanizing force of women's voices to the destructive world of industrial capitalism. An early Mason pamphlet from 1912, *The Divine Discontent*, argued that providing the ballot to women would bring their discontent to public life: "Divine discontent has been responsible for every reformation accomplished in the history of our race. It has furnished the incentive for progress and development. It has led to the purifying of religion, politics and all social institutions."[28] She became involved in efforts to support workers, and began to use her name recognition to take on actions business interests denounced, including organizing an all-female strike. The *New York Times* would later note that her success in that time lay in her ability to "get along with a hard-headed businessman and make him see the light, even if he doesn't want to."[29] She began to draw the attention of national women's groups, including the National Consumers' League (NCL), which would try over the next several years to hire her.

By the end of her tenure at the YWCA, the work had gotten to her; Mason longed for a more effective forum for accomplishing change. She confessed that "the weight of the sodden human beings that fill these states, economically, intellectually, socially, educationally, spiritually, depressed almost to the bottom of the scale—white and Negroes—the one holding down the other—fears inhibiting, social vision lacking—politics dirty, narrow, selfish—it gets you." She continued, "There is so far to go, so comparatively little to work upon. And an industrial system that is practically another kind of slavery."[30] When the NCL called again, Mason was ready and became its executive secretary in 1932, replacing Florence Kelley, and moved to New York City. At Kelley's request, she spent much of her four years with the NCL addressing the dire economic conditions of the South and the brutality of Southern leaders and business owners' efforts to repress workers; Franklin Roosevelt's National Emergency Council labeled the region as the nation's "number one economic problem." She traveled throughout the region, working to persuade state leaders to adopt protections for workers. She didn't see much success in this time, noting, "Virginia killed every social and labor bill except a mutilated amendment to the child labor law."[31] But she continued to build a reputation as a charming but effective advocate for labor. And she formed a strong relationship with Eleanor Roosevelt—and through her with President Roosevelt, whose friendship she would call on later as she returned to the South.

Mason's effectiveness could be attributed to many things, but ultimately it was her ability to see the humanity of the individuals on both sides of the negotiating table. The tendency to demonize the opposition and canonize the poor is a common pitfall for social justice workers. Mason, however, was able to maintain an openness that enabled her to see and address the humanity of the opposing sides. She did not view them as enemies; they simply held differing opinions. Because of that empathy, Mason was usually able to find common ground for negotiation. Her pedigree got her in the door with business owners, but her ability to listen to their concerns kept her there.

But as successful as she was, there were some areas that continued to frustrate her best efforts.

As she traveled throughout the South, Mason sensed a change in industrialists' response to labor, and this shift caused her to reevaluate the National Consumer League's approach to protective legislation; she began to appeal to expediency as the context changed. Mason seemed to sense that she should appeal to the "common sense" of the public and raise support for more progressive labor measures despite the resistance of business and government. She would later report, "I must warn you that the South is completely unresponsive to national organizations. During my five years with the League I think I added about sixty Southern members to the list."[32] By targeting the opinion makers in the South, she thought she might gain adherents for the cause of labor. Despite her respected reputation, Mason herself grew frustrated with the lack of progress with the NCL and longed to return to the South to engage more deeply in changing her home. She planned to use her appeal and lineage to the advantage of her cause. She left the Consumer League that year never to return.

Mason's desire to work in her home region in support of organized labor directed her next profession. Mason's focus on the South indicated a redefinition of the concept of "home." In an early writing, Mason declared, "women of the privileged classes are wakening to their duty to other less fortunate women and to all who are oppressed and over driven. They see the glaring inequalities of life, the placid acceptance of the double standard of morals." She asserted that "women are filled with divine discontent because the potential motherlove in them cries out to correct these evils, to make the world a sweeter, kinder place and to guarantee to the weak as well as the strong fair opportunity for an honest, free, and happy life."[33]

Like many of her colleagues, Mason understood the Christian precept of witnessing as a dictate to work in one's own community. The precept encourages believers to remain in one place and exemplify the substance of Christianity. Mason returned again and again to areas that resisted her activities, even though she could have continued to work at the national level. She believed her purpose was closely connected to working in the South. Indeed, in her first letter to Southern ministers as the CIO "roving ambassador," Mason expressed that, "I am writing you as one southerner to another. . . . My love of the South and deep concern for its orderly progress and development led me to take up this work."[34] The CIO allowed Mason the opportunity to focus her "motherlove" on the South's working class, the group that had first held her attention in Richmond. She would bring to that task techniques that would allow her to target the power structure in the South in order to support workers and end racism. Mason mentioned to her brother-in-law, Taylor Burke, that she would like to go South, "where I could work with organized labor and interracial groups. I was particularly concerned with the status of Negroes in the new unions."[35] Her sister-in-law arranged a meeting with John L. Lewis, a friend of her husband's and a leader of the newly created federation of industrial unions, the CIO. Impressed with Mason, Lewis saw the advantages of having a Virginia aristocrat organizing in the South. He appointed her to the position of public relations representative for the CIO in the South,[36] and a new chapter in her life began.

Virginia Durr, a friend of Mason's known for her progressive work, wrote: "As [a] public relations person Miss Lucy would be very disarming. . . . All the fierce police chiefs and sheriffs and newspaper editors would be looking for some big gorilla to come in, and Miss Lucy would appear. She was the kind of perfect Southern lady for whom men would instinctively rise to offer a seat."[37]

The irresistible charm that camouflaged her radicalism and her important connections made Mason very appealing to the CIO. Mason's appointment as a Southern ambassador for the CIO was meant to mitigate the ire of factory owners, ministers, and editors. To many Southern business and religious leaders, the CIO represented a clear and present danger to the Southern way of life. Playing on white Southerners' mistrust of people from outside the region, employers accused these "outside agitators" of communist ties, which was sometimes true, in an attempt to create suspicion of the new organization and maintain their control of unorganized and cheap labor.[38] Most threatening of all, the CIO was known for a commitment to interracial organizations, the guaranteed spark of anti-union ardor.

Mason's job was to organize among elite white people like herself, to get them to accept labor unionism and interracialism in order to smooth the CIO's way in the South. Until she returned home, she "had no idea of the frequency of attacks on people peacefully pursuing legitimate purposes," she later wrote President Roosevelt in 1937. "I am appalled at the disregard of the most common civil rights," she shared, "and the dangers of bodily harm to which organizers often are exposed." Moreover, she was saddened and frustrated by "a conspiracy of silence" from most of the region's newspapers on issues of anti-worker violence and intimidation. In one despairing moment, she described the South as "Fascist," a place in which "the domination of the Negro had made it easier to repeat the pattern for organized labor."[39]

Mason was almost alone as a female organizer in a male arena, and she was highly effective. During Mason's first months in her new position, she received helpful advice from local labor veterans, including Steve Nance. Nance directed a unionization drive in the South by the Textile Workers Organizing Committee. He quickly became Mason's trusted colleague and mentor, giving her confidence but also alerting her that the "only possible way" to achieve lasting results in the region was by relying on "infinite patience and diplomacy."[40]

Mason accomplished a great deal. Still, at times she doubted her own effectiveness. Two months into the job, in a meeting with Nance, Mason said, "My conscience is hurting me. I ought to get off this staff. I ought to make way for a man." Working in an arena dominated by male organizers, Mason believed she had reason to question the value of her assistance to the cause. However, Nance knew her value to the CIO; he reassured her, "Lady, you are doing a real job and don't forget it. You go places and do things the men can't do."[41]

Not all of her colleagues were so supportive. One director, Van A. Bittner, suggested in a meeting that the best "way to take care of civil rights is to have more men with you than against you and to strike before you are struck when the blow threatens." Mason responded, "a safer and surer way is to follow a procedure some of us have been using—to visit the local authorities and point out the rights guaranteed by federal law in a firm but friendly discussion." Given the directness of her response, Mason fully expected to be fired. But in a supreme test, Bittner gave her three civil rights cases in South Carolina to handle. They included "two civil rights cases involving the police and a third case involving a minister who demanded that the textile workers choose between God and the CIO."[42] After she successfully dealt with each case, Bittner asked her to take a special assignment to look after all of their civil rights cases. In time, these cases constituted the bulk of Mason's work for the CIO.

Mason would later caution another colleague that "moderate statements gain more friends than militant ones," and set off on a letter-writing effort to win support for labor's efforts.[43] She went on to elaborate that, "my contacts will be chiefly with editors, ministers, educators, and others who help to make public opinion."[44] Her work garnered a great deal of suspicion. She wrote Eleanor Roosevelt, "a friend heard I am a dangerous person, that I am down here to incite the Negroes to an uprising as part of the CIO program."[45] And she was.

Mason knew that she would have admittance to these seats of power; her conscious use of that access to organize elite whites informed her organizing strategy. It is not coincidental that Mason informed Franklin Roosevelt of her plans. She would call for his intervention in the years to come, when resistance to a particular strike became violent or a union organizer disappeared; in some instances, she would receive his help. In 1940, for example, the president responded to Mason's request for assistance in a situation in Gadsden, Alabama. Roosevelt had someone investigate a local plant owner's adherence to Defense Commission labor policies,

Lucy Randolph Mason speaks at an early morning union rally and organizational meeting near Buffalo Springs, South Carolina. Lucy Randolph Mason Papers, David M. Rubenstein Rare Book & Manuscript Library, Duke University.

"in order to protect labor's rights," and secured a promise from the owner that policies would be followed.[46]

Mason felt an affinity for the people in the region, from factory workers to mill owners, and she used that knowledge of a particular place and its people to part the veil between the South and the rest of the country. In an early circular letter to 425 Southern ministers, she introduced herself as a Southerner, a child and grandchild of Episcopal ministers, and "an interpreter of the organized labor movement."[47] Those first letters had the "desired effect," according to her biographer. Several ministers responded, some simply to agree to meet with her, but others offering support. She had hoped to just "get her foot in the door" in order to lobby for the importance of the CIO's role in the South.[48] That role of translation and advocacy would be continually tested.

Mason knew that the Southern labor movement "was being built from the bottom up, by and for Southern folk," but she believed that movement would be meaningless without the "corresponding national movement."[49] Mason served as an important connector and interpreter of grassroots organizers to national leaders. She assessed the needs in the labor movement, imploring business and civic groups to support the movement, then translated the needs of both and the tensions between the two to national listeners, who could then intervene.

Early in her work for the CIO, the kidnapping of a union organizer measured Mason's ability to negotiate between local, state, and federal spheres of influence. In April 1938, anti-CIO garment workers kidnapped Jimmie Cox, a union representative working in Tupelo, Mississippi. A colleague notified Mason, and after requesting more information, she began to contact a variety of officials, including those in the White House and at the FBI, "appeal[ing] for immediate action in behalf of Cox."[50] His kidnappers returned him, beaten but alive; Mason and the CIO feared continued problems in Tupelo and urged Cox to file statements against those who had held him. Mason continued to monitor the case in July, urging the FBI to protect the organizers in Mississippi.[51] Working with local union supporters, she "arranged a short-term scholarship to the Highlander Folk School for him, and had helped support his family while he was away."[52] Highlander was the training location for liberals and progressives in the South, founded by educator Myles Horton and boasting such graduates as Septima Clark, Rosa Parks, and Martin Luther King Jr.

Officials in Mississippi took notice of Mason. One sheriff in Jackson attempted to track Mason down, implying to a YWCA representative that she was "a subversive character." Mason later noted that the representative refused to take the bait and "the baffled sheriff gave up hope of discovering a dangerous character in the shape of an elderly white-haired woman." Mason concluded, "I have not heard from him since."[53]

Letter campaigns helped Mason develop working relationships with an important contingent of liberal newspaper editors. She regularly corresponded with Ralph McGill of the *Atlanta Journal-Constitution*; Hodding Carter of the *Delta Democrat-Times* in Greenville, Mississippi; and Virginius Dabney of the *Richmond Times Dispatch* in Virginia. She grew especially close to Jonathan Daniels of the Raleigh *News and Observer*; Daniels would write Mason often for clarification of labor issues, and he attempted to introduce her to other editors, although he admitted that "I wish I could provide you safe conduct to more of my editorial colleagues but I am afraid the number of them that would trust even George Mason's descendent in connection with labor unions in the modern South is strictly limited."[54] The rapport she developed with these journalists aided her work; as John Egerton related, "her name got her in the door but once she was there no man could resist her charm. She reminded them of the white-haired little lady who sat in the pew in front of them in church."[55] "Be a good girl now," Grover Hall, the editor of the *Montgomery Advertiser* warned Mason facetiously, "and do not stab any textile executives."[56] Another colleague noted that Mason was "a good advocate for the CIO." "Feeling a bit flattered," Mason asked why. "You look mild," he said.[57]

Mason's strategies and tactics through several major organizations became consistent. She worked to build relationships with those who were most marginalized by economic forces as well as those in power who benefited from those inequalities. She then sought to be a connector, educator, and persuader to economic interests, to appeal to sense of mutual human concern as a reason for creating safer and more equitable working conditions. She sought to lift up the voices of workers as she simultaneously worked to open the ears of those in power who most needed to listen. This kind of bridge building was often unique, especially in the male-dominated CIO, which preferred a more aggressive and often alienating approach.

But Mason had come to learn what many social justice advocates had not. In order to prick the conscience of moneyed interests so that they would begin to help reset inequitable systems, she first had to change the way they interacted with workers, in ways that were respectful and opened possibilities for dialogue and understanding. And she understood clearly that those opportunities would not emerge if those in power felt attacked and vilified. It was this kind of work at the heart level that was Mason's opening tactic for social change. It was not an end point but rather a way to introduce and reinforce an understanding that the problems facing the region and the nation were not problems only at the level of individuals but instead were grounded in inequitable systems that would have to be reformed or replaced.

Even though Mason continued to hone her ability to secure the assistance of state and federal authorities, her successes did not come easily. Instead, they were the direct result of dogged determination. On learning of the exploitation of prison labor and the sale of prison goods in South Carolina, Mason wrote South Carolina's Commission of Labor as well as the governor of the state. Gaining no response from these men, she wrote an editor of the state paper in Columbia.[58] Repeated attempts to elicit a positive response from the governor failed. Mason continued writing him, as well as members of the South Carolina state senate and members of the press. Finally, she assisted South Carolina unions in passing resolutions favoring prison reforms. The combination of pressure from South Carolina voters also in unions, publicity, and Mason's appeals eventually encouraged the governor to call for prison reform by prohibiting the sale of prison-made goods and preventing the privatization of prisons.[59]

Mason did not forget the governor's support. In August 1940, an active Ku Klux Klan presence threatened the state and especially union activity. At the governor's request, Mason summoned help from the White House. She reported to Mrs. Roosevelt that "the Governor feels that the Klan is as much his enemy as the union's. He more than welcomes federal intervention provided he is not in the position of seeking it."[60] Thus Mason simultaneously assisted the unions, secured the gratitude of the governor of South Carolina, and prevented further Klan violence, all the while circumventing the Southern mentality that typically cut off federal intervention to spite its own face.[61]

In 1942, Mason turned sixty. The years of traveling and intervening in stressful civil liberties cases began to take their toll. Illness circumscribed the last ten years of her work for the CIO. She focused on encouraging interracialism. In her official capacity as public relations representative for the CIO, Mason turned her attention to the election of officials who were sympathetic to labor. Given the even greater obstacles to unionization in the postwar period, Lucy Mason's ability to appeal to owners, government officials, police, ministers, editors, and other opinion makers was especially important and offered the greatest potential to Southern labor organizing in the postwar period. Ultimately, however, few resources, pervasive racism, and anti-union fervor would overwhelm her contributions. Those deterrents would also defeat the CIO's Operation Dixie. The change was reflected in labor unions backing away from civil rights activity and interracial work in response to their Southern members increasingly joining newly forming White Citizens' Councils. The CIO stopped short of pushing for racial equality, because such methods alienated their white constituency. However, as the CIO relaxed its commitment to racial equality, Mason redoubled hers. Unable, perhaps, to achieve these ends through the labor movement, she supplemented her work with the CIO by participating in other organizations that were directly engaged in efforts to change white opinion in the South.

Race relations captured Mason's attention most fully in this period. She participated in a variety of initiatives dedicated to eradicating racism and increasing interracial cooperation. She seemed to understand that education and intervention by whites were crucial to improved racial interactions. To that end, she worked with the National Council of Churches on race issues, as well as with the Southern Regional Council (SRC).[62] Of the latter, she said, "I regard the SRC as the most important organization dealing with the whole matter of promoting justice, understanding, and opportunity for the Negro people in our region."[63]

Mason retired from the CIO in 1953 and died in 1959. Through relationship building, moral suasion, and an active campaign of publicity that used her access to an elite white base of power, Lucy Mason was able, for a time, to help aid the cause of labor and racial reconciliation in the South. While she was able to sway the opinions of some, much work remained in the South. On the day that Mason passed away, the *Atlanta Journal-Constitution* published the report of a black man's lynching in Poplarville, Mississippi.[64] The coincidence is striking. Mason had once written, "a Mississippian said to me many years ago, 'The CIO will never organize the South; Negroes just won't join unions; and the white people won't work in the same unions with Negroes.'" Mason labeled him "a false prophet," and yet the accusation inherent in a tragic episode of racial violence in the "middle of the iceberg" made the Mississippian's charge ring true.[65] It would fall to a new generation to test the truth of Mason's prediction that whites and blacks could work together.

RICHARD TWISS

(1954–2013)

Richard Twiss. Photo courtesy of Katherine Twiss.

Standing Tall

Richard Twiss, a Witness to Native American Humanity

Soong-Chan Rah

On the eve of a February 2013 National Prayer Breakfast in Washington, DC, Richard Twiss suffered a massive heart attack and collapsed in a hotel lobby. Several days later, "encircled by his wife, Katherine, and sons Andrew, Phillip, Ian and Daniel," he died. "Richard was fifty-eight."[1]

Many American Christian communities may not recognize his name, but Richard Twiss served as a significant prophetic witness, a Native American missionary to American Christianity. In his eulogy of Malcolm X, Ossie Davis declared of his legacy, "Malcolm was our manhood, our living, black manhood," pointing to the example of a strong and fearless presence in the face of a society that sought to diminish it. In a similar way, Richard Twiss stands as a testimony of a strong, fearless man and gracious witness to the humanity of Native Americans in a world that often diminished them.

I was with Richard a week before he died. He, Vince Bantu, and I spoke at Gordon College, a stalwart evangelical institute of higher education. Founded at the close of the nineteenth century in rural Massachusetts, Gordon College's student body, faculty, and administration reflect the white, suburban, middle-class ethos of twentieth-century American Christianity. Rigorously defending the key tenets of evangelical Christianity, Gordon College holds a high view of Scripture and emphasizes Jesus's sacrifice on the cross.

Richard, Vince, and I had forged a friendship over the years as we traveled in the same ministry circles and oftentimes spoke at the same events. The event that now brought us together at Gordon College was titled "Beyond Color Blind" and intentionally combined the perspectives of a Native American, African American, and Asian American scholar.

After our first evening presentation, the three of us were joined by pastoral friends in the Boston area. We headed over to the blue-collar neighborhood of East Boston—a place not exactly known for ethnic diversity—to a local bar for late-night eats.

As our ethnically diverse group entered the bar, we were seated at a large table toward the middle of the room. Richard was noticeable whenever he entered a room with his six-foot-four-inch frame and long black hair, usually tied back into a ponytail. That night, Richard wore a long leather jacket and a feather jutting atop his hair. He towered over most of our group, as well as over pretty much every other patron in the bar. As we were enjoying our pizza, sausages, and beer, the bar began to fill up. The Boston Bruins game had just let out, and frustrated fans were coming in to drown their sorrows.

As the booths filled around us, we found ourselves surrounded by neighborhood locals of a pale variety. It was at this moment that Richard decided to share a story. He began using a measured but confident tone without any concern about who was sitting at the surrounding tables.

So, I'm part of a pastors' group in the Portland area.

The group is half black and half white and I'm the one Native guy. We meet regularly to share honest conversation among the pastors.

So one time, these three young hipster church planters show up. They're three young white guys from a conservative, fundamentalist Bible college in the Midwest. None of them could have been over thirty years old. They had just planted a church together in an inner-city neighborhood in Portland.

One of my buddies in the group, an older African American pastor, walked over to them and asked, "So why are you planting a church in Portland?"

They responded that they had a passion for the gospel of Jesus and wanted the gospel to be preached in Portland.

The pastor asked again, "I want to know why you planted a church in that specific neighborhood of Portland."

They again responded that they had a passion for the gospel of Jesus and wanted the gospel to be preached in Portland.

The pastor took another pass at the question, "I want to know why you planted a church in my neighborhood and down the block from my church where I've been pastoring for the last several decades."

They again muttered something about their passion for the gospel of Jesus and wanting the gospel to be preached in Portland.

At this point, Richard raised his voice to reflect the raised voice of his Portland pastor friend: "Well, fuck you!" he shouted. "Fuck you white people. Fuck you white church planters. Fuck you and your white Jesus. Fuck you and your white gospel. Fuck you!"

As Richard's voice cut through the din of the bar, I tried to disappear into my chair. I was simultaneously laughing hysterically and scared shitless. But Richard never blinked. Surrounded by drunk, working-class, East Boston white people, Richard was still Richard.

A week later, when I received news of Richard's heart attack, I remembered that scene as he smiled and calmly but assertively dropped the f-bomb in the middle of an East Boston bar. I thought for sure his fighting spirit would cause him to miraculously rise up from that hospital bed.

*   *   *

Richard Twiss was born on the Rosebud Sioux Reservation in South Dakota. His parents met on his father's reservation, the Pine Ridge Reservation, but Richard's mom returned to Rosebud before Richard was born. Rosebud Reservation was created in 1889 and covers close to 900,000 acres in south-central South Dakota, which represents a small fraction of the 7.7 million acres of Sioux lands confiscated by the US government after the Plains Wars of the 1870s.[2] A representative experience on the Rosebud Reservation was "marked by land dispossession, economic marginalization, and a reservation community suffering poverty and disease."[3]

Before beginning any public talk, Richard would offer up the following statement as a marker of his identity as a Native American: "My father is an Oglala Lakota from the Pine Ridge Reservation in South Dakota and my mother is Sicangu Lakota, from the Rosebud Sioux Reservation also in South Dakota. And I was born among my mother's people in 1954." Richard unashamedly claimed his Native heritage from both parents, but he also asserted that he had "Scottish-English and French blood polluting—I mean coursing through my veins." Richard did not meet his father until he was in his thirties. He grew up with an alcoholic stepdad who physically abused his mom and the children. "My vision in life as a little boy," he later said, "was to be big enough to get a baseball bat to beat the '*shnikees*' out of him. But they divorced before I was old enough and brave enough to do that. So then I grew up without a dad after age nine or age ten, and typical wild kid, early 60s, drugs and alcohol and peace, love, dove, and all that kind of stuff."[4]

A long-term impact of his teenage rebellion was a brutal car accident that Richard described this way: "The empty beer bottle I had just tossed out the rear window of the speeding '66 Chevy Impala SS had whistled off into the dark, rainy night. I was drinking beer and smoking marijuana with a carload of friends, cruising the countryside and having a good time. My arm was still outside the window when our car suddenly went airborne, and my stomach catapulted into my throat as we became momentarily suspended in midair. . . . All at once, glass was flying everywhere, and I heard a horrible, grinding metal sound."[5] The accident left Richard's left arm disfigured, and his damaged arm later became the source of a festering infection, which he likened to the festering infection of a genocidal history against Natives that could destroy the foundations of American society.

It is easy to explain Richard's rebellion years as typical of teenagers in the United States. However, the Native American context of his upbringing provides an additional layer. Richard lived in a society that diminished Native lives and belonged to a church that elevated white, Western expressions of Christianity. His teenage rebellion was not merely an expression of a wild, untethered life but a rebellion against the powers and principalities that sought to diminish Native existence. The troubled history of the Native American story serves as the festering wound that needed to be addressed in the testimony and ministry of Richard Twiss.

To understand Richard's deep concern over dehumanized Indian lives and Native American existence is to understand the societal context tracing back to the very "discovery" of the North American continent. At the dawn of the age of exploration and European imperialism, a series of papal bulls that came to be known as the Doctrine of Discovery were employed as theological justification for the European conquest of the world. The Doctrine of Discovery asserted that Europeans were the true image-bearers of God and that any people and lands they encountered were discoverable, since the inhabitants of that land were not the full image-bearers of God. Africans could be deemed less than human and therefore taken captive as slave laborers for European expansion. Christopher Columbus could discover a continent that was already inhabited by millions of people and thousands of civilizations. The Doctrine of Discovery allowed the European explorer and colonizer to see the New World's inhabitants as savages rather than humans made in the image of God. The long history of conquest, broken treaties, and genocide reflect a diminished value of Native lives. The Doctrine of Discovery informed the European Christian worldview that contributed to a severely dysfunctional theological imagination.

Theologian Willie Jennings asserts that theology is the "imaginative capacity to redefine the social."[6] The reality of a broken world, however, means that Christians often engage in dysfunctional theological imagination. The dysfunctional theological imagination of Europeans as image-bearers of God went unchallenged by the American church, and as a result, the ongoing relationship between the white American church and the Native community affirms the assumption of European superiority and Native inferiority. As the church bought into the dysfunctional imagination, Natives in the American church often discovered that they were portrayed and perceived as the most rejected and despised people group in a society that depends on dysfunctional imagination to sustain its broken social system.

Native Americans experience a disproportionate level of social injustice, Richard would say. And his presentations never shied away from depicting the difficulties and challenges of the reality of Native life. Richard noted that before Columbus's arrival in 1492, there were approximately twenty million Natives. "When Columbus arrived, [Native] civilizations and cultures, they're flourishing. . . . [A] short time later came colonization, Christianity and civilization. . . . By 1900 only 237,000 Native people were left in the United States. . . . Approximately 200 Native tribes have become extinct,"[7] he wrote in his book *One Church, Many Tribes*. Nor did Richard hesitate to identify the faulty relationship between Christianity and the American government as a source of the Native American genocide. "We go from 20 million to 200,000. . . . That's what Christianization brought. That's what the Constitution brought. That's what the Bill of Rights brought. That's the kind of freedom and liberty and justice for *all* that came to our people."[8]

Richard pointed out that the diminishing of Native lives coincided with the elevation of white lives. White Christians "appropriated all of these Genesis themes of deliverance so they became the chosen people, coming to *their* promised land, escaping persecution, only to bring it to us. . . . So we became the Canaanites, the Jebusites, the Hittites, the Perrezites, who stood in the way of they, 'the chosen people' coming to the New World to inherit the *promised land*."[9]

Richard Twiss pointed toward how this dysfunctional worldview impacted Native self-perception. To Richard, because of the assumed supremacy of the white American Christian, Christianity became associated with whiteness, and the white world brought it to the Native communities.

For Richard, short haircuts forced on Native children revealed the assumption of Western, white supremacy by the American church. Richard's original title for *One Church, Many Tribes* was *500 Years of Bad Haircuts*. After five hundred years of missionary efforts, he said, the most salient difference among Native Americans was shorter hair. "[These] haircuts symbolized an attempt to civilize Native American young people and turn them into good little Englishmen, Dutchmen, Frenchmen, etc. Bad haircuts were but one example of forced changes and the replacement of traditional clothing, language and culture—changes that were a denial of a people's God-given identity and existence. If I can be so bold, this approach to missions could legitimately be viewed as a kind of cultural genocide."[10] Later in his life, Richard identified the beauty and worth of Native culture when he delved into contextualized ministry among Native Americans, embodying and encouraging spiritual cultural expressions such as long hair, Native regalia, and Native rituals.

*　　　*　　　*

In 1968, when Richard was fourteen years old, the American Indian Movement (AIM) emerged from a collection of various Indian activist groups from Minneapolis, with a particular focus on urban Indian concerns. "AIM attracted attention and emboldened local Indians by protesting against demeaning treatment in public schools. . . . AIM also demonstrated Indian power during this time by protesting injustices against Indians nationwide."[11] In 1972 AIM leaders conferred with Sioux leaders on the Rosebud Reservation. They reviewed the long history of broken treaties by the US government against the indigenous community. AIM began to organize a march on Washington "to be called the 'Trail of Broken Treaties.' . . . After arriving in Washington on November 1, 1972, the march participants stayed in a cramped and unsanitary church basement due to a lack of advance planning. Only as an afterthought did the group the next day decide to seize the BIA [Bureau of Indian Affairs] building, which it renamed the 'Native American Embassy.'"[12]

Richard Twiss was eighteen years old when he joined AIM on the Rosebud Reservation.[13] Richard described how "six hundred of us took over this big federal building surrounded by riot police and dogs and teargas and federal marshals. And we were protesting the federal government's breaking of all of these treaties. . . . When the white man came, we had all the land and they had the Bible. Now we have the Bible and they have all the land."[14] The takeover of the building made national news and illuminated a prolonged injustice perpetrated upon the Native American community. "I stood four stories up on the roof of the Bureau of Indian Affairs (BIA) office building in Washington, DC. We had forced all the BIA employees to leave; then we had chained the doors and taken control of the building. . . . This well-worn stone building represented to us the centuries of governmental injustice, oppression and impoverishment Native people had experienced in America."[15]

Participation in the countercultural protest movement of AIM allowed Richard to express his outrage toward the systemic injustice perpetrated against his community. "We had exploded with long pent-up bitterness, anger and frustration. . . . Native Americans had stored up generations of anger and frustration, and some of us were prepared to take whatever actions might seem necessary to bring about change in Indian America."[16]

As the Indian Health Service attests, "Native Americans have long experienced lower health status when compared with other Americans. Lower life expectancy and the disproportionate disease burden exist perhaps because of inadequate education, disproportionate poverty, discrimination in the delivery of health services, and cultural differences. These are broad quality of life issues rooted in economic adversity and poor social conditions."[17] In response to these injustices on reservations, many Native Americans were rising up in protest through AIM.

Despite those efforts, Richard's involvement in AIM, even the takeover of the BIA building, did not prove to be satisfying. "I found myself both disillusioned and disappointed with AIM. I saw the same hypocrisy among the leaders of AIM that I had seen in the lives of other political and spiritual leaders. . . . I began drifting deeper into drug and alcohol abuse."[18] The pattern of substance abuse only found its end when Richard converted to Christianity.

*   *   *

After spending most of his teen years in the Pacific Northwest, Richard left for Hawaii after an arrest and facing a court-mandated drug rehabilitation program. In Hawaii, Richard acknowledged: "I was drawn to the Eastern religions: Buddhism, Taoism, Hinduism. Still searching for meaning in my life, I practiced yoga, prayed metric prayers and sought enlightenment through the use of hallucinogenic drugs. I spent many nights praying and sleeping under the stars. But the combination of drugs, Eastern religion, my Catholic upbringing and Native American spirituality only led to further confusion. . . . I felt empty inside."[19] Richard's search for meaning culminated in a supernatural experience.

> One day, I had eaten numerous magic mushrooms . . . and at 2:30 in the morning, I found myself completely engulfed in paranoia and the fear of dying or losing my mind. I tried my Eastern meditations and prayers for relief, but to no avail. . . . It was a horrible moment mentally and emotionally. At last feeling the worst, I literally yelled at the top of my lungs, "Jesus, if You're real . . . then I want You to come into my heart and life and to forgive me for the wrong I've done!" The effect of the drugs left, the fear disappeared, and the most incredible sensation of peace flooded my being from the top of my head to the bottom of my feet. . . . I became a follower of the Jesus Way.[20]

Not only did he convert to Christianity; Richard tried to adapt to norms associated with American Christianity and the confusing categories that emerged as he delved deeper into his faith. "I spoke in tongues. . . . Then I became a Presbyterian. Then a Pentecostal. Then a Nazarene. Then an Assembly of God. Then a Methodist. And on the list went, because Christianity got very complicated for me."[21]

In the process of trying to fit into dominant-culture Christianity, Richard aspired to honorary white-person status. At his funeral, the image and photo that elicited the most laughter was of Richard in a wide-lapel brown suit, short hair, and huge glasses: Richard attempted to fit into the mold of white evangelicals.

Richard's adaptation into white American evangelicalism was short-lived. As he traveled through the wide world of Christianity, he recognized the captivity of American evangelicalism to the standards and values of Western, white culture. He recognized that blending the ideology of nationhood, the Christian religion, and the presupposition of American exceptionalism was a clear expression of syncretism.[22]

Richard asked himself: "Have we, as First Nations believers, been taught to have too small a view of God? Are we worshipping an apparently culturally anemic God if we can't see Him already working among the tribes of North America long before the European missionaries arrived?"[23] Richard chafed under the American-church belief that Native American spiritual expressions were somehow suspect. "Then the church said that he doesn't like your drums because they're used for demonic Indian ceremonies. So no more drums. No more pow-wows. No more dancing. No more ceremonies. No more rituals. No more sage. No more sweet grass."[24] As Richard embraced the spiritual expressions of his people, he found God in the midst of indigenous expressions. American Christian worship was a contextualized expression of faith. In the same way, Richard advocated for the use of Native implements and practices as an expression of true Christian worship: hand drums for Sunday morning worship, as well as "eagle feathers, rattles, whistles, sweat lodges, etc."[25]

Richard's awakening paralleled the experiences of other Native North American contemporaries increasingly aware of the need for a decolonizing, indigenous theology. He became part of a group of Native North Americans embarking in doctoral studies at Asbury Theological Seminary. The group included Terry LeBlanc, Randy Woodley, Adrian Jacobs, and Ray Aldred, and together with Richard they formed a community that pursued higher education together. Much later they remarked that "in Richard's first week of school we had no fewer than seven serious discussions about him quitting the program. Yet, in the end, the experience brought us together."[26] In 2011, Richard successfully attained his doctorate from Asbury Seminary.

The development of a community around the work of contextualization spurred the formation of the North American Institute of Indigenous Theological Studies (NAIITS): "in 1999, the controversial issue of contextualization of theology by and for Native North Americans prompted a small group of Native evangelicals to explore ways to address the issue. . . . Finding little in print that addressed the theological and biblical issues at hand, this small band determined to gather a group of people together to explore and write on the issue of contextualization—of culture and faith." NAIITS provided a safe place for indigenous leaders to engage in the challenging task of decolonization, and Richard served as one of its founders and longtime board members. NAIITS "pressed forward believing that the Christian community had essentially written them (and their culture) out of the story of the church centuries ago during colonization. . . . They emphasized the inclusion of an indigenous worldview."[27] Serving as an important incubator of Native American theology and place of intersection for evangelicals with Native American Christian leaders, NAIITS also served as a critical place of development for Richard's vocation as a Native American activist and advocate as well as public theologian.

*   *   *

Over the years and with overlapping speaking engagements, my friendship with Richard deepened, and he became a mentor in my life. As a board member of the Christian Community Development Association (CCDA), I recommended Richard Twiss for the board of this organization that worked on issues of compassion and justice in the United States. CCDA's values and vision relied heavily on the narrative of its founder, John Perkins, an African American evangelical who lived through the civil rights movement and bore the scars of a beating at the hands of the police, and then embodied the possibility of healing between the races.[28]

When Richard Twiss walked onto the platform at the 2011 CCDA National Conference, he presented one of the most significant talks in the ministry's history. To a largely evangelical audience he introduced the narrative of Native American Christians, presenting his perspective with humor as he challenged US Christian captivity to white supremacy: "And the Bible says when you come . . . to Christ, you become a new creation. All things pass away and all things become white. Amen. . . . So I was thinking, what should I call white people? . . . I could say Caucasian, Euro-American, Anglo, Euro-centric, Paleface, Honkey, Q-tip, I could like come up with a whole bunch of words. . . . So God gave me a politically correct term for white people. It's pigmentally challenged."[29]

One conference attendee reported she was laughing so hard that she didn't realize that she had been surgically cut to the core of her beliefs. Richard confronted the Christian academic world's theological allegiance to old, dead, white reformers. And he reminded the audience that Christians were complicit in the formation of boarding schools that contributed to the cultural genocide of the Native American community and the severe abuse of Native American children, with multigenerational implications.[30]

What Richard did that day was make visible the formerly "invisible" story of humanity and culture of the Native American community. Richard then asked: "How do we collectively rescue theology from the metaphoric cowboy? The one who goes with a sense of entitlement to live his or her destiny out in the name of the Lord at the expense of others, with no consideration for who they are and what they want?"[31] Calling the white evangelical world into a position of learning from Native Americans, Richard spoke out for respect and honor for Native Americans as he stood tall and proud before the listening audience.

*   *   *

When I learned of Richard's death, I was wrapping up a session at a conference on the topic of multiethnic churches. While my co-speaker was presenting his perspective on the value of diversity, my phone buzzed. I left the sanctuary and went out into the hallway to answer the call. I learned that they had taken Richard off of life support and that he had died. Arrangements were being made to take his body back to the West Coast. His family was preparing to leave DC. Richard was gone.

By the time I reentered the sanctuary, the conference had wrapped up. Most folks had already made a beeline for the parking lot; they had already spent enough time discussing diversity and race issues. My co-speaker rushed over to me as I entered the sanctuary. He had just gotten off the phone. For a second I thought he had also received a phone call regarding Richard's death, but he had just gotten off the phone with a representative for Rick Warren. He was excited as he came up to me and declared that Rick Warren might offer a video message for his upcoming conference. "What a great moment," he said, "for the multi-ethnic church."

Still raw from the news of Richard's death, and in the spirit of Richard, I blurted out: "That's bullshit! Richard Twiss just died. He flew all over the country to speak on racial reconciliation. He literally died for the ministry of racial reconciliation. He was never invited to this conference, but you're getting all excited about white pastors who have no clue about racial reconciliation. That's bullshit," I said again. After my initial rant, I reverted to my Asian American stereotype and mumbled an apology for my language.

*   *   *

The American evangelical world operates under a narrative of triumphalism and exceptionalism: The exceptional nature of the American church reflects the exceptional nature of American society. The enslavement of African bodies for the growth of the American economy and the genocide of the Native American community for the territorial expansion of the New World reflect an underlying belief that America is a truly exceptional nation with a Manifest Destiny, all of which is rooted in the American Christian imagination of white supremacy. The mediating narrative of white supremacy and power are evident in the desire to

"Make America Great Again"—to return to a previous state when it was dominated by white Christians.

Profoundly captive to the wanton lust for power in American society and politics, American evangelicals are identified as those willing to compromise moral values in their candidates for the sake of partisan victories and secular power, an unfettered and perverse pursuit of worldly political power that emerges from the narratives of exceptionalism and triumphalism.

Richard—his life, voice, message, and physical presence—was a prophetic intrusion into the dysfunctional Christian imagination of white American Christian exceptionalism and triumphalism. Richard offered an embodied lament of a community whose narrative had long been suppressed and denied.

For many evangelicals of color who seek to bring a message of racial reconciliation and the holistic message of the gospel, Richard was our humanity. Richard stood tall as a Native American with a troubled past, a dramatic conversion, a theological awakening, and a deepening of his academic work. He spoke prophetic words to a community enamored with the latest hotshot white superstar pastor. Yet Richard held fast to his convictions even as he faced opposition from all sides. Richard stood tall.

DANIEL BERRIGAN

(1921–2016)

Daniel Berrigan. Bob Fitch Photography Archive, Department of Special Collections, Stanford University Libraries.

I See What I See

Daniel Berrigan's Witness to Christ,
Gospel, and Sanity Itself

David Dark

I have an extended image that changed everything for me at the age of sixteen. I beheld it on a movie screen. A man tied to a cross is carried down to a river, placed within it with no apparent regard 'for whether he'll remain on top or flip over, and then left to stream down to certain death by way of a raging waterfall. In under two minutes, Christianity was placed before me as a problem, a terror, and a thing of beauty. It was the trailer for *The Mission*. And as a distracted, full, and profoundly stretched young man, I experienced it as a kind of calling.

Weeks later when the film was released, I couldn't find a single peer who wanted to take it in with me, so I had to go to the theater by myself. And here they were: *Jesuits*. They lived and worked and loved life among the indigenous Guarani of South America in the eighteenth century. Jeremy Irons's oboe-playing Father Gabriel brought his gospel with music, vulnerability, and, once he'd learned their language, words. Robert De Niro's mercenary slaver Mendoza repented of his lived monstrousness, joined the Society of Jesus and read 1 Corinthians 13 aloud. They were in it for life, bodily invested in a community of mutual enrichment that helpfully rebuked my understanding of missions as an exchange that separated those who do the ministering from those allegedly being ministered to. Very movingly playing for keeps, these Jesuits remained with the Guarani as they were being gunned down by Portuguese soldiers whether it meant dying while celebrating Eucharist or dying returning their fire with fire of their own. The whole thing blew my mind. I stumbled out of the theater into a heavy downpour and wept in my car as I tried to process it all.

I'd never get over it. I felt somehow inspired and chastened all at once. I wanted in. Here was a communal culture with a centuries-old witness of long-suffering love, and little did I know that the most elderly Jesuit in the film, a diminutive, silver-haired man with a penetrating stare and who'd uttered hardly a word, was played by a real live Jesuit who was also an on-set adviser to director, cast, and crew, perhaps the most well-known Jesuit of his time: Daniel Berrigan. I'd be quite a ways into my twenties before I read his words or heard tell of his own beleaguered witness outside the world of cinema, but like *The Mission*, he would remain a guiding standard in my thinking concerning the Christianity that is the real deal. Real-deal life. Real-deal righteousness.

When Berrigan died in 2016 at the age of ninety-five, his appearance on the front page of the *New York Times* for the first time in decades served as one more reminder of how profoundly his life defies categorization and, relatedly, how tragically a culture of for-profit news cycles so haplessly ignores a witness as rare and joyful and direct as his. Where do you put the poet-priest who passed his years as a hospice volunteer, a college professor, a fugitive from the law, an incarcerated medical assistant, and a prophetic voice against American war-making? Shall we decree him religious or political? Bound as they are to cater to our haste, our preference for oversimplification, and our avoidance of life-giving nuance, the content cookers of media outlets are at the mercy of our oft-limited attention spans when it comes to testifying to such a life. Are we still capable of following a story as varied as his?

If conservative means conserving as much human thriving as possible, Father Berrigan was as conservative as they come. If liberal refers to liberation, few have sought space for freedom of thought, word, and deed for neighbor near and far in so costly and self-sacrificial a manner as Berrigan. The labels—as if we needed reminding—never really worked that well to begin with. Perhaps Kurt Vonnegut puts it best: "For me Father Berrigan is Jesus as a poet. If this be heresy, make the most of it."[1] We'll have to let the word signal more expansively than usual, but *poet* might do the trick. And like that other very apt word, *prophet*, we can let it refer to the whole of Berrigan's life. Poetry, in this sense, names a vocation of lived thoughtfulness, a deep inquiry into every form of human activity, an aliveness to the making and unmaking of meaning in our everyday words and actions. This is the poetry—the prophecy too—that challenges our preferred boundaries, exposing them as arbitrary, unmasking them as orchestrated. Poetic and prophetic consciousness is without borders. It issues its call to awareness into every nook and cranny, every moment in fact, because it believes and knows that lives are at stake in the way we imagine ourselves and others.

If we can begin to credit Berrigan, from the outset, as a pioneer of human seriousness, we can better discern the trajectory of an award-winning poet who would eventually find it morally necessary to burn draft files, dig graves on the White House lawn, and pour blood on weapons blueprints in a General Electric plant. But let's not get ahead of ourselves.

The youngest of six boys growing up during the Great Depression in a Catholic family in Syracuse, Berrigan learned early on that power is always more fluid and meaning more up for grabs than either let on. One episode in particular was peculiarly formative in this regard. In his autobiography, *To Dwell in Peace*, he recalls a moment in fifth grade when a nun walked among the children, overseeing strict classroom decorum. One girl, stricken with polio, could not help but protrude her foot out slightly into the aisle between the desks. In a sudden fit of pique, the nun stopped and ground her heel deliberately against the child's foot.

As Berrigan tells it, "It was an act of cruelty so gratuitous as to rattle the chain of command. The links rattled, a few fell apart." Somehow, the fact of all eyes and ears on the sheer meanness of what occurred brought all hands on deck and consensus of courage. Children bore witness, the girl's parents addressed the nun's superiors, "and one day, as unthinkable as the Last Day of All," all parties appeared before the class, and the nun apologized. For Berrigan, it had the force of a revelation: "The grip of authority could never again rub so cruelly. . . . They were fallible, those great ones, those Olympians. . . . But more wonderful by far, they could be held accountable for their sin."[2]

This is one of many instances in which Berrigan, as a young man, watched the given script of power get decisively flipped. The weight of *the way things are* proved again and again to *not* be the way things have to be. A sense of the fluidity of authority was ever before him. As he recounts, he had an oft-dejected and oft-bullying father who, were it not for his mother's relentless advocacy, would have broken his sons in the same way his own spirit had been broken. A sense of moral solidarity developed around her and brought that cycle to a kind of halt. Within their household, Dorothy Day was a long-distance friend to his family insofar as the *Catholic Worker* newspaper was shared and read aloud, calling into question the perceived have-to's of the world at home and at large with grace and wit.

And at school, he would encounter rare teachers for whom children were genuinely a joy, teachers who appeared before him as human beings among human beings. It was with a sense of the righteous connivance of certain Catholics who had gone before him and the training to be had as a discerner of spirits that he entered a Jesuit seminary near Poughkeepsie and later continued his studies in Baltimore. In history and literature, he spied a company of thoughtful people living and dead, a great cloud of witnesses among whom he could find his own way.

While he would eventually join well-known figures like Sister Corita Kent, A. J. Muste, Thomas Merton, and Martin Sheen in various coalitions of nonviolent protest of state-sanctioned violence, his path to viewing this work as an actual call to be answered by all Christians and other people of goodwill was neither direct nor inevitable. There's an especially telling passage from a recently published letter he sent to his brother Philip, whose experience as an active serviceman with the Air Force, both at home and overseas, had left him in the throes of a vocational crisis. Daniel is hoping he might persuade his brother that, despite the complications, they're each seeking God's kingdom and righteousness in their own way:

> The soldiering of this war is a vocation too. . . . To believe our Lord wants you as surely in a field Artillery or Air Force just as surely as he wants fifteen years of study and sweat from me— that's a grand faith and trust and high outlook that will solve a great deal, clear up a lot of moral issues, turn the whole situation (which is otherwise a pure mess) into part of a great plan to bring souls back to God their maker—the only thing that counts in life. And your part is to play the game (as you are doing superbly) looking on Him Who was a good Soldier—unto death.[3]

The letter is dated September 15, 1943. As moved as we might be by one brother's attempt to allay another's anxiety through a heartening read on life under God and how to live it, we can also note how unconvincing this spiritualizing of war would later strike both of them. In time, the institutional racism and the unexamined faith in the strategic use of lethal force at work in military culture would lead Philip to disavow the very game Daniel here believes can be played in good faith as a part of the grander plan of God's reconciliation of souls.

Daniel's conversion was gradual. A voracious reader throughout his life, he recalls being struck by Ronald Knox's book *God and the Atom*, which argues that the United States could have easily opted to drop the atomic bomb on an uninhabited Pacific island as a show of force instead of incinerating thousands of people in Hiroshima and Nagasaki. Mulling over this idea as a schoolteacher in the late forties, he decided to voice it aloud to a classroom full of fifteen-year-olds at St. Peter's Prep in Jersey City. Might there have been another way?

The room erupted. "We did good! . . . It was them or us!" the children exclaimed. It was as if the needful violence that fate had decreed must never be questioned, and entertaining alternatives to the path of annihilation was tantamount to treason. In a room full of young thought police, he began to realize that a very different catechesis than the one he hoped to build on had been long ago ingrained. Their minds had been enlisted for some time. Berrigan was himself receiving an education. Such exchanges with students, parishioners, and superiors would continue throughout his life. The perceived necessity of violence was everywhere in the air. It was a question of deep identity: "We . . . knew who we were . . . in the act of war. Ancestors were, first of all, warriors; in that degree only, they merited honor. Ancestor to child; it was presumed that violence needed no teaching, it took care of itself. It was nonviolence, civility, that required discipline and instruction, and was under perennial assault."[4]

*   *   *

Civility, we know it feelingly, is the rarer happening in human history, and Berrigan came to understand that there was a mobile mythology of endless war afoot, at home and abroad, that would have to be engaged in long-haul fashion if he was to be a minister of Jesus's good news concerning God's peaceable empire. The myth of redeeming violence, he saw, is a costly and well-funded faith more widespread than any other "world religion," and its most self-satisfied manifestation is—and was—the vision of Pax Americana that sought, like the false gods of Scripture, to hold the entire world in thrall.

Berrigan would see the unacknowledged religion of blind nationalism exposed further as he lived and worked among Jesuit communities around the globe in France, South Africa, and the former Czechoslovakia. In their embrace of the wider cultures within which they lived and worked and dwelt with an affirming alertness to every form of human thriving, they were a live demonstration that a different way of being in the world was possible. What he spied among them, at their most exemplary, was "the gift of conscience alive; of life lived to the hilt . . . a unity of the human." But even at its most faithful, he saw the Jesuit vision as a kind of baseline for any student of Jesus's gospel. The Jesuit ethic, in this sense, is "nothing more remarkable than the common calling of Christians."[5]

With this observation, Berrigan strikes a posture similar to that of Dorothy Day, who bristled at the suggestion that a sense of otherworldly saintliness should be affixed to Christian norms as basic as hospitality, love of enemy, and caring for the poor. Decreeing these straightforward practices radical, extreme, or unique to women and men who take up vows is often an evasion, a way of dismissing the moral demand that comes to any and every human life, a refusal to acknowledge oneself as whole and a part of a greater whole, a person among persons. As Berrigan saw it, God loves and saves the world through people who behave as Jesus did, as Jesus taught everyone to behave, giving expression to the good news of God's order in all things.

Like Day, Berrigan also took as common sense Dostoevsky's adage that it's beauty that saves the cosmos. To see and insist on God's order is to always ask what right recognition of the beauty of God's world and of one another demands of us; what behaviors, policies, and postures arise when God's love is the standard by which we measure human activity. Aesthetics and ethics, in this sense, are one. Berrigan's poetic vocation was, again, no separate issue from the work of prophetic witness, because beauty is never a means to some other end, never a side issue. It's the gift of God summoning our witness. Beauty beckons us, calling us out of cold calculation, out of any habits of mind that would reduce people, places, or things to their alleged use value and into a saving sense of ourselves and others, the saving covenant of beauty. A rose, he once argued, is its own credential.[6] Resisting the means-end thinking of fear, competition, hoarding, and other false covenants becomes a matter of regarding the world that is—the world that we are—beautifully; thinking beautifully, speaking beautifully, and acting beautifully, to re-enchant spaces of disenchantment. He described the task of true witness as an always-to-be-embodied-anew process: "Constantly exploring and enlarging the known frontiers of the Kingdom, the visible geography of spirit, so that the Kingdom is not a limbo of the restless disembodied, but a community of incarnate consciences."[7]

This thinking (penned in 1967) arose from an array of experiences that included his participation in the march on Selma, his involvement alongside Abraham Heschel and John Neuhaus in the founding of Clergy and Laymen Concerned about Vietnam, a burgeoning friendship with the likes of Peter Maurin and Ivan Illich, and his growing dismay with church communities that believed they could watch from the sidelines in the face of social catastrophe by way of an abstraction called "politics." This vision of the church as a community of incarnate conscience was also the fruit of his ongoing deliberation with his unstintingly socially active brother Philip (a Josephite Father since 1950) over what real Christianity consists of. As he asked him in a brainstorm enclosed in a letter in 1965: "What is the form of the cross for adults in the world?"[8] What heretofore unimagined and still unattempted feats of attentiveness and sanity would a community of true faithfulness need to undertake?

As the Vietnam War escalated, the drama of 1968 would begin in January with an invitation from Hanoi. Serving as a chaplain at Cornell, Berrigan received a call from Tom Hayden detailing an offer on the part of the North Vietnamese government to release three American prisoners of war in celebration of the Buddhist Tet holiday. Two representatives of the peace movement would travel to Hanoi and conduct them back to America as a joint goodwill gesture. The historian Howard Zinn was his partner in international peace crime.

Upon arrival, Berrigan received an immersive experience in geopolitics that would shape his thinking for the rest of his life: "How is one to convey the atmosphere of a city rendered alien as another star by the mythology of our words, by distance, by bombs? It was like stepping out upon the threshold of a new planet."[9] They held babies, hid in bomb shelters, and visited an art museum. He was forever disabused of the notion of America as an innocent or even mostly well-intentioned actor on the world stage. Certain inextricable connections between a foreign policy of murderous despair, the listlessness of the American electorate, and the suffering of the many on the wrong side of one nation's perceived self-interest were rendered undeniable. For Berrigan, "the mythology of our words" would become his mission field, his writing assignment, and his moving target in all his thinking and doing. Whether it surfaced in the pronouncements of public officials, the truncated visions of newspeak, or the ease with which Americans were made to view an entire civilian population as a lethal threat through image and rhetoric, this mythology would have to be engaged by the countermythology—the living culture—of God's civilization. God's civics spies a neighbor to be loved where the US government sees a threat to be exterminated. As a welcomed guest in Hanoi, Berrigan saw feelingly the fact of kinship with the alleged enemy like never before: "Like any Vietnamese peasant or worker, I cowered under the savage bombardment of, so to speak, my own air force. It was a momentous education. I learned my lesson."[10]

Before the trip was over, Berrigan's chastened imagination would be confronted once more by how fluid a thing power could be—or even had to be—for those who presumed to wield it in the name of certain toxic ideas. While the US government could not afford to be seen obstructing the liberation of American POWs in Hanoi, they could nevertheless de-escalate the breaking news of servicemen seeing release through the efforts of the peace movement. Berrigan and Zinn were stopped in Laos by US Ambassador William Sullivan, who insisted that the soldiers be returned home in an Air Force plane, thus preventing the PR disaster that would ensue if someone other than the military were viewed as the primary agents of liberation. It was a return to the militant catechesis that confronted him in a Jersey City classroom. The military-industrial complex would not allow itself to be upstaged even an inch. The script was written long ago and would permit no deviation: violence alone can save. The metanarrative—funded by the American taxpayer—would always have stage managers on hand to try to insure that, ultimately, war and war alone would be venerated as truly revolutionary. Thus Berrigan witnessed anew the power of stagecraft, the power to form and deform public perception. How might the violence at the heart of our republic be rightly perceived, understood, and repented of? What's a developing community of incarnate consciences to do? What would a response worthy of adults look like?

* * *

"I was in danger of verbalizing my moral impulses out of existence."[11] This is Berrigan's articulation of the meaning crisis he had to confront following his trip. Perhaps it's a common crisis for anyone who lives with the worry that their alleged devotion to the love of God might prove to have been all talk, but Berrigan, the priest and an increasingly public figure, felt especially alive to this ethical pinch. Then as now, at home and abroad, "The abnormal was being normalized."[12] And then as now, it fell on the people of God to be a faithful witness to God's saving wisdom whether it turned the tide in the short term or not. The Day of the Lord attested to by the prophets (Isa. 2:12; Amos 5:18–24) and the reign of God that Jesus proclaimed and taught his hearers to seek and pray for (Matt. 6:9–13) are equal parts sign, promise, and awareness campaign, a long witnessing work, poetic and prophetic, that is never quite done. What good is a church community if it offers no question, quarrel, or even a point of clarification when the government of the land of its sojourn enlists its citizenry in the labor of mass destruction in the name of peace? Without a lived witness, is it right to say that the church exists at all?

Noting that poverty and racism and war can't be rightly conceived or even helpfully discussed until they're understood biblically as profoundly related phenomena, Martin Luther King Jr. once declaimed that the Vietnam War was "a demonic destruction suction tube."[13] For a multitude of Americans in the late sixties, this was both prophecy and description, and to put it this way was not to isolate an issue, attempt a distraction, or stage a publicity stunt; it was to make plain the social fact of a moral disaster among us, the kind, then and now, that breaks the world people of righteous faith insist God *so* loves.

Even before the trip to Hanoi, Berrigan had been consistently admonished by his superiors for his energizing presence among alleged agitators. He came to be associated with the story of Roger Laporte, a twenty-two-year-old resident of a Catholic Worker community, who—modeling himself on Vietnamese monks who had given up their lives in a similar gesture—had tried to burn himself alive in front of the United Nations building to voice his opposition to the war.[14] Laporte died in a hospital days later. When a Eucharist was held by the Catholic Worker community, Berrigan didn't hesitate to eulogize him. He of course spoke of the tragedy of suicide, but he also noted that it wouldn't be fitting or appropriate to insist that Laporte's decision demonstrated *only* despair. As he asked years later: "What if the death reflected not despair, but a self-offering attuned (however naively or mistakenly) to the sacrifice of Christ?"[15] This probing of the mystery at work in one human will was the kind of nuanced speech that would put him in the crosshairs of just about every breed of institutional authority at one time or another. In the case of his proximity to the figure of Roger Laporte, a rebuke arrived from his Jesuit superiors in the form of a months-long exile to Latin America.

There was also the matter of his brother Philip, who was increasingly convinced that being a true minister of God's Word and sacrament necessitates direct action. In the American context, this meant confronting in some way the illegitimacy of state-sponsored violence, the US government's trespasses on human life, with actions that call the alleged justice of officialdom into question in the name of higher law. Like Mandela, Gandhi, or Thoreau, Philip believed actively refusing recognition of unjust rule and accepting, without plea bargaining, whatever comes from doing so was essential in engaging any tyranny that holds human beings in thrall. For Philip, the most immediate name for that tyranny was idolatry. Having watched younger men refuse induction into their own military and suffer imprisonment for it, he saw fit to walk into Baltimore's Selective Service Board at the Custom House with the artist Tom Lewis, the poet David Eberhardt, and the minister Jim Mengel, who handed out copies of the New Testament while the other three opened draft files and poured blood over them.[16] They also passed out leaflets that included a statement concerning the meaning of their action: "This sacrificial and constructive act is meant to protest the pitiful waste of American and Vietnamese blood in Indochina."[17]

At this point in time, Daniel was in prison for his involvement in a mass protest at the Pentagon, but the two brothers kept in close contact over the details of the action as decisions were made, as well as the criminal prosecution that followed. In what came to be known as the trial of the Baltimore Four, the proceedings highlighted a question that would be recited again and again in similar actions and trials that would follow them: How might the reality of the kingdom of God be amplified in an interface between the communities that witness to it and the governing authorities of the present world? As Philip recounted in a letter dated April 10, 1968: "His Honor made it clear that the law could not consider subjectivity, which in effect meant, it could not consider the reality prompting us to move. In a word, the court will allow no indictment of the government or itself . . . which strengthens our hand rather than weakening it."[18] He would eventually receive a six-year sentence and be the first Roman Catholic priest in American history to be tried and imprisoned for a political crime.[19]

The reality that prompted them to move—their own subjectivity, their experience, their witness, their own powers of perception when it came to what's true and needful—was viewed as inadmissible. This was indeed a showing of hands that would be played again and again, and Daniel would come to describe the stronger hand with a simple evangelical formula: "Christ, gospel, sanity itself."[20] How to be accountable and responsible to these three in the work of seeing and loving the sweet old world and those who inhabit it was the question ever before him.

The seriousness of the question intensified when Philip traveled to Cornell with a proposal. In advance of the trial for his action in Baltimore a few days before, he wanted to raid another draft board. Upon procuring the files and getting them outdoors, it would be fire this time, but it would again be "a moral assault on purportedly sacrosanct territory."[21] It was not at all clear to Daniel that he would be right to join the undertaking, but he assured Philip he would pray and meditate over the matter for twenty-four hours.

An assurance came to him, "a certainty deeper than logic. . . . Suddenly, my hands and heart lifted, and I knew." It was as if "in choosing, I could now breathe deep, and call my life my own. . . . I didn't want to do it, but I couldn't *not* do it." On May 17, 1968, following much prayer, they walked into a draft board in Catonsville, Maryland, with seven other activists and removed papers with the names of young men scheduled to be conscripted. They then took the draft files outside and burned them with homemade napalm, this liturgy concocted according to the specifications of another: a US Army Special Forces manual. "Some property," they argued referring to the paperwork, "has no right to exist."[22] Apologizing for their fracture of what they could no longer abide as "good order," and noting that they were no longer able to say "Peace, peace" when there is no peace, they observed aloud that they thought it fitting to burn paper instead of children: "We could not, so help us God, do otherwise."[23] As the fire burned, they emphasized the reality that had prompted the action by reciting the Lord's Prayer.

Praying that God's kingdom would come to this particular plot of public property in Catonsville while burning these government issued claims on American and Vietnamese lives explicitly clarified God's claim on what the state decrees sacrosanct. How would the reality that prompted them be received in court now? Power and authorization is ever in play if God's kingdom, power, and glory are to be understood as definitive and binding. They brought the liturgy of Christ, gospel, and sanity to bear on the liturgy of war. Their *transparent* liturgy would serve to disrupt and destabilize, even if only in one neighborly instance, the *unacknowledged* liturgy of the draft.

What came of it? Prison sentences, both brothers' faces on the cover of *Time* magazine, and, at least for a time, the public was aghast: "The revulsion could only be called ecumenical. All sides agreed—we were fools or renegades or plain crazy."[24] Similar actions would be undertaken and continue into our day, often under the moniker of the Plowshares movement, and pose again and again, as prophetic expression always does, the question of authority. For now, the Catonsville Nine had confronted and dramatized the reigning dysfunction of their day. By confronting and dramatizing taxpayer-funded liturgy at home and abroad, the action sought to bring an awakening to the American parish, positing a sacred sense of reality counter to reigning disorder, making plain the brutal arbitrariness of "the way things are," creating a scene of recognition in which the habitual devaluing of life appeared a little less inevitable:

> I tried, in response, to put matters biblically. That there was a history for acts such as ours. In such biblical acts, results, outcome, benefits, are unknown, totally obscure. The acts are at variance with good manners and behavior. Worse, they are plainly illegal. More yet: everything of prudence and good sense points to the uselessness and ineffectiveness of such acts. . . . And yet, and yet, it is also said: The poor mortal is to go ahead; in spite of all. To go ahead, in faith; which is to say, because so commanded. . . . One had very little to go on; and went ahead nonetheless. Still, the "little," I reflected ruefully, had at least one advantage. One was free to concentrate on the act itself, without regard to its reception in the world. Free also to concentrate on moral preparation, consistency, conscience. Looked at in this light, the "little" appeared irreducible, a treasure. . . . So, despite all, a history of sorts was launched on a May morning in 1968. Also, a tradition was vindicated, at least to a degree. Or so I believe to this day.[25]

On the one hand, Berrigan and his brother can appear very alone at this stage in their community of incarnate conscience, but on the other, it's the tradition of Jesus and the prophets they have behind them, a tradition, as Daniel notes, made *more* viable to the watching world in view of the risk they've taken on. Nevertheless, a raging defensiveness had been awakened. In the months preceding his prison sentence, the chapel in which his Cornell community gathered was firebombed, and he found that the more he grounded his explanations of the Catonsville action in Scripture, the less sympathy he received from self-described Christians in America. And yet he became more enamored with a kind of popular unsuccess as an essential form of faithfulness. Witness as truthfully as you can, and let the chips fall where they may: "The creation of a scene is not done by coaching actors and painting scenery. It is by getting on stage, tragicomedian, improvising the script, and allowing the outcome to grow as naturally as yeast or a baby. Grace under pressure. Prison with freedom."[26]

The job is to ring as true and truthfully as one can, in every human exchange, and to then let it go. He would hold to this principle when he was actually *in* prison when it came to relationships and an alertness to what true neighborliness requires at all times: "The means are so important because we have to live with them—so do others. . . . I don't mean anything mild by this. I mean sanity: right order of means so the end is always as concrete and compelling as my treatment of a single person."[27] Both brothers would conduct Bible studies, continue postal correspondence, and hold to the disciplines of their vows in and among their fellow inmates. True neighborliness, for Berrigan, *is* sanity.

*   *   *

But before entering prison, Berrigan surprised himself with an act of noncooperation. There were perhaps many avenues yet to be discerned for renewed witness in spite of a court's decree. In view of the continued escalation of violence at home and abroad and his sense of the ongoing illegitimacy of the US government, he opted for a different course: "I went underground. It was a delaying tactic. It was to call more attention to the war and, in the process, give Mr. Hoover a headache."[28]

It started out modestly. Well aware that he was being surveilled by the FBI, he climbed out of a first floor window on Cornell's campus and went to a waiting car that took him to a wooded residence where he purposed to read and meditate on a Bonhoeffer biography. When plans arose for an antiwar rally at Cornell, it was proposed that he might address the audience and then surrender himself to the agents in attendance.

But then an opportunity arose. Berrigan made his speech in the context of a reenactment of the Last Supper put on by the Bread and Puppet Theater. Then a darkness descended between sets and a member of the troupe asked if he'd like to make an exit. With his consent, the papier-mâché head of an apostle was placed on his head, and he marched out with the cast. Having tried to shine a light on the geopolitical nightmare the US government was imposing on neighbors at home and foreigners abroad in Catonsville, he would now up the ante further by dramatizing his dissent.

As a nonviolent hero now at large, he would become a problem for the Nixon administration through his constant and unpredictable appearances in the news cycle. While underground, he would appear in documentaries, and his play *The Trial of the Catonsville Nine* premiered in Los Angeles. NBC would air an interview with him conducted in a motel room. He would preach sermons here, there, and yon. He would even communicate with the Weather Underground, offering qualified admiration for their work while also counseling them against their taking up of arms: "A revolution is interesting insofar as it avoids like the plague the plague it promised to heal."[29]

His reading, speaking, and extended interviews occasioned a space for his own reflection as well as months on end in which the American public were treated to the phenomenon of a living outlaw of righteousness. What to make of a government that viewed an unarmed poet-priest as a threat to national security? The question of whether or not he was being consistent with his own principles was popularly bandied about and served as a constant reminder that the claims of church and state, God and government, aren't always easily distinguishable. In a book-length conversation with Robert Coles conducted during these months, Berrigan observed that this was to the point. The military-industrial-incarceration-entertainment complex, he observed, must maintain the uncritical consent of the people. The show *has* to go on: "I *have* to be caught, you see. . . . The whole point of all these weeks underground is to stand witness all over. . . . Caesar and Mammon are everywhere. So, it is everywhere they have to be confronted."[30]

His final stop on his underground tour was Block Island, where he resided at the home of William Stringfellow and Anthony Towne before being picked up by federal agents posing as bird-watchers. The three of them (Towne, Stringfellow, and Berrigan) had long comprised a mutual admiration society in which each served as among the other's closest readers and celebrants of one another's work. Towne offered this assessment of Berrigan's (and our) plight: "It is my considered opinion that any society that locks up priests is sick, and any society that imprisons poets is doomed."[31] More than a little like Dorothy Day, Towne argued that poetry serves as an enlivening assertion of norms, that its end is, in the most life-giving sense, "normal living," which, "if there is any love in it, is one long gorgeous and, no doubt, subversive conspiracy."[32] Poet practitioners, like prophets, are the caretakers of words, of what we do with words, or, borrowing Berrigan's phrase upon beholding war-torn Hanoi, our mythology of words that often takes the form of murderous abstractions. And the creation of righteous norms calls for specificity and more specificity. "Poets," Towne maintained with an eye on the criminal poet-priest in his midst, "are the most specific people on earth. That is what poetry is all about."[33]

Just as William Blake announced that anyone who hopes to love well will have to labor well the minute particulars, Berrigan insists that our consciences become incarnate when we learn to be more concrete in word and deed. As he notes in *The Trial of the Catonsville Nine*: "The great sinfulness / of modern war is / that it renders concrete things abstract." In the burning of draft files, the task of the poet and the aspiring prophet are one: "I was trying to be concrete / about death because death is a concrete fact / as I have throughout my life / tried to be concrete about the existence of God / Who is not an abstraction / but is someone before me / for Whom I am responsible."[34]

Berrigan's responsibility to the God whose reigning reality prompted Catonsville and to whom he hoped to bear faithful witness his whole life long posed a constant legal challenge to dominant American culture. To even *say* what he saw was to engage in a conspiracy as a prophetic subversive. His poem "Prophecy" lays it out beautifully:

> The way I see the world is strictly illegal
> To wit, through my eyes
> Is illegal, yes;
> to wit, I live
> like a pickpocket, like the sun
> like the hand that writes this, by
> my wits
> This is not permitted
> that I look on the world
> and worse, insist that I see
> what I see
> —a conundrum, a fury, a burning bush.[35]

*   *   *

For Berrigan, there was no unseeing what he was being shown of the country he loved, the violence that so often seems to possess its very core, and the good news of God's kingdom and righteousness. The two years in prison Berrigan served for the Catonsville action did not in any way lessen his resolve, his wit, and his capacity for truth-telling—a telling made incarnate, he understood, in action or not at all. Faith without action is not, as it turns out, faith in the first place.

"Understand," he insisted, "that it is not God who through some magic or other will beat swords into plowshares; it is yourselves. It is you. . . . Disarm. Take care of the widow, the orphan, and the poor."[36] Our dreams for the world, our hungering and thirsting for righteousness, will have to put on flesh if we're to be as Christ in the world. A merely theoretical faith is a dead one. The call to discernment is the call to embodiment. There's always more awareness to be had, more human persons to seek fellowship with, and more beauty to be apprehended and attested to.

The joy of always more was recently recalled by the journalist Jeremy Scahill, founding editor of *The Intercept*, who grew up with parents for whom the Berrigan brothers were a constant inspiration and an essential resource for the kind of social consciousness they hoped to pass on. In the summer of 1995, Scahill traveled as a college student to Washington, DC, unaware that participants in the peace movement were also descending on the capitol to commemorate the fiftieth anniversary of the bombings of Hiroshima and Nagasaki.

Upon arriving at the Pentagon, he found Daniel Berrigan standing among the gathered with his sister-in-law Elizabeth McAlister. Sensing that Scahill was starstruck, she asked him if he'd be willing to accompany Daniel to the bathroom. Because this was years before the September 11 attacks, the public could enter the Pentagon and use the facilities with ease and few restrictions.

Upon walking in, people in uniform, accustomed to seeing him at protests, greeted Berrigan with deep warmth and affection, which he duly returned. Once they were in the bathroom, Berrigan had some history to share. As Scahill recounts, he began to muse aloud: "You know . . . in the 1940s when Roosevelt authorized the building of this place there was talk of it being converted to a hospital when the war was over. . . . And you know in a way they kept their word. . . . It's the largest insane asylum in the world."[37]

This good-humored assessment of the planet's largest office building manages mirth and seriousness simultaneously. We might also recall that Berrigan's well-known love of ice cream landed him a panel in a Ben & Jerry's advertisement, that he delighted watching Al Pacino on stage and screen, and that he often spent nights in jail with Martin Sheen. And if you imagine he might prove a downer in the presence of anyone implicated in the afore-

Daniel Berrigan. Daniel and Philip Berrigan Collection, #4602. Division of Rare and Manuscript Collections, Cornell University Library.

mentioned military-industrial-incarceration-entertainment complex (that would be most of us), consider this description of the community he means to embody and find his own life within: "We want life. We want it even for those who work against it, who kill,

who believe in killing as an act of social usefulness, personal en-
hancement, political savvy; those also who do the works of death
(safely at a distance from the results): that phalanx of researchers,
scientists, engineers, for whom bomb-making is a 'living.' I long
to enlarge the scope of life until it includes everyone from soldiers
to priests, a spectrum by no means arbitrary or easily entered."[38]
There's so much here. There's a very specific longing for very
specific kinds of people, and there's even a bit of kick at the end
that suggests this communion of the living can't be accessed without a constant change of thought habits; as if no one gets saved
without changing their minds. But there's also an appeal, a hospi-
table humor that won't settle for anyone getting left out.

The context of the passage above is a book-length meditation
on being present to dying people as a hospice volunteer. It's all
jokes, anecdotes, and the occasional foray into film, art commentary, books people are reading, or something happening on television. As he begins to note the way he's watching and imagining
people while also recalling that Walt Whitman was a hospital orderly, he makes an observation concerning himself: "Catholics, I
think, are people who are freer to go crazy than practically anyone
I know."[39]

As one who took seriously the liberty afforded by this near-
anarchic creative license, Berrigan ended up writing on just about
everything, and each book was a kind of patchwork of musings
circling around the Word of God as a movement of relentlessly
human interest. His longest project, still in this vein, would be his
numerous biblical commentaries. He wrote books on almost every
book of the Bible (sometimes dedicating a volume to a genre), and
they're intensely personal, homing in—especially with the prophets—on the work of really hearing the Spirit of the Lord in every
corner of the human barnyard. His midrash includes items as varied as Wendell Berry poems, a statement from the Revolutionary
Association of Women of Afghanistan, and a letter to a newspaper
editor from a woman widowed on 9/11 begging her elected leaders

to not fight terror with more terror. "Human one, do you see what they are doing?" Berrigan asks the reader by way of Ezekiel quoting God's question to Ezekiel himself.[40] Each volume is a dizzying read, but it puts us squarely into the thick of things (inspiration, authority, God's love), inviting us to imagine life in Christ as Berrigan does, a life of ceaseless dialogue and endless hospitality.

His time in prison, exile, and underground often afforded him occasions to reflect on the why and how of those who opposed or sidelined him. And he was especially eloquent concerning what he took to be the perceived offense, the scope, of what he'd taken on: "We were challenging certain myths and assumptions concerning the human itself, its capacities, drives, needs, appetites, spirituality. How is the human to be defined in a most inhuman time? What might a prohuman politics look like?"[41]

Berrigan's witness looks hard—and would have us look hard—at the given, the facts on the ground of a given time or season, the opportunities that arise within the context of the daily. The work to be done is to live in search of "the larger yes," the wider human affirmation in any given circumstance, "and live according to the slight edge over death."[42]

And despite his eloquence, his unassailable credibility in the peace movement, and the encouragement his witness was to the watching world, Berrigan still very often felt to himself like a ridiculous person. "What is a clown like me doing, blundering about the earth?"[43] he once asked in a journal. An anxiety over his own effectiveness haunted him in spite of it all. Given the boldness of his action and speech, we might imagine him waving away such insecurity as unworthy, debilitating nonsense. And yet, there it was.

But if the rose is its own credential, goodness is its own end, Christ, gospel, and sanity are their own reward. Results? Impact? Not to be worried over overly. Berrigan spied a different logic and advised a different path: "The good is to be done because it is good, not because it goes somewhere. I believe if it is done in that spirit it will go somewhere, but I don't know where. I don't think the Bible grants us to know where goodness goes, what direction, what force. I have never been seriously interested in the outcome. I was interested in trying to do it humanly and carefully and non-violently and let it go."[44]

Do it humanly. In doubt and fear and trembling, don't shut your eyes to your own confusion, your dawning sense of complicity, if you sense it, in the larger culture of which we're each a part, your nascent intuition of good work to be done. Enter the community of thoughtfulness that appears before you whatever form it might take. When we think of Daniel Berrigan as one of many artisans of human honesty, a film like *The Mission*, my own entry into this community, becomes one of many offerings within his decades-long orbit of witness. These lives and their creative offerings are there as a resource of courage and inquisitiveness. As they are, so are we in this world. We get to open our eyes, again and again, to our own scenario, and take up their witness as our own.

MARY STELLA SIMPSON

(1910–2004)

Sr. Mary Stella Simpson in full habit, circa 1950s. Photo: Daughters of Charity Provincial Archives, Emmitsburg, Maryland. Courtesy of Daughters of Charity Province of St. Louise, St. Louis, MO.

A MIDWIFE OF GRACE

Mary Stella Simpson and the
Transcendence of Accompaniment

M. Therese Lysaught

There's no way around it: the only way to Moses is through the midwives. They stand at the front door of the book of Exodus, poised, smiling, and immoveable like an executive admin barring access to a CEO's office. With feigned innocence, Shiphrah and Puah shrewdly foil Pharaoh's orders, refusing to kill the baby boys born to their Hebrew sisters. God rewards them, we are told, building up families for them and doing the one thing Pharaoh feared the most—multiplying the Hebrew people. Fear drives Pharaoh and his fellow Egyptians to loathe the Hebrews, doubling down on their oppression: "So the Egyptians reduced the Israelites to cruel slavery, making life bitter for them with hard labor, at mortar and brick and all kinds of field work—cruelly oppressed in all their labor" (Exod. 1:13-14 NABRE). And while they're not looking, with the help of the midwives, God slips Moses into the river.

It might be tempting to think that Moses is the true hero of this story and the midwives are optional or accidental. But the deliverance of the Hebrews from the land of Egypt begins with the quiet, patient, mundane work of the midwives. It is through their hands that God opens the door to the liberation and healing and flourishing and justice that unfolds through the pages of Exodus. It is here that the miracle begins.

This is how God generally seems to work, especially in situations of darkness and oppression. Occasionally God sends a Moses or a Martin Luther King Jr., but mostly God sends midwives. Sometimes these midwives are metaphorical; sometimes they're actually licensed. This chapter tells the story of one: Sr. Mary Stella Simpson.

*　　　*　　　*

On Monday, November 27, 1967, Sr. Mary Stella Simpson wrote a letter to her Sisters back home at her community in Evansville, Indiana. She wrote from Mound Bayou, Mississippi, where generations of African Americans had often sung of the connections between their lives and those of the ancient Israelites:

Today was my [first] day for home visit. I go on Monday, Wednesday, and Friday, if possible. We see all new obstetric patients in the home. This affords an opportunity to discover anyone else who lives in the home and needs health care. I started out with my guide and made five visits. On the very first one, I had to come back to town to get milk for a baby. He had finished his last bottle. It has gotten really cold and the 14 people in that family all congregate in one room around a small wood-burning stove. I had to go through a front room which was like a deep-freeze. The floor was slick with ice where water had been tracked in and then froze. The children were all barefoot, therefore could not go to school. The parents have no way of getting shoes for them since they have no income.

Another family was freezing, too. Although they had a fire, there were holes in the walls so big that the cats came and went as they liked. A year-old baby was very ill with diarrhea—had it for a week. So I had to drive the mother with all six children in to the clinic. The baby had to be hospitalized. Again, the children were not in school because they had no shoes.[1]

On this particular evening, Sr. Mary Stella Simpson had been in Mound Bayou for a week. She had been called to help launch one of the most innovative experiments in health care for the poor in US history—the Tufts-Delta Health Center. Here, in 1967, this nurse-midwife who had previously pioneered radical changes in obstetrics care across the United States turned to face the pharaoh of the Jim Crow South. The cruel oppression of slavery—at least in its most visible form—was a century behind the African American people of Mississippi. A few decades earlier, a group of ex-slaves founded Mound Bayou, a nascent promised land that initially flourished economically, politically, and culturally. Yet the effects of the racialized politics, economics, and medicine of the mid-twentieth century had exceeded even pharaoh's vision: when Sr. Mary Stella arrived, 59 percent of all the babies born in Bolivar County, Mississippi, were dying every year, girls and boys alike. But as the story of Shiphrah and Puah attests, God works grace through those who defy the pharaohs of the world. The Israelites multiplied and grew very numerous. Sr. Mary Stella, in her six years in Mound Bayou, never lost a baby.

*   *   *

How was it that Sr. Mary Stella—one of the leading nurse-midwives of the twentieth century—found herself in Mound Bayou, Mississippi, in November 1967, at the age of fifty-seven? If there was ever a path with no straight lines, hers was one. Her story—a story of ongoing conversion—begins in Mount Ada, Arkansas, in 1910.[2]

Granddaughter of a Creek Indian, Mary was raised in a one-room log cabin located on a homestead farm ten miles from the nearest town. Apart from the death of her father when she was eight, Mary's childhood was a combination of happiness and hardscrabble farming. She had three younger brothers and eventually five stepbrothers. Her childhood responsibilities included milking six cows every morning and afternoon and working the cotton fields on leased river bottomland. These chores bookended the three-mile walk to and from school. Poverty, hard work, and fortitude were built into her marrow from the beginning.

Mary was raised a Baptist deep within the Bible Belt, thoroughly immersed in Baptist culture and ethos. Yet she was born with a capacity to challenge social norms and to patiently wait them out if need be. By her own testimony, she could quote the Bible backward and forward, but over time she was put off by her denomination, which she found negative and judgmental. "Every time I'd go there," she said, "there'd be some minister who'd lambast somebody. I felt I'd be better off reading the Bible at home."

On graduation from Baptist Academy at the age of seventeen, Mary declared her lifelong intention: to become a nurse. Due in part to Charles Dickens's portrayal of the sloppy, incompetent, and often drunk nurse Sarah Gamp in his novel *Martin Chuzzlewit*, as well as the ways in which nurses transgressed stereotypical social roles for women prior to World War II, nurses were considered by many to be immoral. Mary's mother, Georgia, was horrified at the prospect of her only daughter becoming a nurse and insisted that she wait until she was twenty-one, hoping that instead she would take a liking to teaching school. Obediently, Mary earned her teaching certificate and patiently taught kindergarten for four years, and then, at the age of emancipation, she enrolled in a nurse training program at a small hospital in Hot Springs, Arkansas.

About a year after she began her studies, new regulations for nursing schools promulgated by the American Nurses Association led to the closing of the program. At the recommendation of a Catholic physician, she transferred to a Benedictine hospital, St. Bernard's, in Jonesboro, Arkansas. Again, her mother blanched. "My mother," Mary remembers, "did not want any part of a Catholic hospital, so she told me to forget about it." But Mary persisted.

Up to that point in her life, Mary had never even heard the word "Catholic," much less seen a nun. "So of course," she says, "I was quite curious. I thought they [the nuns] looked very strange with their long veils and cloaks, since I was still a practicing Baptist." Suddenly, here she was, immersed in the vibrant materiality, community, and history of Catholicism. Every morning, she was awakened at 4:30 a.m. by the Sisters praying the Divine Office. Though she was initially aggravated because they interrupted her sleep, "in time their chanting began to sound sort of like music." Like her contemporary Dorothy Day, Mary found the tangible aspects of Catholicism intriguing, and she started "wondering what made these Catholic people tick." Her roommate, who was "born and bred Catholic" had little knowledge of her faith, leading her "to believe Catholics didn't think for themselves." But she was impressed by the depth of the Catholic tradition and immersed herself in the hospital library, reading everything she could about the history of the Catholic Church.

What drew her to Catholicism most of all was the powerful witness of the Sisters' work with the sick. Here, in the grueling yet ordinary work of touching and being present to the sick, Mary knew that she encountered transcendence. She tells of an "experiment" she ran on one Catholic practice that particularly perplexed her—holy water:

> While I was [at St. Bernard's Hospital School of Nursing], I became interested in the Church because of the work the Sisters did with the patients and with people and all of that. But, I had to have things proven. . . . I'd see Sisters put their hands in holy water and make the sign of the cross, and I'd thought, "what makes that water holy anyway?" . . . And so, one night, I was on night duty, and the hallway went right into the chapel . . . by the holy water font. And so I emptied the holy water font one night and just put plain water in it. I wanted to see if the Sisters knew the difference the next morning when they came in. And they didn't. And so I went to Sister a week or so later, and told her what I had done, and I said, I just want to know what the differ-

ence is. She said, well, first of all, that water had been blessed, and secondly, I would like to think that when we put our hands in it, it made it holier than water that we hadn't had our hands in. That made sense to me, because I had seen them work and knew what they did. So my lessons came one at a time like that. (Matousek interview)

For Mary and the Sisters, their work made holiness tangible, communicable, almost infectious. Later in her life, when told that serving in a delivery room was unsuitable for a nun, she responded, "If God isn't present at the birth of a child, He Isn't" (Matousek interview).

Shortly after completing her nurse training, Mary converted to Catholicism. Not surprisingly, this made her mother very unhappy. "I'm sure she prayed her Baptist friends would never find out," Mary recalled. Her conversion created a two-year rift with her mother, broken only when Georgia became gravely ill. Summoned to Los Angeles, where her mother and stepfather had moved, Mary found forty-three-year-old Georgia under the care of a quack who had diagnosed her distended abdomen as yet another pregnancy. Mary and Georgia both knew better. Convinced that a Catholic hospital would provide her mother with the best care, Mary had her admitted to St. Vincent Hospital within two days.

Though no skeptic about medicine, Mary considered what happened next to be as close to a miracle as one might get. They had arrived the day before Thanksgiving, and the Sister in charge was not optimistic about finding a doctor. Yet within minutes, in walked two of the best physicians on staff, who had trained at the Mayo Clinic. They confirmed Mary's diagnosis that her mother was riddled with cancer, "of the ovaries and the uterus and the omentum, and everything." Surgery was followed by postoperative X-ray treatments, but the physician saw these interventions as mostly palliative, giving Georgia at best six months to live. At the end of the treatment, the doctor called Mary in to his office. Mary recalled that conversation:

"She has no sign of cancer." And he said, "You know, we couldn't remove it all because it had metastasized everywhere. But it's not there." He said, "We have either a miracle here or an X-ray that does good work." And I said, "well the two together should be enough. We'll say we had both." (Matousek interview)

Georgia lived another forty years, dying of a stroke at the age of eighty-eight. She never knew that she'd had cancer.

At St. Vincent's, Mary met the Daughters of Charity—a women's religious order founded in France in 1633 by priest St. Vincent de Paul and widow St. Louise de Marillac to meet the pressing needs of the sick—particularly of the poorest and most abandoned individuals in Paris and throughout France. Unlike most religious congregations at the time, the first twelve members of the community were peasant girls rather than people from higher socio-economic tiers. They were one of the first apostolic orders for women—granted permission in 1668 by Pope Clement IX—to not be cloistered so that they could live among and minister to the poor in their own communities.[3] The Daughters of Charity first arrived in the United States in 1816 and were instrumental in helping to establish the robust infrastructure of Catholic health care in the US.[4] They opened the first hospital in Los Angeles, St. Vincent Hospital (now St. Vincent Medical Center), in 1856.[5]

Mary worked in obstetrics at St. Vincent's during her mother's course of treatment in order to help pay for her mother's medical bills. At St. Bernard's, she had felt called to become Catholic in order to be the best nurse she could be. Working at St. Vincent's, God pushed the call one step further: she now knew that she wanted to become a Sister as a way of pursuing excellence and serving the poor. In the Daughters of Charity, she found a community, which she entered in 1936. Georgia, who "said she'd rather die than have me become a Sister," was dealt yet another blow. If the cancer didn't kill her, at this rate Mary just might.

Their rift, healed by illness, was opened anew. For three years, mother and daughter again did not speak, even though Mary wrote to Georgia once a month. In 1939, Georgia finally visited Mary in St. Louis, where she had gone for her novitiate and where she was now working as a nurse. Meeting at the train station on Georgia's arrival, they faced each other across a clear divide. Georgia declared: "I came to take you home." Mary stood resolved: "I am not leaving, and if you can't accept that, you might just get back on the train" (Matousek interview).

Georgia did not get back on the train. She stayed and was introduced to this strange new world of Catholicism. The Sisters, she discovered, were a delight. She was astonished to discover how much the community loved them. People came up to Mary repeatedly, handing her money, giving her and her mother free ice cream and ferry tickets, and thanking them for their good work. In the most delicious twist of all, before the visit was out, Georgia asked if she could attend Mass with Mary and her community.

*　　　*　　　*

Over the next eighteen years, Sr. Mary Stella served as a labor and delivery nurse in a series of hospitals owned by the Daughters. In one institution after another, bedecked in her long, white nurse's habit and cornette, she helped improve care processes and achieve stunning outcomes. She excelled in both clinical care and nurse management, whether she was tending to abandoned children and unwed mothers in Chicago or eliminating neonatal deaths caused by diarrhea in St. Louis. She rose quickly to the top of her trade.

Where Mary Simpson had defied her mother at every turn to pursue her vocation, *Sister* Mary Stella was under a vow of obedience. Those in religious life, especially women, were often "missioned" where needed per the judgment of community leadership, often without their input. So it was that in 1957, Sr. Mary Stella learned that she was to be sent to the Catholic Midwifery Institute in Santa Fe, New Mexico. She initially took umbrage at her Mother Superior's directive: "You mean to tell me that I have been in obstetrics for twenty-two years and now I'm going to go away to learn how it's done?" (Matousek interview). Sr. Mary Stella had never heard of nurse-midwives, so she couldn't have guessed that they would transform the trajectory of her life and of obstetrics care in the United States.

Sr. Mary Stella was not alone in never having heard of nurse-midwives. While professional midwifery and nurse-midwifery had flourished in Europe, it met significant opposition from the medical establishment in the US in the early part of the twentieth century. Medicine sought to establish itself as a profession in large part by disenfranchising all non-allopathic care providers. As a result, by the time Sr. Mary Stella left for Santa Fe, nurse-midwifery had only been practiced in the US for about twenty-five years.

The Catholic Maternity Institute (CMI) School for Nurse-Midwifery was one of the first five nurse-midwifery schools in the United States and the first such Catholic institution. Opened in 1944, it was established through a cooperative effort of the archbishop of Santa Fe, the School of Nursing Education at Catholic University of America, the New Mexico State Department of Health, and the US Children's Bureau to provide "a complete maternity service for the Spanish-speaking population of the territory surrounding [Santa Fe]."[6]

The leaders of the CMI were members of the Society of Catholic Medical Missionaries, a community of nuns better known as the Medical Mission Sisters (MMS). The MMS was founded in 1925 by a laywoman physician, Anna Dengel, to provide medical and nursing care where needed, primarily in India. Like the Daughters of Charity, the Medical Mission Sisters lived in community but did not take public vows. Until 1936, Sisters who took public vows were not permitted by the Catholic church to practice medicine, surgery, or obstetrics—or even, as Sr. Mary Stella noted earlier, to handle babies.[7]

Missioned to Santa Fe for six months, Sr. Mary Stella stayed a year. From the outset, her experience at CMI transformed her approach to her vocation. CMI trained its students by sending them into the homes of poor Hispanic women. In these spaces, centered on the women and their families, different rules applied. In the hospital, she recalled, nurses never knocked at a door—they just walked right in. And nurses called the shots; mothers didn't have any say in the care of their babies. That was normal there. But not at CMI. As she recalls:

> So in Santa Fe, you talk about an eye opener. I almost had to have treatment for shock! I went out the first day, there were two of us that went out together . . . and they knock at the door and wait to be asked in, they wait for somebody to tell you where to put your bag. . . . They don't do anything in that home without the mother's or somebody's permission to do it. That really knocked me for a loop! I thought, "We are really heathens in the OB world, at our place." (Matousek interview)

To her horror and chagrin, she realized almost immediately that her previous twenty years of nursing care—in which she had been hailed as a managerial whiz and thought of herself as giving good OB care—had been designed primarily to serve the needs of the hospital, the medical staff, and the nurses. It minimized or ignored the perspective and needs of the mother as well as the rest of the family. This realization bothered her to no end.

The homes of the women served by CMI stretched in a forty-mile radius. Here she was introduced to the practice of making home visits—driving to the furthest reaches of the Santa Fe area, often with one of her colleagues, to attend to women in their own settings. Each patient received two to three prenatal home visits prior to delivery. One thing she learned was that, given the poverty of her patients, these visits could not be limited simply to prenatal care. "You become acquainted with other members of the family, going in two or three times," she recalled. "We got to know them so well. We were also taking in the home conditions. You'd never be able to deliver babies in some of those conditions" (Matousek interview). As a result, she began to be trained to attend not only to her patients' medical needs but also to the practical conditions of their lives.

Home visits also immersed her in the wondrous spirituality of childbirth. Siblings in the home or community would be summoned after the delivery for a blessing ceremony, a Spanish custom. The father would bless the baby on the forehead and then pass the baby around to everyone in the room—children, relatives, nurse-midwives—and each person would bless the baby. Then they'd kneel and pray. Not only did this deepen her sense of the spiritual nature of her work; it gave her new on-the-ground insight into the centrality of the family: "That home give and take was wonderful—something we never saw in the hospital. We never saw the family, ever. . . . That Santa Fe just turns your life around professionally and personally. It just turns your life around. And home deliveries—there's nothing that will ever replace it" (Matousek interview).

Her time with CMI converted her to a new vision of obstetrics care that she would carry into both the regimented, aseptic world of state-of-the-art hospitals and to a series of poor communities across the country. She was trained to attend to what we now call the social determinants of health. She learned how to teach mothers to breastfeed—which was almost unheard of in the United States. She learned the importance of childbirth and childcare classes for parents. And she was schooled in the importance of the relationship between mother and father, something she had never seen in the delivery room. "The year in Santa Fe," she noted, "was the best year of my life because it prepared me for the rest of my life" (Matousek interview).

In Santa Fe, Sr. Mary Stella was midwifed by the MMS and a community of poor Hispanic women into her new vocation as a midwife. Although she had never heard of it until 1957, it answered her deepest calling: "In my heart I always knew I wanted to be able to deliver babies, poor babies, because there were so many of them; they had nothing; they had no care" (Matousek interview).

She returned from the desert transformed.

*   *   *

There was no going back. At the end of her year in Santa Fe, Sr. Mary Stella was torn. She wanted to continue her work with poor women in poor communities but knew that the Daughters wanted her back in hospital administration. "I was so sure I could never go back to a hospital like I left," she averred. She made clear to her superiors that she was not the same person who had left for Santa Fe, that the experience had transformed her, and that if she was going to be put in charge of an obstetrics department in a hospital, things were going to have to change. "I said I want you all to understand this because you're going to get a lot of flak about that sister that left there—a good OB supervisor; I was really a mechanic, that's all—and I said, now I'm coming back and I'm not going to live like that and they [the parents] aren't either" (Matousek interview). To her surprise, they gave her the green light.

They returned her to St. Mary's Hospital in Evansville, a new facility with a large maternity department. In the midst of the baby boom, St. Mary's was delivering about one thousand babies per year when Sr. Mary Stella arrived, a number that doubled the next year.

She knew that implementing her new vision of family-centered care would not be easy. Culture change—even in one hospital, let alone on a national scale—is never easy. So she said to herself,

"'Go easy.' So where do I start? Labor and delivery. Labor room the best of all. I couldn't do it all at once so I'll do it a piece at a time" (Matousek interview). And she did. Within a week, she was giving last-minute instructions to patients in labor, which they welcomed enthusiastically. This piqued the interest of nurses, whom she began to train one by one. Then she made the big move: she sat down with the chief of the obstetrics staff and said, "You know, doctor, I think we should try something different in OB. We're far behind the times already; let's not get any further behind." She made her case for allowing fathers in the labor and delivery room. He responded, "It's fine with me" (Matousek interview). She never expected it would be so easy.

From here, quietly, and amazingly with little opposition (except from the occasional postpartum nurse or hospital receptionist), Sr. Mary Stella began a crusade that transformed maternal-infant health care in the US. From Evansville, she took her show on the road, making the case for what became known as family-centered maternity care. She was the first health care provider in the United States to encourage fathers to be present at the birth of their children.[8] Labor and delivery classes for the parents, permitting fathers to be in the delivery room and to visit their wives whenever they wanted, centering care on the mother's needs and wishes rather than on that of the hospital staff—for five years, she took this vision for maternity care nationwide, traveling the lecture circuit nonstop to "every state in the US except Washington and Oregon."

She spent time at various hospitals in the Daughters of Charity system—St. Louis, Chicago, Detroit, Los Angeles—helping local staff implement this new vision. She created two films that made her famous, "Family-Centered Maternity Care" and "All My Babies." In 1963, she was elected President of the American College of Nurse-Midwives (ACNM), serving two terms as well as six years on the executive board.[9] She also convinced the Daughters to mission her to care for poor women, and she was sent to El Carmen, Texas, to serve Mexican immigrants who spoke little or no English.

"Nurse midwifery," she noted, "puts you at the front line of those who have nothing."

Shortly thereafter, she received a call from the American Nurses Association. An organization was "looking for one nurse midwife who was to set up and supervise a maternal-child health clinic in a very rural area" (Matousek interview).[10] A short visit convinced her that this was the place for her. The doctors, social workers, and staff were already working in the community, not only tending to medical issues but also working on substandard housing, putting in window screens and plumbing, and more. She learned that the infant mortality rate was 59 percent.

> They said: "That can be stopped don't you think?" I said, "It better be!" And he said, "Do you want the job?" I said: "Yes, I want the job. I'd be glad."
>
> I said, "I'm a country person anyway, I'm rural, I grew up poor, that's no news to me, and it's fine if I do this. I'll be glad." (Matousek interview)

In November 1967, with the support of her religious community, she left for Mound Bayou, ready to defy pharaoh.

*   *   *

Turning off old Highway 61 two hours south of Memphis, Sr. Mary Stella found herself at the outskirts of Mound Bayou, a stranger in a strange land. It would be easy to miss the exit, lulled by the endlessly flat, green expanse of the cotton and soybean fields of the Mississippi Delta, broken only by distant stands of trees and the translucent haze of the searing heat. The potholed main road that led to the heart of the mile-square hamlet was edged by scrubby, yellow grasses.

Tired, tiny homes with broken windows and automobile carcasses on cinder-block stilts cried out for repairs. Boarded up remnants slouched over what for a time was the bustling downtown of a promised land. Mound Bayou's main intersection was too quiet to require a stoplight. Yet here Sr. Mary Stella stopped, in front of the former Taborian Hospital, and read the historical marker witnessing the town's storied place in African American history:

> Mound Bayou—Largest U.S. Negro town: settled July 12, 1887 by ex-slaves of Joe Davis, who conceived idea before Civil War: Isaiah T. Montgomery (member of 1890 state convention) & his cousin, Benjamin T. Green.[11]

Montgomery and Green had been slaves of Joseph Davis, brother of Confederate president Jefferson Davis. After years of planning and negotiations, they purchased 840 acres of land in Bolivar County, twenty-five miles from the winding Mississippi River alongside the path of the New Orleans and Texas Railroad, establishing a haven for former slaves. But this was not quite a land flowing with milk and honey, at least to the immediate eye: "Thick woods of cottonwood and cypress trees, cane stalks and briar-patches, with streams, bayous, and pools of stagnant water, made the land almost impenetrable. Many of the trees stood over 130 feet tall, while cane stalks grew to over 25 feet. Poisonous snakes, especially water moccasins, wolves, panthers, and bears endangered adventurers brave enough to travel through the Delta or settle there."[12]

Within a mere twenty years, the original inhabitants carved Mound Bayou out of this wilderness to create a prosperous, self-governing community that for all of its history has been upward of 98 percent African American.[13]

By 1907, Mound Bayou had become the seat of African American culture and power in the country. It ranked as the largest cotton producer in the world. It boasted a population of roughly eight hundred families who owned upward of tens of thousands of acres of land. In addition, "the town had three schools, 40 businesses, a half-dozen churches, a train depot, a post office, a newspaper, three cotton gins, a cottonseed oil mill, a zoo, a Carnegie public library, and a swimming pool, all African American owned, operated, and patronized." President Theodore Roosevelt, on a whistle-stop tour in 1900, christened Mound Bayou "the Jewel of the Delta."

Completely self-governing, it was also a sanctuary from segregation. Though Mound Bayou was embedded in a world of legislated oppression, "inside the town limits there were no racial codes. . . . White visitors to town stayed in homes, and none of the businesses maintained separate facilities, as was commonly done in the rest of the state. Blacks entered the front doors of restaurants rather than through the back, and the mayor, aldermen, constable, and town marshal were all duly elected." The only exceptions were the Jim Crow signs at the train station built by the railroad company. In a delicious twist, the "Colored" waiting room at the depot was larger and finer than that for the "Whites."

Mound Bayou was also a haven from discriminatory health care practices. Under Jim Crow, African Americans were required to enter hospitals through the back door, if they were allowed to enter at all. One story is told of a man whose surgery was performed in the hospital boiler room, as that was the only place a black person was allowed. In response, the black fraternal organization, the International Order of Twelve Knights and Daughters of Tabor, founded the Taborian Hospital in Mound Bayou in 1942. This fifty-bed facility not only openly provided health care for blacks in Mississippi; it also introduced a key innovation into US health care: it was the first health maintenance organization (HMO) in the country.

Mound Bayou prospered until the early 1920s, when it was hobbled by a series of economic setbacks: a sharp sell-off in cotton prices around 1920, the Great Depression of 1929, and two fires that devastated the business district in 1926 and 1941. The white regulatory and business interests of Mississippi took advantage of these crises to obstruct the town via economic discrimination, crippling its ability to recover.

By the time Sr. Mary Stella arrived in 1967, both the infrastructure and the health status of the area were profoundly devastated. She discovered, as she notes in the introduction to her letters, that "many people in the area had never visited a doctor in their lives" and "virtually every family we cared for needed much more than obstetrical and newborn care." Her letters also hold many choice words for the former Taborian Hospital (which by 1967 had been renamed the Mound Bayou Community Hospital). Two nights after she arrived, she sent an eighteen-year-old woman in active labor

to the Mound Bayou Hospital, such as it is. (They do not have an admitting clerk. Oh, it would take me all night to describe *that* situation!) The doctors (surgeons, internists, and pediatricians) gave all of the prenatal patients to Miss Johansen and me—the two nurse-midwives. They are scared to death of a pregnant woman. . . . The surgeon has no compassion for the poor. I hope to work him over—quietly, that is. (Wednesday, November 22, 1967)

Later in the year, her ire over the obstructionist attitudes and substandard care at Mound Bayou's only main health center continued to flare:

The hospital here is still inadequate despite the improvements I told you about some time ago. I could say other things about it that would not look good on paper. They just sent us a letter saying they could not take any more unwed mothers. Why? They don't want to "get a bad name for themselves." I could be arrested for what I'm thinking! (Sunday, April 28, 1967)

Yet despite its economic troubles, Mound Bayou remained an epicenter of black self-empowerment, and it is credited by many as the birthplace of the civil rights movement. In 1951, Dr. T. R. M. Howard, the first chief surgeon of Taborian Hospital, started a grassroots civil rights organization, the Regional Council of Negro Leadership (RCNL). Howard was friends with Martin Luther King Sr. and had a significant influence on his son. He hired the recent college graduate Medgar Evers to direct the organization, which launched one of the first economic boycott initiatives. (For this purpose, they also invented that ubiquitous billboard of American culture: the bumper sticker.) Annual meetings of the RCNL in Mound Bayou between 1952 and 1955 attracted crowds of ten thousand or more, including national leaders of the civil rights movement. Mound Bayou was the training ground for many of the future leaders of the movement.

This activism, combined with the Supreme Court's 1954 decision in *Brown v. Board of Education*, incited the emergence of the White Citizens' Councils—a network of white supremacist organizations, founded in Indianola, Mississippi, just forty miles from Mound Bayou. Ostensibly eschewing the violent tactics of the Ku Klux Klan, they claimed to opt for economic and political means of intimidation, retaliation, and discrimination. They were nonetheless known for inciting violence.

Yet during the 1950s and 1960s, while Mississippi was burning and "the rest of the Delta was a hornet's nest of intimidation and violence," Mound Bayou stood as an engine and refuge for civil rights activists. Mamie Till—mother of Emmett Till, a fourteen-year-old boy visiting the Delta from Chicago, who was lynched, it was said, for whistling at a white woman—stayed in the home of Dr. Howard when she came in 1955 to testify in the trial of those who murdered her son; she was not considered safe anywhere else in the Delta. Many others found it be a safe haven as well. As one longtime resident explained: "If a black person was running away, got in trouble, they knew if they ever made it to Mound Bayou, they wouldn't be bothered." It was reputed to be the one town in Mississippi that the Klan refused to enter. Some attribute this protection to the arsenal of firearms allegedly stored in Dr. Howard's home. Oral tradition credits the women of the town and the power of the Spirit. The Rev. Dr. Otis Moss III tells this story: "The Night Riders would come riding their horses and the horses would get to the boundary [of Mound Bayou] and just stop and throw the riders off. . . . What they didn't know was that there was a circle of praying sisters who prayed all around the boundaries of Mound Bayou, Mississippi, and prayed for Mound Bayou, Mississippi, that we place a hedge of protection around this city that [God] would protect our children and our children's children."[14]

Horse and rider, once again, were thrown into the sea—this time back into the sea of racial violence.

*   *   *

Sr. Mary Stella stepped out of her car in front of the convent at St. Gabriel's Church, where she would live with the African American nuns for the next six years. She breathed deeply and felt like she was home. "Having been born and having lived for 20 years in rural Arkansas," she recalled, "I was very familiar with the kind of poverty we found in Mound Bayou."[15] She had finally gotten to the place where she could really work with poor people, which was the reason she had originally followed the vocation to become a Sister. And Mound Bayou gave her the opportunity to implement and expand the model of community-based, home-based, family-centered care she had learned in Santa Fe and developed in El Carmen.

She had come to help launch the Tufts-Delta Health Center (TDHC), one of the most important innovations in health care for the poor in the US. The TDHC was not simply yet another clinic for the poor. In 1965, physician-activist H. John Geiger, who at the time was on faculty at Harvard Medical School, pitched a groundbreaking proposal to the US Office of Economic Opportunity (OEO), part of Lyndon Johnson's War on Poverty. Geiger's vision was inspired by his work in the 1950s with a novel community health center in Pholela, South Africa, funded by the Rockefeller Foundation. Geiger had spent the summer of 1964 in Mississippi with the Freedom Riders, leading the Medical Committee for Human Rights, whose goal was "eradicating and replacing the southern segregated and discriminatory health care system with an egalitarian one."[16] The similarities between South African apartheid and segregated Mississippi were too glaring for Geiger to ignore.

With two colleagues, Geiger proposed that the OEO launch two national health centers, one urban, one rural, to be opened as demonstration projects for an approach to health care that addressed medical needs as well as environmental factors affecting individual and community health, including sanitation, nutrition, basic preventive care, and substandard housing; that advanced economic development by employing community residents as day care or after-school workers, health aides, and community outreach workers; that partnered with local community colleges to help community members gain advanced degrees; and that involved community members and patients in the planning and oversight of the centers via community organizing.

The project was accepted, and in 1965 the OEO launched the first two National Health Centers (NHC) in the US, one in Mound Bayou and the other at Columbia Point in Massachusetts. Mound Bayou was selected due to its historical importance for the African American community and its terrible poverty.[17] As anticipated, the TDHC met stiff opposition from the white community in Mississippi. Geiger's proposal to the OEO was opposed in vocal and vigorous terms by state officials including the governor, the head of the Mississippi Department of Health, and local physicians. Yet through wily strategizing too long to recount here, the TDHC was funded and went forward. It proved to be a great success, even more than the urban center.[18] By the end of 1968, when the building was finally completed, the clinic was seeing between 150 and

175 people per day with another 30 to 40 receiving visits in their homes. These numbers are particularly extraordinary considering the local population was 14,000.

And Sr. Mary Stella was at the heart of it. When she arrived, she was the lone nurse-midwife on staff; the clinic was working from rented space in an old Baptist parsonage, and she taught her parenting classes in an abandoned movie theater. (The new facility would not be completed for a year.) Every evening, "regardless of the hour," she wrote letters to her community back in Evansville, Indiana, detailing her work and the challenges that she encountered. Her first letter, written November 21, 1967, opens,

> My very dear Sisters, The grace of our Lord be with us forever! Well here I am in Mound Bayou. . . . I came directly to the convent of St. Gabriel, where I will be staying. I knew if I stopped at the clinic, I would be there for hours. I don't think we will have to worry about case-finding. I hear that the cases just appear— some patients walking for miles, sleeping under the stars the night before they are seen.

Although familiar with poverty, she was taken aback by the desperate conditions of the community residents, which seemed more like a developing country than Arkansas where she grew up:

> I saw an 11-month old baby who was almost dead from starvation at clinic yesterday. I have seen pictures of these little starved ones from India and Viet Nam, but the actual face-to-face encounter is really an experience. . . . The little one doesn't know how to eat. The mother had taken him to two other doctors, and they did nothing for him. She lives quite a distance from us but heard about our good doctors. (Thursday, April 4, 1968)

Her letters detail her regular visits to the homes of families with twelve, fourteen, fifteen, or more children, whom she finds barefoot with "heads that are masses of matted hair from ring-worm and sores. They wear rags for clothes. When the rags fall off them, they look for more rags. Really!" (Friday, November 24, 1967). Families lived in wooden sharecropper shacks at the ends of rutted dirt lanes that veered off the gravel paths that cut between the cotton fields. Raised off the ground on stilts or posts, the shacks were stiflingly hot in the summer even with their wide front porches. They had no heat in the winter, leaky roofs, walls with holes traversed by dogs and cats, and no running water or sanitation.

Mothers who had to choose between taking a sick child to the doctor and feeding their families often resorted to home remedies, as trips to see a doctor were often futile. "I used to be so frustrated when I'd get home at night; I'd be exhausted because I'd been angry most of the day!"[19]

But she was no angry activist. In her letters and recorded interviews, she recounts her tale with a lilting voice shot through with lightness and constant good humor. She seems to draw from a deep well of peace and joy. Still, she was a savvy, canny actor, smiling and steely as she challenged givens and helped to dismantle institutional structures that exacerbated both segregation and mortality. Her imposing physical presence may have helped. Perhaps it was not easy to say no to this six-foot-tall woman with a square, cheery face, high cheekbones, and laughing eyes. She had the robust build and "big hands" of a country farm girl. Armed with her public health bag or delivery bag and bedecked in one of her two calf-length cotton "Catholic dresses" (as one of the locals called her many-layered habit), she soon became a familiar and valued presence in the five-hundred-square-mile catchment area for the TDHC.

In addition to attending patients and driving them to the TDHC and elsewhere, she spent days mustering clothes and diapers, cleaning supplies, soaps and shampoos, cardboard boxes for crafting bassinettes, jugs of water, food, and more to take to her patients. She taught basic life skills, makeshift solutions, and breastfeeding to mothers in their homes, as well as parenting classes in the abandoned movie theater downtown.

Outfitted first with a white Ford and later with a beige Volkswagen "nearer the color of mud," she clocked 150 to 200 miles per day visiting homes between the cotton fields, soybean fields, and wastelands. Finding them could be a challenge in itself as they were often located ten to fifteen miles apart:

> They give you such strange directions: "Three hickory trees down the road, then turn right at the dead tree." When you start looking, all the trees look alike and there are many dead ones. We usually find the place—eventually. Sometimes I have to park the car half a mile away and walk to the house because the roads have tire ruts so deep that the car hangs up on the center ridge. (Monday, January 29, 1968)
>
> [I] went for miles and miles down in the country, in the mud.... I wore knee boots and these oil slickers.... It rained all the time.... And I drove a bug, a Volkswagen, because I knew that it was light enough that if I had to push it, I could push it. And I did have to push it a lot of times. But I always got back, there was always somebody come along who would help. Everybody knew who I was after a while. And people would always help me. They'd change my tires if I had a flat, and so on.... The presence down there was great. (Matousek interview)

The stiflingly humid Mississippi air spilled its heaviness with alarming frequency, often pouring all night long. Muddy water stood in puddles and filled the deep drainage ditches around the villages and fields, complicating both walking and driving. One January evening after a long day on the road, muddied to the knees, she confided to her Sisters: "You know, after today, I really have respect for the mini skirt and wish I had one to wear."

Through these home visits, she came to know not only her patients and members of the community; she was also brought face-to-face with the pernicious structures of Jim Crow that exacerbated poverty and often shocked her. On these she brought to bear the same patient, good-natured guile honed through her decades of undermining structures of sexism and medicalism. A local postmistress, she discovered, would wait days to give black families their small welfare checks. She investigated, made some contacts, and a month later wrote, "Remember that postmistress we reported for holding back welfare checks from black people? She is now enjoying retirement. Poor Mississippi will never be the same with all these health center people occupying the Delta area. Things really are a-changing!" (Wednesday, June 19, 1968).

She had been in Mound Bayou almost a year before she discovered a family whose children—ages eleven, twelve, and thirteen—had never been to school because they had not been issued birth certificates. "I couldn't see how any state law or school regulation could be so stupid, so I went to see the principal of the elementary school to ask about it. He was very nice and said this was an enforced regulation, passed long ago to prevent blacks from going to school. (Most are born at home and do not have that lily white piece of paper)" (Tuesday, October 23, 1968). She succeeded in getting them enrolled in school the following week.

One by one, she pulled the threads of Jim Crow that she encountered, unraveling in small ways the fabric of oppression. She became particularly incensed when she encountered segregated medicine. In Jackson, Mississippi, where the TDHC would sometimes take patients, she was aghast to find "a waiting room for blacks, waiting rooms for whites, cafeterias for blacks, cafeterias for whites, *nurseries* for blacks, and *nurseries* for whites. I thought 'NO. I haven't lived long enough to see this!'" (Matousek interview). She and her colleagues used the economic lever of government funding to slowly pry apart these structures. They would threaten to withhold their government-funded patients from segregated clinics or physician's offices and send them elsewhere. Often they received a familiar response: "Well, we never thought about it. It's always been this way" or "We can't help it! It's just the way it is!" But, as she notes, "It didn't take long [to get them to come around and change things] because all that money was going to other doctors who only had one waiting room" (Matousek interview).

She became particularly industrious over the segregated entrances at a clinic in Clarksdale:

> So I went to Clarksdale one night and I saw this sign: white entrance, on the other side, black entrance. So when I went in . . . I said, "Doctor, I am shocked."
>
> He said, "Why, Sister?"
>
> I said, "You still, in this day and age, have a post out there that says 'white entrance' and over there it says 'black entrance'?" I said, "I can't believe that."
>
> He said, "It's not my clinic, Sister."
>
> I said, "Don't pass the buck." I said, "you work here, you pay rent here, so it is your clinic."
>
> He kind of smiled and didn't say anything.
>
> I said to the Sister [who was with me] that the next time I come up here at night to bring a baby that is sick or something, I'm going to pull those posts up. And I did. And I took them home with me! . . .
>
> So then I had to go see the doctor, and I went to him purposely to see if he said anything. When I came in, I went into his office, he started to laugh, and he laughed and he laughed. I wasn't sure what he was laughing at. He said: "Well, you got your way, didn't you."
>
> And I laughed and said: "Yes, and I'm going to use it for firewood!"
>
> Oh my. Those were the days. But I enjoyed them. . . . If somebody doesn't do that, who's going to do it? (Matousek interview)

*   *   *

Sr. Mary Stella loved the people of Mound Bayou, loved the work, and certainly loved bringing joy, grace, and a little bit of God's righteous justice every so often. "My only regret," she later said, "is that I didn't stay young long enough to do it forever" (Matousek interview).

> I was happy to go [to Mound Bayou] because it was such a challenge. It was marvelous. . . . I learned more about pediatrics there than I ever learned in school, but most of all I learned about faith. I never had to spread the Gospel to the people there—in spite of all their hardships, their faith in God was unshakeable. . . . I think God was with me all the way. Because I didn't really have to sit down and think about what to do next.[20]

In her six years with the TDHC, she never lost a baby or a mother. Nor did she during her year in El Carmen. These outcomes are nothing short of astonishing, seeming to defy the laws of biology or poverty or reality. How could one woman, with her team, make such a difference? We hear stories of astounding healings in Scripture or in the stories of the saints, healings that are referred to as miracles. Generally, we enlightened modern readers dismiss such stories as exaggerations, myths, or hagiography. But in the case of Sr. Mary Stella, we know that the story is true. Does the fact that we might know the mechanism—dedicated women seeking out the poor in their homes, being present with them as persons with dignity, connecting them with health care, and attending to the social determinants of their health—make it any less of a miracle? Or is this how grace actually works in the world?

*　　　*　　　*

Sr. Mary Stella's story launched me on a seven-hundred-mile pilgrimage through Mississippi—a place this Midwestern white woman never had any reason to go. Immersed in the suffocating heat of a Mississippi July, I walked the streets of Mound Bayou through sites made holy by the blood of the civil rights martyrs and the witness of those who stood with them. Although sharecropping has been replaced with agribusiness, I could sense the silent but vigilant racism that still weaves the state's physical and social fabric and that watched me warily as I traversed soybean fields and small towns. What Midwesterners like me often consider history is still alive and active in the South; the ghosts of pharaoh's army still ride, and much work remains to be done.

Looking around at the dusty dry bones of Mound Bayou, I thought of Sr. Mary Stella and wondered: who could tell such a miracle had occurred? Although the sharecropper shacks and Jim Crow signs are gone, Mound Bayou looks much the same today as it did in the late 1960s. Health outcomes in Bolivar County remain grim, with the premature death rate at almost twice the national average and almost half of the county's children living in poverty.[21] In 2016, Mississippi had one of the highest rates of infant mortality in the US, with rates twice as high in black communities as white, Bolivar County being among them.[22]

This is nothing new. After the parting of the Red Sea, the Israelites still had ahead of them a long sojourn in the desert. I'm sure Bethlehem and Galilee looked little-changed even after the incarnation. And in Mississippi, pharaoh's cruel slavery continues to take its toll. Yet God continues to call midwives of grace to walk with the beautiful, enduring people caught in those places where the violence of poverty, racism, and oppression continue to deal death in its myriad forms.

The witness of Sr. Mary Stella Simpson, the story she tells, is that it's not impossible; in fact, it's really not that hard. If we face pharaoh as midwives rather than as Moses, we'll find that our small part in bringing miracles to birth will be one filled with joy and laughter, and surely justice will eventually roll down.

For Further Reading

CESAR CHAVEZ

Levy, Jacques E., Jacqueline M. Levy, and Fred Ross Jr. *Cesar Chavez: Autobiography of La Causa*. Minneapolis: University of Minnesota Press, 2007.

Pawel, Miriam. *The Crusades of Cesar Chavez: A Biography*. New York: Bloomsbury, 2014.

HOWARD THURMAN

Thurman, Howard. *Disciplines of the Spirit*. New York: Harper & Row, 1963.

——. *Jesus and the Disinherited*. New York: Abingdon-Cokesbury, 1949. Reprinted with a foreword by Vincent Harding. Boston: Beacon, 1996.

——. *A Strange Freedom: The Best of Howard Thurman on Religious Experience and Public Life*. Edited by Walter Earl Fluker and Catherine Tumber. Boston: Beacon, 1998.

Yuri Kochiyama

Fujino, Diane C. *Heartbeat of Struggle: The Revolutionary Life of Yuri Kochiyama*. Minneapolis: University of Minnesota Press, 2005.

Kochiyama, Yuri. *Passing It On*. Los Angeles: UCLA Asian American Studies Center Press, 2004.

Howard Kester

Dunbar, Anthony P. *Against the Grain: Southern Radicals and Prophets, 1929-1959*. Charlottesville, VA: University of Virginia Press, 1981.

Egerton, John. *Speak Now Against the Day: The Generation Before the Civil Rights Movement in the South*. New York: Knopf, 1994.

Martin, Robert Francis. *Howard Kester and the Struggle for Social Justice in the South, 1904-1977*. Charlottesville: University of Virginia Press, 1991.

Ella Baker

Day, Keri. *Unfinished Business: Black Women, the Black Church, and the Struggle to Thrive in America*. Maryknoll, NY: Orbis Books, 2012.

Grant, Joanne. *Ella Baker: Freedom Bound*. New York: Wiley, 1999.

Ross, Rosetta E. *Witnessing and Testifying*. Minneapolis: Fortress, 2003.

DOROTHY DAY

Miller, William D. *Dorothy Day: A Biography.* San Francisco: Harper & Row, 1984.

Troester, Rosalie Riegle. *Voices from the Catholic Worker.* Philadelphia: Temple University Press, 1993.

JOHN A. RYAN

Broderick, Francis L. *Right Reverend New Dealer John A. Ryan.* New York: Macmillan, 1961.

Gearty, Patrick. *The Economic Thought of Monsignor John A. Ryan.* Washington, DC: Catholic University of America Press, 1953.

Ryan, John A. *Social Doctrine in Action: A Personal History.* New York: Harper & Brothers, 1941.

WILLIAM STRINGFELLOW

Stringfellow, William. *A Private and Public Faith.* Grand Rapids: Eerdmans, 1962.

———. *Suspect Tenderness: The Ethics of the Berrigan Witness.* New York: Holt, Rinehart & Winston, 1971.

MAHALIA JACKSON

Best, Wallace. *Passionately Human, No Less Divine: Religion and Culture in Black Chicago, 1915-1952.* Princeton, NJ: Princeton University Press, 2007.

Harris, Michael W. *The Rise of Gospel Blues: The Music of Thomas Andrew Dorsey in the Urban Church.* New York: Oxford University Press, 1992.

Schwerin, Jules. *Got to Tell It: Mahalia Jackson, Queen of Gospel.* New York: Oxford University Press, 1992.

LUCY RANDOLPH MASON

Goldfield, Michael. "Race and the CIO: The Possibilities for Racial Egalitarianism during the 1930s and 1940s." *International Labor and Working-Class History* 44 (1993): 1–32.

Mason, Lucy Randolph. *To Win These Rights: A Personal Story of the CIO in the South.* New York: Harper & Brothers, 1952.

Salmond, John A. *Miss Lucy of the CIO: The Life and Times of Lucy Randolph Mason, 1882–1959.* Athens, GA: University of Georgia Press, 1988.

RICHARD TWISS

Twiss, Richard. *Rescuing the Gospel from the Cowboys: A Native American Expression of the Jesus Way.* Downers Grove, IL: InterVarsity Press, 2015.

Twiss, Richard, and John Dawson. *One Church, Many Tribes.* Minneapolis: Chosen Books, 2000.

DANIEL BERRIGAN

Berrigan, Daniel. *Essential Writings.* Edited by John Dear. Maryknoll, NY: Orbis Books, 2009.

———. *Isaiah: Spirit of Courage, Gift of Tears.* Minneapolis: Fortress, 1996.

Forest, Jim. *At Play in the Lion's Den: A Biography and Memoir of Daniel Berrigan.* Maryknoll, NY: Orbis Books, 2017.

For Further Reading

MARY STELLA SIMPSON

Farren, Suzy. *A Call to Care: The Women Who Built Catholic Health-care in America*. St. Louis: Catholic Health Association of the United States, 1996.

Simpson, Mary Stella. *Sister Stella's Babies: Days in the Practice of a Nurse-Midwife*. New York: American Journal of Nursing, 1978.

Ward, Thomas, Jr. *Out in the Rural: A Mississippi Health Center and Its War on Poverty*. New York: Oxford University Press, 2016.

Contributors

Carlene Bauer is the author of the memoir *Not That Kind of Girl* (Harper, 2009) and the novel *Frances and Bernard* (Houghton Mifflin Harcourt, 2013). Her work has been published in *The Virginia Quarterly Review*, *n+1*, *The New York Times Book Review*, and *Elle*.

David Dark is the author of *Life's Too Short to Pretend You're Not Religious* (InterVarsity Press, 2016). He teaches at the Tennessee Prison for Women and Belmont University, where he is assistant professor of religion and the arts in the College of Theology.

W. Ralph Eubanks is the author of *The House at the End of the Road: The Story of Three Generations of an Interracial Family in the American South* (Harper Collins, 2009) and *Ever Is a Long Time: A Journey into Mississippi's Dark Past* (Basic Books, 2005).

Nichole M. Flores is assistant professor of religious studies at the University of Virginia. She is a contributing author at *America: The Jesuit Review of Faith and Culture* and has published essays in the *Journal of Religious Ethics* and the *Journal of the Society of Christian Ethics*.

331

Susan M. Glisson is cofounder and partner of Sustainable Equity, which works with communities, schools, and corporations to foster effective historical dialogue in order to build inclusive and equitable communities. She was the founding director of the William Winter Institute for Racial Reconciliation.

Grace Y. Kao is professor of ethics and codirector of the Center for Sexuality, Gender, and Religion at Claremont School of Theology. She is the author of *Grounding Human Rights in a Pluralist World* (Georgetown University Press, 2011) and the coeditor of *Asian American Christian Ethics: Voices, Methods, Issues* (Baylor University Press, 2015) and *Encountering the Sacred: Feminist Reflections on Women's Lives* (T&T Clark, 2018).

M. Therese Lysaught is professor of Catholic moral theology and health care ethics at the Neiswanger Institute of Bioethics and Healthcare Leadership, Loyola University Chicago Stritch School of Medicine, and the Institute of Pastoral Studies at Loyola University Chicago. She is the coeditor of *Catholic Bioethics and Social Justice: The Praxis of US Health Care in a Globalized World* (Liturgical Press, 2018) and of the third edition of *On Moral Medicine: Theological Perspectives on Medical Ethics* (Eerdmans, 2012).

Charles Marsh is Commonwealth Professor of Religious Studies and director of the Project on Lived Theology at the University of Virginia. He is the author of *Strange Glory: A Life of Dietrich Bonhoeffer* (Knopf, 2014) and numerous books on religion and social justice.

Donyelle C. McCray is assistant professor of homiletics at Yale Divinity School. Her book, *The Censored Pulpit: Julian of Norwich as Preacher*, is forthcoming from Fortress Academic.

Soong-Chan Rah is Milton B. Engebretson Professor of Church Growth and Evangelism at North Park Theological Seminary. He is the author of *The Next Evangelicalism* (InterVarsity Press, 2009) and *Prophetic Lament* (InterVarsity Press, 2015).

Daniel P. Rhodes is clinical assistant professor of social justice and coordinator of contextual education at Loyola University Chicago and editor in chief of *The Other Journal*. He is coauthor of *Organizing Church: Grassroots Practices for Embodying Change in Your Congregation, Your Community, and Our World* (Chalice, 2017).

Peter Slade teaches courses in the history of Christianity and Christian thought at Ashland University in Ohio. He is the author of *Open Friendship in a Closed Society: Mission Mississippi and a Theology of Friendship* (Oxford University Press, 2009) and coeditor of *Lived Theology: New Perspectives on Style, Method, and Pedagogy* (Oxford University Press, 2016).

Becca Stevens is an author, a priest, and the founder and president of Thistle Farms, a global community of survivors of trafficking and addiction that includes justice enterprises. For her work as an entrepreneur and justice advocate, Becca has been named a White House Champion of Change and a CNN Hero. She holds numerous honorary doctorates, and her most recent book, *Love Heals*, was published by Thomas Nelson in 2017.

Charles H. Tucker is cofounder and partner of Sustainable Equity, where he serves as a facilitator and community builder and helps nurture national and international partnerships. He is also a freelance writer and photographer.

Shea Tuttle is editorial and program manager at the Project on Lived Theology. She is currently writing a book about Mister Rogers, to be published by Eerdmans.

Heather A. Warren is associate professor of religious studies at the University of Virginia and an Episcopal priest. She is the author of *Theologians of a New World Order: Reinhold Niebuhr and the Christian Realists, 1920-1948* (Oxford University Press, 1997).

Notes

1. Dietrich Bonhoeffer, *Letters and Papers from Prison* (New York: Touchstone, 1971), 275.

2. Christopher Rowland, *Radical Christianity: A Reading of Recovery* (Eugene, OR: Wipf and Stock, 2004), 161.

3. "St. Mathetes Epistle to Diognetus," *Apostolic Fathers* (London: Lightfoot & Harmer, 1891).

4. Albert J. Raboteau, "American Salvation: The Place of Christianity in Public Life," *Boston Review*, April/May 2005.

5. Thomas Merton, "Events and Pseudo-Events: Letter to a Southern Churchman" in *The Failure and the Hope: Essays of Southern Churchmen*, ed. Will D. Campbell and James Y. Holloway (Eugene, OR: Wipf and Stock, 1972), 91. Merton's essay first appeared, in slightly different form, in *Katallagete—Be Reconciled*, the journal of the Committee of Southern Churchmen, in 1966.

CESAR CHAVEZ

1. Peter Matthiessen, *Sal Si Puedes: Cesar Chavez and the New American Revolution* (New York: Random House, 1969), 6.

2. Jacques E. Levy, *Cesar Chavez: Autobiography of La Causa* (New York: W. W. Norton and Company, 1975), 37.

3. Quoted in Matthiessen, *Sal Si Puedes*, 148.

4. Fred Ross, *Conquering Goliath: Cesar Chavez at the Beginning* (Keene, CA: El Taller Grafico Press, 1989), 143.

5. Miriam Pawel, *The Crusades of Cesar Chavez: A Biography* (New York: Bloomsbury Press, 2014), 7.

6. Pawel, *Crusades of Cesar Chavez*, 8–9.

7. Levy, *Cesar Chavez*, 17.

8. Richard Griswold del Castillo and Richard A. Garcia, *César Chávez: A Triumph of Spirit* (Norman: University of Oklahoma Press, 1995), 7.

9. Ronald B. Taylor, *Chavez and the Farmworkers* (Boston, MA: Beacon Press, 1975), 61.

10. Levy, *Cesar Chavez*, 26.

11. Levy, *Cesar Chavez*, 25.

12. Levy, *Cesar Chavez*, 18–19.

13. Levy, *Cesar Chavez*, 27.

14. Frederick John Dalton, *The Moral Vision of César Chavez* (Maryknoll, NY: Orbis Books, 2003), 40–41.

15. Levy, *Cesar Chavez*, 66.

16. Pawel, *Crusades of Cesar Chavez*, 16.

17. Levy, *Cesar Chavez*, 74.

18. Cesar Chavez, *An Organizer's Tale: Speeches*, ed. Ilan Stavans (New York: Penguin, 2008), 25.

19. Pawel, *Crusades of Cesar Chavez*, 467.

20. Pawel, *Crusades of Cesar Chavez*, 93.

21. Levy, *Cesar Chavez*, 99.

22. Chavez, *Organizer's Tale*, 17.

23. Levy, *Cesar Chavez*, 4.

24. Levy, *Cesar Chavez*, 3.

25. Castillo and Garcia, *César Chávez*, 34–35.

26. Matthiessen, *Sal Si Puedes*, 58, 87.

27. Levy, *Cesar Chavez*, 42.

28. Chavez, *Organizer's Tale*, 14. Originally coauthored by Cesar, Helen, and Luis Valdez, the "Plan of Delano" was first published in the union's newspaper, *El Malcriado*, on March 17, 1966.

29. Miriam Pawel, *The Union of Their Dreams: Power, Hope, and Struggle in Cesar Chavez's Farm Worker Movement* (New York: Bloomsbury Press, 2009), 10.

30. For instance, Mark Day reports that a Bank of America subsidiary, the California Land Company of Visalia, began absorbing smaller farms in the 1930s until they controlled 90 percent of the ranches around the

San Joaquin Valley town of Delano (Mark Day, *Forty Acres: Cesar Chavez and the Farm Workers* [New York: Praeger, 1971], 27). Similarly, Ronald Taylor notes that other titans such as Wells Fargo, the United Fruit Company, J. G. Boswell Co., Purex, and Tenneco were key players in the industry. The Tenneco conglomerate alone held 1.4 million acres in California and Arizona, a true industry behemoth (Taylor, *Chavez*, 39).

31. An account of the history and development of agribusiness in California with special attention to its impact on workers can be found in Carey McWilliams, *Factories in the Field: The Story of Migratory Farm Labor in California* (Boston, MA: Little, Brown, 1939; repr., Hamden, CT: Archon Books, 1969).

32. Taylor, *Chavez*, 38–39.

33. Castillo and Garcia, *César Chávez*, 28–29.

34. Pawel, *Union of Their Dreams*, 10.

35. Pawel, *Union of Their Dreams*, 15.

36. Castillo and Garcia, *César Chávez*, 36.

37. Levy, *Cesar Chavez*, 175.

38. Castillo and Garcia, *César Chávez*, 38.

39. Pawel, *Crusades of Cesar Chavez*, 101.

40. Pawel, *Crusades of Cesar Chavez*, 101.

41. Pawel, *Crusades of Cesar Chavez*, 105.

42. Levy, *Cesar Chavez*, 184.

43. Castillo and Garcia, *César Chávez*, 42–44.

44. Pawel, *Crusades of Cesar Chavez*, 106.

45. Mattheissen, *Sal Si Puedes*, 137.

46. Levy, *Cesar Chavez*, xxiii.

47. French philosopher and former Jesuit Michel de Certeau argued that the strong enjoy a certain geographical advantage, deploying strategies of domination based on their superior vantage point and thus on their ability to dictate the structure of the spatial dimension of relations. The weak, by contrast, he theorized, make use of more ad hoc tactics that play on time in order to resist domination. Michel de Certeau, *The Practice of Everyday Life*, trans. Steven Rendall (Berkeley: University of California Press, 1988), 34–39.

48. *El Malcriado*, no. 21 (1965), 10–11.

49. *El Malcriado*, no. 23 (1965), 3.

50. *El Malcriado*, no. 23 (1965), 5.

51. Dalton, *Moral Vision*, 86.

52. de Certeau, *Practice of Everyday Life*, 119–20.

53. de Certeau, *Practice of Everyday Life*, 210.

54. Chavez, *Organizer's Tale*, 10–11.

55. Cesar Chavez, foreword in Pat Hoffman, *Ministry of the Dispossessed: Learning from the Farm Worker Movement* (Los Angeles: Wallace Press, 1987), vii.

56. Levy, *Cesar Chavez*, 217.

57. Castillo and Garcia, *César Chávez*, 53.

58. Castillo and Garcia, *César Chávez*, 53–54.

59. Levy, *Cesar Chavez*, 223.

60. Levy, *Cesar Chavez*, 226.

61. Levy, *Cesar Chavez*, 226.

62. Levy, *Cesar Chavez*, 227.

63. Castillo and Garcia, *César Chávez*, 56.

64. Joan London and Henry Anderson, *So Shall Ye Reap: The Story of Cesar Chavez and the Farm Worker's Movement* (New York: Thomas Y. Crowell, 1970), 159–60.

65. Levy, *Cesar Chavez*, 272; Castillo and Garcia, *César Chávez*, 84.

66. Cesar Chavez, letter to the National Council of Churches, February 20, 1968, San Joaquin Valley Farmworkers Collection, Fresno State University Library; reprinted in Winthrop Yinger, *Cesar Chavez: The Rhetoric of Nonviolence* (Hicksville, NY: Exposition Press, 1975), 108–9.

67. Levy, *Cesar Chavez*, 272.

68. Pawel, *Crusades of Cesar Chavez*, 159.

69. Stephen R. Lloyd-Moffet, "The Mysticism and Social Action of César Chávez," in *Latino Religions and Civic Activism in the United States*, edited by Gastón Espinosa, Virgilio Elizondo, and Jesse Miranda (Oxford: Oxford University Press, 2005), 35–51.

70. Chavez, *Organizer's Tale*, 47–48.

71. Dalton, *Moral Vision of Cesar Chavez*, 121, and Castillo and Garcia, *César Chávez*, 47.

72. Day, *Forty Acres*, 115.

73. In her critical biography of Chavez, Miriam Pawel depicts how this stubborn side of him created rifts in the movement and even among those who had long worked in its leadership. See Pawel, *Crusades of Cesar Chavez*.

74. Yinger, *Cesar Chavez*, 37.

75. Chavez, *Organizer's Tale*, 47–48.

76. Castillo and Garcia, *César Chávez*, 91.

77. Castillo and Garcia, *César Chávez*, 92–93.

78. Pawel, *Crusades of Cesar Chavez*, 207–8.

79. Levy, *Cesar Chavez*, 325.

80. Written by Cesar Chavez. Available at the Cesar E. Chavez Foundation website at https://www.chavezfoundation.org/uploads/Prayer _of_the_Farm_Workers.pdf.

HOWARD THURMAN

1. Kenneth T. Jackson, *The Ku Klux Klan in the City, 1915–1930* (New York: Oxford University Press, 1967), 173.

2. Howard Thurman, *With Head and Heart: The Autobiography of Howard Thurman* (New York: Harcourt Brace Jovanovich, 1979), 49.

3. Thurman, *With Head and Heart*, 7.

4. Thurman, *With Head and Heart*, 8–9.

5. Thurman, *With Head and Heart*, 5.

6. Thurman, *With Head and Heart*, 5.

7. Thurman, *With Head and Heart*, 6.

8. Howard Thurman, "Horn of the Wild Oxen," sermon preached at Marsh Chapel, Boston University, Feb. 28, 1954, Howard Thurman Collection, Howard Gotlieb Archival Research Center at Boston University.

9. Thurman, *With Head and Heart*, 12; Howard Thurman, "Human Freedom and the Emancipation Proclamation," *Pulpit Digest*, December 1962, 13–16, 66.

10. Thurman, *With Head and Heart*, 253.

11. Thurman, *With Head and Heart*, 15.

12. Thurman, *With Head and Heart*, 15.

13. Thurman, *With Head and Heart*, 16.

14. Thurman, *With Head and Heart*, 28.

15. Thurman, *With Head and Heart*, 241.

16. Howard Thurman, *The Luminous Darkness: A Personal Interpretation of the Anatomy of Segregation and the Ground of Hope* (New York: Harper & Row, 1965), x.

17. Thurman, *With Head and Heart*, 115.

18. Orlando Patterson, *Slavery & Social Death: A Comparative Study* (Cambridge, MA: Harvard University Press, 1982), 63. Patterson argues that being treated as a perpetual minor is one dimension of enslavement.

19. Thurman, *With Head and Heart*, 116.

20. Howard Thurman, *Jesus and the Disinherited* (Nashville: Abingdon, 1949; Boston: Beacon Press, 1996), 13.

21. Howard Thurman, *Deep River and the Negro Spiritual Speaks of Life and Death* (Richmond, IN: Friends United Press, 1975), 16.

22. Thurman understands freedom to consist of a sense of alternative. He explains, "The essential word here is 'sense'; for it is the sense of alternative that guarantees the freedom." Howard Thurman, "Human Freedom and the Emancipation Proclamation," *Pulpit Digest*, December 1962, 15.

23. Claude McKay, "If We Must Die," in *Complete Poems*, ed. William J. Maxwell (Champaign: University of Illinois Press, 2004), 177–78.

24. Thurman, *With Head and Heart*, 109.

25. Howard Thurman, "Notes on Homiletics Course," October 13 [no year]. Howard Gottlieb Archival Research Center, Boston University, box 16, folder 47.

26. Howard Thurman, "The Preacher as a Religious Professional," prayer given at Golden Gate Baptist Theological Seminary, February 8–12, 1971. Howard Gottlieb Archival Research Center, Boston University, box 10, folder 28.

27. Thurman, *With Head and Heart*, 152–53.

28. Thurman, *With Head and Heart*, 19–20.

29. Thurman, *With Head and Heart*, 20.

30. From the Howard Thurman Collection, Howard Gotlieb Archival Research Center at Boston University, box 104, folder 15.

31. From the Howard Thurman Collection, Howard Gotlieb Archival Research Center at Boston University, box 104, folder 15.

32. While at Morehouse College, Howard got to know Martin Luther King Sr., "Daddy King." Sue and Alberta King met at Spelman's high school and developed a lasting friendship. Thurman, *With Head and Heart*, 254.

33. Thurman, *With Head and Heart*, 254–55.

34. Thurman, *With Head and Heart*, 255.

35. Thurman, *With Head and Heart*, 224.

36. Howard Thurman, *My People Need Me, June 1918–March 1936*, vol. 1 of *The Papers of Howard Washington Thurman*, ed. Walter E. Fluker, Kai Jackson Issa, Quinton H. Dixie, Peter Eisenstadt, Catherine Tumber, Alton Pollard III, and Luther E. Smith Jr. (Columbia: University of South Carolina Press, 2009), 215–16.

37. Oswald W. S. McCall, *The Hand of God* (New York: Harper &

Brothers, 1939), 66–67; Howard Thurman, *The Growing Edge* (New York: Harper, 1956), 87.

38. Julian of Norwich, *Revelations of Divine Love*, trans. Elizabeth Spearing with an introduction and notes by A. C. Spearing (London: Penguin, 1998), 147.

39. Thurman, *With Head and Heart*, 255.

YURI KOCHIYAMA

1. Yuri Kochiyama, "My Creed . . . 22," in *Passing It On: A Memoir*, 2nd ed. (Los Angeles: UCLA Asian American Studies Center Press, 2004), xxiv–xxv.

2. Diane C. Fujino, *Heartbeat of Struggle: The Revolutionary Life of Yuri Kochiyama* (Minneapolis: University of Minnesota Press, 2005), xvi. Approximately six hundred additional Japanese Americans were arrested on the day following the attack, with some three thousand total by March 1942.

3. Yuri Kochiyama, *Fishermerchant's Daughter: Yuri Kochiyama, An Oral History* (New York: St. Mark's in the Bowery, 1981), 1:9.

4. Fujino, *Heartbeat of Struggle*, xx.

5. Kochiyama, *Fishermerchant's Daughter*, 1:9.

6. As Yuri's biographer has noted, Seiichi's cause of death has been a source of great speculation, with some family members suspecting that he was not administered his diabetes medication, others believing that he had been physically abused, and Yuri herself concluding that whatever the particulars, her father died prematurely as a result of inadequate medical attention while imprisoned. His death certificate lists "duodenal ulcer" and "hypertropic cirrhosis of liver" as the cause of death, while the FBI files note that he died in the family home of "natural causes." See Fujino, *Heartbeat of Struggle*, xx–xxi.

7. T. A. Frail, "American Incarceration: The Injustice of Japanese-American Internment Camps Resonates Strongly to This Day," *Smithsonian Magazine*, January 2017, https://www.smithsonianmag.com/history/injustice-japanese-americans-internment-camps-resonates-strongly-180961422/.

8. Kiran Ahuja, "Honoring the Legacy of Yuri Kochiyama," June 6, 2014, https://obamawhitehouse.archives.gov/blog/2014/06/06/honoring-legacy-yuri-kochiyama.

9. The May 19, 2016, Google doodle can be viewed at https://www
.google.com/doodles/yuri-kochiyamas-95th-birthday.

10. For more information about the nomination, see http://rising
womenrisingworld.com/portfolio-items/1000-women-for-the-nobel
-peace-prize-project/. For Yuri's other notable recognitions, see Kathlyn
Gay, ed., *American Dissidents: An Encyclopedia of Activists, Subversives, and
Prisoners of Conscience* (Santa Barbara, CA: ABC-CLIO, 2012), 2:354–58.

11. Yuri's admiration for revolutionaries remains one of the most
controversial aspects of her legacy. She was drawn to Maoist philosophy
after having received *The Little Red Book: Quotations from Chairman Mao
Tse-tung* as a gift; supported the Peruvian militant communist group Shining Path; and favorably compared Osama bin Laden to Malcolm X, Che
Guevara, Fidel Castro, and several others for fighting against US imperialism. See Fujino, *Heartbeat of Struggle*, 194–95; Kochiyama, *Passing It
On*, chap. 14, "People's War in Peru"; Tamara Kil Ja Kim Nopper, "Yuri
Kochiyama on War, Imperialism, Osama bin Laden, and Black-Asian
Politics," *The Objector: A Magazine of Conscience and Resistance*, October
17, 2003, http://la.indymedia.org/news/2003/10/89393_comment.php.

12. Yuri spent three out of fifteen chapters in her memoir, *Passing It On*,
talking about political prisoners and has called those willing to be jailed in
furtherance of justice the "heartbeat of struggle." Her official biographer,
Diane J. Fujino, also concurs that Yuri's "most steadfast area of struggle"
was her support for those imprisoned on account of their political beliefs
and activities. See Fujino, *Heartbeat of Struggle*, xxiii.

13. Many historians and educators, as well as many Japanese Americans, use different terminology than bureaucratic language to describe
what Japanese Americans endured during World War II out of their conviction that the official language minimizes what actually happened. The
permanent exhibit about Japanese Americans and World War II at the National Museum of American History uses and suggests the following sub-
stitutions: "eviction" (instead of exclusion), "forced removal" (instead of
evacuation), "incarceration" (instead of internment), "inmate" (instead
of internee), "temporary detention center" (instead of assembly center),
and "incarceration camp" (instead of relocation center). The Smithsonian
also notes the controversy surrounding the proposal to designate "internment camps" as "concentration camps" given the term's close association
with the Nazi "death camps." See http://americanhistory.si.edu/righting
-wrong-japanese-americans-and-world-war-ii/language-incarceration.

14. The following month, Congress passed Public Law 503 on March 21,

1942, with unusual speed, to authorize enforcement of the Executive Order's provisions. To be clear, Japanese Americans were not the only ones forcibly exiled and imprisoned during World War II: (1) President Roosevelt's Executive Orders 2526 and 2527 also led to detentions for smaller numbers of German Americans and Italian Americans, (2) the United States also worked in conjunction with thirteen Latin American countries to forcibly relocate more than 2,200 Latin American citizens and residents of Japanese ancestry into US concentration camps, and (3) Aleutians, an indigenous people, were also involuntarily removed from their homes after Japan invaded and occupied the westernmost islands of Alaska's Aleutian Chain in June 1942 and likewise placed in camps in Juneau.

15. Yuri recalls some Japanese American communities being given only forty-eight hours to pack, and then only what they could carry—thus requiring them to sell nearly everything they owned for "almost nothing" to the "vultures" who descended to take advantage of their situation. Her family was thus comparatively fortunate for having both a month's time to get their affairs in order and trustworthy neighbors who rented out their home and looked after their personal effects in their absence. The Nakaharas were able to hold onto their house but not Seiichi's small business, because the banks froze his account upon his arrest. See Kochiyama, *Fishermerchant's Daughter*, 1:11.

16. Kochiyama, *Fishermerchant's Daughter*, 1:13.

17. Kochiyama, *Fishermerchant's Daughter*, 1:14.

18. Yuri Kochiyama, quoted in Fujino, *Heartbeat of Struggle*, 59.

19. Yuri reproduced that creed in a May 7, 1944, group letter to her class. See Fujino, *Heartbeat of Struggle*, 51.

20. Kochiyama, "Mothers and Daughters," in *Discover Your Mission: Selected Speeches & Writings of Yuri Kochiyama*, eds. Russel Muranaka and Tram Nguyen (Los Angeles: UCLA Asian American Studies Center, 1998), 31. Yuri reports here and elsewhere returning to this pearl of wisdom throughout her life.

21. Quoted in Fujino, *Heartbeat of Struggle*, 50. Yuri wanted the youth to remain optimistic and neither develop a "terrible feeling against the government" nor "try to revenge themselves on the people who made us go into camp." See her *Fishermerchant's Daughter*, 1:17. According to Valerie J. Matsumoto, *City Girls: The Nisei Social World in Los Angeles, 1920–1950* (New York: Oxford University Press, 2014), Nisei women were known for playing morale-boosting roles in the camps. Thanks to Chrissy Yee Lau for alerting me to this reference.

22. Fujino, *Heartbeat of Struggle*, 49.

23. Fujino, *Heartbeat of Struggle*, 49.

24. Fujino, *Heartbeat of Struggle*, 44–45.

25. Fujino, *Heartbeat of Struggle*, 70–71.

26. See Kochiyama, *Passing It On*, xxiii; Fujino, *Heartbeat of Struggle*, 7, 32–33; Yuri Kochiyama, "The Impact of Malcolm X on Asian-American Politics and Activism," in *Blacks, Latinos, and Asians in Urban America: Status and Prospects for Politics and Activism*, ed. James Jennings (Westport, CT: Praeger, 1994), 134.

27. Internal Security Act of 1950, Pub. L. No. 81-831, 64 Stat. 987.

28. See Masumi Izumi, "Alienable Citizenship: Race, Loyalty, and the Law in the Age of American Concentration Camps, 1941-1971," *Asian American Law Journal* 13, no. 1 (2006): 1–30; Fujino, *Heartbeat of Struggle*, 261–62.

29. Quoted from a CJA newsletter as reproduced in Fujino, *Heartbeat of Struggle*, 262. Ironically, even a senator of Japanese heritage, Samuel Ichiye ("S. I.") Hayakawa—but one who had not himself been incarcerated during World War II because he had been living in the Midwest—had called for Iranian Americans to be detained en masse during the hostage crisis. Hayakawa also claimed that the forcible removal and imprisonment had been "good" for Japanese Americans and had called Nisei requests for reparations both "ridiculous" and something that filled him with "shame and embarrassment." See Emily Hiramatsu Morishima, "S. I. Hayakama," in *Asian American History and Culture*, vols. 1–2, ed. Huping Ling and Allen Austin (New York: Taylor & Francis, 2010), 409–10.

30. Nevertheless, during the hostage crisis, the Carter administration had subjected all Iranian students to immediate deportation if they had violated the terms of their visas (all Iranian students had to report to immigration officials to have their visas checked for irregularities) and also temporarily suspended the issuing of new visas for Iranians. See David Farber, *Taken Hostage: The Iranian Hostage Crisis and America's First Encounter with Radical Islam* (Princeton, NJ: Princeton University Press, 2005), 151.

31. While isolated demands for redress by Japanese American individuals date back to the 1940s, the birth of the organized, community-wide calls for redress began decades later when community efforts to commemorate their incarceration began intensifying with the emergence of the Asian American movement in the late 1960s and when the Japanese American Citizens League (JACL) entertained a proposal for reparations at their national convention in 1970.

32. Fujino, *Heartbeat of Struggle*, 263. This grassroots movement eventually led to the formation of the East Coast Japanese Americans for Redress in September, 1981—another organization, of which both Yuri and Bill were prominent members, that played a role in securing redress for Japanese Americans.

33. Fujino, *Heartbeat of Struggle*, 267. Yuri's rationale for reparations and her clever means of communicating it to others is best seen in the "Song for Redress/Reparation" she composed to the tune of "Battle Hymn of the Republic." The song spoke of a presidential order that made "incarcerees of a single ancestry," Japanese Americans being victims of "hysteria and . . . bigotry," and the necessity of restitution, justice, and compensation for "120,000 wronged," Kochiyama, *Passing It On*, 194.

34. Unfortunately, the legacy of the infamous Korematsu decision is in dispute as seen in the majority and dissenting opinions in *Trump v. Hawaii*, 585 U.S. ___ (2018) concerning the constitutionality of restricting travel into the United States from foreign nationals of several countries with Muslim majorities ostensibly to prevent infiltration by foreign terrorists.

35. United States Congressional Commission, "Personal Justice Denied: Report of the Commission on Wartime Relocation and Internment of Civilians" (Washington, DC: Civil Liberties Public Education Fund; Seattle: University of Washington Press, 1997). As the JACL activist Fred Hirasuna has acknowledged, these findings were socially reparative in "restor[ing] our faith in the US and what the Constitution really means." As law professor Eric K. Yamamoto recounts, they were also psychologically cathartic: "Former internees could finally talk about the internment. Feelings long repressed, surfaced. One woman, now in her sixties, stated that she always felt the internment was wrong, but that, after being told by the military, the President, and the Supreme Court that it was a necessity, she had come seriously to doubt herself. Redress and reparations . . . had now freed her soul." See Fred Hirasuna as quoted in Alice Murray, *Historical Memories of the Japanese American Internment and the Struggle for Redress* (Stanford, CA: Stanford University Press, 2007), 439; Eric K. Yamamoto, "Friend, Foe or Something Else: Social Meanings of Redress and Reparations," *Denver Journal of International Law and Politics* 20 (1992): 227.

36. Civil Liberties Act of 1988, 50 U.S.C. § 4211; Ronald Reagan, "Remarks on Signing the Bill Providing Restitution for the Wartime Intern-

ment of Japanese-American Civilians," August 10, 1988, reproduced in Gerhard Peters and John T. Woolley, *The American Presidency Project*, http://www.presidency.ucsb.edu/ws/?pid=36240. Yuri and Bill were publicly acknowledged for their leadership efforts in the 1988 redress celebration in New York, subsequent National Day of Remembrance commemorations in New York and Los Angeles (1993, 1996), in several widely attended pilgrimages to former camp sites (1971, 2002), and in the aforementioned official White House tribute to Yuri, among other occasions. See Fujino, *Heartbeat of Struggle*, 271; Kochiyama, *Passing It On*, 187 and appendix 18.

37. Fujino, *Heartbeat of Struggle*, 113–28.

38. Yuri credits her friendship with Malcolm X for helping her to move beyond an internal US frame toward a more expansive concern for human rights, people's self-determination, and the liberation of various "Third World" peoples. Though their relationship was cut short by his assassination, his influence on her cannot be underestimated. For details, see Yuri Kochiyama, "The Impact of Malcolm X on Asian-American Politics and Activism," in *Blacks, Latinos, and Asians in Urban America: Status and Prospects for Politics and Activism*, ed. James Jennings (Westport, CT: Praeger, 1994), 129–41.

39. Fujino, *Heartbeat of Struggle*, 180–83.

40. Kochiyama, *Fishermerchant's Daughter*, 2:15. Yuri had herself come under FBI surveillance beginning in 1966 because of her association with black nationalists. She was incorrectly identified as a "Red Chinese agent," and the New York FBI office had also placed her on the Security Index, Category II, which meant that she would be subject to immediate arrest and detention in an emergency, just as her father had been in 1941. See Fujino, *Heartbeat of Struggle*, 174–75. A congressional investigation into COINTELPRO led by Senator Frank Church in the mid-1970s found that the FBI had engaged in a number of unconstitutional activities, including illegal wiretaps, warrantless physical searches, and other dirty infiltration tactics aimed at defaming, and in some cases blackmailing, political dissidents. See Senate Select Committee on Intelligence Activities, *COINTELPRO and Other Intelligence Activities Targeting Americans, 1940–1975* (Ipswich, MA: Mary Ferrell Foundation Press, 2008); Ursula Wolfe-Rocca, "Why We Should Teach about the FBI's War on the Civil Rights Movement," *The Zinn Education Project*, March 1, 2016, https://zinnedproject.org/2016/03/fbi-war-civil-rights-movement/.

41. Diane C. Fujino, "The Black Liberation Movement and Japanese

American Activism: The Radical Activism of Richard Aoki and Yuri Kochiyama," in *Afro Asia: Revolutionary Political and Cultural Connections between African Americans and Asian Americans*, eds. Fred Ho and Bill V. Mullen (Durham, NC: Duke University Press, 2008), 187–88.

42. Fujino, *Heartbeat of Struggle*, 183.

43. Fujino, *Heartbeat of Struggle*, 185.

44. Fujino, "The Black Liberation Movement and Japanese American Activism," 185.

45. Fujino, *Heartbeat of Struggle*, 49. See also Melissa Hung, "The Last Revolutionary," *East Bay Express*, March 13, 2002.

46. Fujino, *Heartbeat of Struggle*, chap. 3.

47. Kochiyama, *Passing It On*, 127. As Fujino notes, at times Yuri "prioritized the struggle for global freedom and justice above the needs of her own family," and doing so occasionally came at great cost to the latter. *Heartbeat of Struggle*, 219. As Yuri has herself maintained, "all mothers wish the best for their children," but they must consider "priorities of needs," for when "other children starve and suffer," how can a mother "be only preoccupied that her child 'have the best' of anything?" "Mothers and Daughters," 34.

48. Fujino, *Heartbeat of Struggle*, xxiv.

49. Yuri has essentially affirmed the definition provided by the Jericho Movement, an organization founded in 1998 to free all political prisoners: those "brothers and sisters, men and women who, as a consequence of their political work and/or organized affiliations were given criminal charges, arrested or captured, tried in criminal courts and sent to prison." Quoted in Fujino, *Heartbeat of Struggle*, 206. In *Passing It On* and elsewhere, however, Yuri has also wanted to expand the definition to include what the Jericho Movement would consider to be "politicized" prisoners instead—those who were not originally incarcerated for their political activities but who became politically active when serving time.

50. All twenty-nine activists were arrested for trespassing on federal property but freed on minimal bail the following day, likely due to the four-hundred-plus demonstrators who had appeared at the police station demanding their release. See Fujino, *Heartbeat of Struggle*, 229. See also Karl Jagbandhansingh, "Yuri Kochiyama on the Occupation of the Statue of Liberty in 1977," https://archive.org/details/YuriStatueOfLiberty1977KarlOct2009.

51. Fujino, *Heartbeat of Struggle*, 228.

52. The oldest of Yuri's six children, Billy, had ended his life after

spending three years in and out of hospitals following a serious car accident that ultimately cost him his leg. See Kochiyama, *Passing It On*, 163; Fujino, *Heartbeat of Struggle*, 222-24.

53. Fujino, *Heartbeat of Struggle*, 227. Yuri acknowledges that when polled, only a small minority of Puerto Ricans want independence. She attributes this small number to the situation of colonial dependence that the US has created for Puerto Rico, where Puerto Ricans are US citizens but "have no control over customs, postal, monetary or judicial systems" and thus have become "powerless to develop their own destiny, their own politics, their own decisions." See Yuri Kochiyama, "Expand Our Horizon; Decolonize Our Mind; Cross Our Borders" in *Discover Your Mission*, 37.

54. Jimmy Carter, "Andres Figueroa Cordero Announcement of the Commutation of Mr. Figueroa Cordero's Prison Sentence," October 6, 1977, reproduced in Gerhard Peters and John T. Woolley, *The American Presidency Project*, http://www.presidency.ucsb.edu/ws/?pid=6757.

55. Jimmy Carter, "Puerto Rican Nationalists Announcement of the President's Commutation of Sentences," September 6, 1979, reproduced in Gerhard Peters and John T. Woolley, *The American Presidency Project*, http://www.presidency.ucsb.edu/ws/?pid=32827.

56. Kochiyama, *Passing It On*, 144.

57. For details of Wong's case, see Steve Fishman, "He Got Life," *New York Magazine*, June 13, 2005; Maurice Possley, "David Wong," *The National Registry of Exonerations*, https://www.law.umich.edu/special/exoneration/Pages/casedetail.aspx?caseid=3763.

58. David W. Chen, "An Inmate's Family of Strangers: Bonds Sustain 12-Year Quest for a New Murder Trial," *New York Times*, March 28, 1999.

59. See Chen, "An Inmate's Family of Strangers"; Hung, "The Last Revolutionary."

60. Quoted in Fishman, "He Got Life."

61. Quoted in Chen, "An Inmate's Family of Strangers."

62. David W. Chen, "Metro Briefing/New York: Wrongfully Convicted Man Is Deported after Release," *New York Times*, August 16, 2005; DPA, "Hong Kong Man Back Home after Winning Freedom," *Taipei Times*, August 13, 2005, http://www.taipeitimes.com/News/world/archives/2005/08/13/2003267557.

63. Timothy Williams, "Execution Case Dropped against Abu-Jamal," *New York Times*, December 7, 2011.

64. He is so described by Educators for Mumia Abu-Jamal (EMAJ), https://www.facebook.com/groups/109829015700381/about/, an orga-

nization founded in 1995 as a network of teachers and coordinated by Baruch College (SUNY) history professor Johanna Fernandez and Princeton Theological Seminary professor Mark Lewis Taylor.

65. "Mumia Abu-Jamal Spared Death Row Penalty after Prosecutors Drop 30-Year Bid for Execution," *Democracy Now*, December 8, 2011. Academics for Mumia (now EMAJ) also placed a full-page ad in the *New York Times* on May 7, 2000, demanding justice for him with over six hundred signers.

66. Amnesty International, "USA: A Life in Balance—The Case of Mumia Abu-Jamal," February 17, 2000, https://www.amnesty.org/en /documents/amr51/001/2000/en/.

67. Kochiyama, *Passing It On*, 134; Amnesty International, "USA: A Life in Balance," 1, 6. According to the latter's report, the FBI's COINTEL-PRO "appeared to number Abu-Jamal among its targets," and the officers who arrested Mumia—even if they were unaware of his identity—would have "immediately associated him with the organization [MOVE] because of his dreadlocks, a hairstyle adopted by MOVE as part of their beliefs."

68. Quoted from Mark Lewis Taylor's description of Yuri's "clarion call" about Mumia at an April 4, 1996, press conference in the Philadelphia Capitol Building. He recalls her linking Mumia's plight that day to Puerto Rican independence movements and American Indian groups. See Mark Lewis Taylor, "She Has Become an Ancestor: Yuri Kochiyama's Legacy: I Remember," June 3, 2014, http://marklewistaylor.net/blog/she -has-become-an-ancestor-yuri-kochiyamas-legacy-i-remember/.

69. Hung, "The Last Revolutionary"; Elaine Woo, "Yuri Kochiyama Dies at 93; Civil Rights Activist, Friend of Malcolm X," *Los Angeles Times*, June 3, 2014.

70. Kochiyama, *Passing It On*, 134, 136.

71. Kochiyama, *Passing It On*, 187.

72. Mumia Abu-Jamal, "Yuri Kochiyama: A Life in Struggle" (written June 2, 2014), http://www.prisonradio.org/media/audio/mumia/yuri -kochiyama-324-mumia-abu-jamal.

73. Hung, "The Last Revolutionary."

74. Kochiyama, *Passing It On*, 187.

75. Fujino, *Heartbeat of Struggle*, 209–12.

76. Akemi Kochiyama-Sardinha, foreword in Kochiyama, *Passing It On*, xiii.

77. Fujino, *Heartbeat of Struggle*, 259.

78. Fujino, *Heartbeat of Struggle*, 333n54.

79. Thanks to Lerron Wright, Jeongyun Hur, and Jeremy V. Cruz for bibliographic and other assistance; Joshua Mendez and Jorge J. Rodriguez V for helpful information about Puerto Rican *independentistas* and the Young Lords; and Charles Marsh for the invitation to participate in this book project. I owe a special debt of gratitude to two groups of people who gave me helpful feedback on earlier drafts: (1) fellow contributors Donyelle McCray, David Dark, Heather Warren, and editor Shea Tuttle and (2) the members of APARRI 2017 (Asian Pacific American Religions Research Initiative) who came to my precirculated papers session (Tracy Tiemeier, Carolyn Chen, David K. Yoo, Dean Adachi, Esther Chung-Kim, Sharon Suh, Tat-Siong Benny Liew, and Chrissy Lau). All mistakes that remain, of course, are mine.

HOWARD KESTER

1. John Egerton, *A Mind to Stay Here: Profiles from the South* (New York: Macmillan, 1970), 75; James F. Kay, "The Renovation of Miller Chapel," *Princeton Seminary Bulletin* 22, no. 1 (2001).

2. Egerton, *A Mind to Stay Here*, 74.

3. Robert Francis Martin, *Howard Kester and the Struggle for Social Justice in the South, 1904–77,* Minds of the New South (Charlottesville: University Press of Virginia, 1991), 21; John Stark Bellamy, *If Christ Came to Dixie: The Southern Prophetic Vision of Howard Kester* (MA thesis, University of Virginia, 1977), 35.

4. Howard Kester, "Early Life of Howard Kester," 5, in the Howard Kester Papers #3834, Southern Historical Collection, Lewis Round Wilson Special Collections Library, University of North Carolina at Chapel Hill (hereafter cited as Howard Kester Papers).

5. Interview with Howard Kester, July 22, 1974. Interviewed by Jacqueline Hall and William Finger, B-0007-1. Southern Oral History Program Collection (#4007) in the Southern Oral History Program Collection, Southern Historical Collection, Lewis Round Wilson Special Collections Library, University of North Carolina at Chapel Hill, http://docsouth.unc.edu/sohp/B-0007-1/menu.html.

6. *The Message of the Student Christian Association Movement* (New York: Association Press, 1928), 11–12, in David P. Setran, *The College "Y": Student Religion in the Era of Secularization* (New York: Palgrave Macmil-

lan, 2007), 198. It is important to realize the huge influence of the YMCA in this period. In 1920, the YMCA had 764 chapters in colleges and universities across the country with a membership of 80,649 students: one in four male students were members of their college Y. Setran, *The College "Y,"* 4. The YWCA had 600 student chapters with more than 60,000 female members. "YWCA of the U.S.A. Records. Record Group 07. Student Work," Five College Archives and Manuscript Collection, Sophia Smith Collection, Smith College, Northampton, MA, https:// asteria.fivecolleges.edu/findaids/sophiasmith/mnsss292rg7_bioghist .html.

7. Kester, "Early Life of Howard Kester," (1940), 3.

8. Kester, "Early Life of Howard Kester," 4.

9. Edward M. Wayland in his introduction to Kester's papers wrote "By 1931 Kester had come to see his work in terms of three general issues: an attack on the practices and attitudes of racial segregation, an opposition to war and the use of violence, and an opposition to capitalist economics." Edward M. Wayland, "Biography," in *Howard A. Kester Papers, 1923–1972,* ed. Edward M. Wayland (Glen Rock, NJ: Microfilming Corp. of America, 1973), 1.

10. Interview with Howard Kester, July 22, 1974.

11. Kester, "Early Life of Howard Kester," 6.

12. Kester, "Early Life of Howard Kester," 5.

13. Bradley J. Longfield, *The Presbyterian Controversy: Fundamentalists, Modernists, and Moderates,* Religion in America Series (New York: Oxford University Press, 1991), 130–31; Charles R. Erdman, "The Church and Socialism" in volume 12 of *The Fundamentals: A Testimony to the Truth,* ed. R. A. Torrey (Los Angeles: The Bible Institute of Los Angeles, 1917), 116.

14. Erdman, "The Church and Socialism," 119.

15. Egerton, *A Mind to Stay Here,* 74.

16. Egerton, *A Mind to Stay Here,* 74.

17. Egerton, *A Mind to Stay Here,* 75.

18. Ronald T. Clutter, "The Reorganization of Princeton Theological Seminary Reconsidered," *Grace Theological Journal* 7, no. 2 (1986): 196, https://biblicalstudies.org.uk/pdf/gtj/07-2_179.pdf.

19. Kester, "Early Life of Howard Kester," 6.

20. Howard Kester, "The Fellowship of Southern Churchmen: A Religion for Today," *Mountain Life and Work* 15, no. 1 (April 1939): 3, Howard Kester Papers.

21. Kester, "Early Life of Howard Kester," 6.

22. Martin, *Howard Kester and the Struggle for Social Justice in the South, 1904-77*, 30.

23. The YMCA camps were segregated. The white students met at the Blue Ridge Assembly just outside Asheville, North Carolina.

24. Kester, "Early Life of Howard Kester," 6.

25. For a history of the strike see P. C. Cotham, *Toil, Turmoil, and Triumph: A Portrait of the Tennessee Labor Movement* (Franklin, TN: Hillsboro Press, 1995).

26. Anthony P. Dunbar, *Against the Grain: Southern Radicals and Prophets, 1929-1959* (Charlottesville: University Press of Virginia, 1981), 268.

27. Fran Ansley and Brenda Bell, "'No Moanin': Voices of Southern Struggle," *Southern Exposure* (Winter 1974): 129; Angela J. Smith, "Myles Horton, Highlander Folk School, and the Wilder Coal Strike of 1932," 18, http://www.academia.edu/174810/Myles_Horton_Highlander_Folk _School_and_the_Wilder_Coal_Strike_of_19322003; Dunbar, *Against the Grain*, 8.

28. Dale A. Johnson, *Vanderbilt Divinity School: Education, Contest, and Change* (Nashville: Vanderbilt University Press, 2001), 110.

29. Annual Report of Howard Kester, Southern Secretary, Annual Conference of the Fellowship of Reconciliation, October 1933, Howard Kester Papers; Dunbar, *Against the Grain*, 8. There is some question over which night the Kesters stayed in the Graham home. In his reminiscences, Kester implies they were there the night of the murder, but he is explicit in his memory that it was the night before the funeral. There were two days between the murder and the funeral. In one account, Kester writes "On the day after the shooting the author was in Wilder," "A Brief Account of the Wilder Strike," (unpublished manuscript, August 1, 1933), 4, Howard Kester Papers. Kester also reported to the Fellowship of Reconciliation (FOR): "I was in Wilder by 2:30 the following morning." Annual Report of Howard Kester.

30. "Of the seventy-one miles of state highways in Fentress county in late 1930s, State Route 28 was the only paved road; State Routes 52 and 85 were still gravel." "Historic and Architectural Resources of Fentress County, Tennessee," United States Department of the Interior, National Park Service, http://focus.nps.gov/pdfhost/docs/NRHP/Text/64500603 .pdf.

31. Marriage Record of Byron Graham and Daisy (Nickens) Ledbetter, Overton County, Tennessee, November 19, 1926.

32. Howard Kester, "A Brief Account of the Wilder Strike," August 1, 1933, 4, Howard Kester Papers.

33. Howard Kester, "Radical Prophets: A History of the Fellowship of Southern Churchmen" (unpublished manuscript, 1974), 8, Howard Kester Papers.

34. This description is taken from Kester, "Radical Prophets," 10.

35. Dunbar, *Against the Grain*, 7; Martin, *Howard Kester and the Struggle for Social Justice in the South, 1904–77*, 49.

36. Dunbar, *Against the Grain*, 1.

37. J. J. Lorence, *A Hard Journey: The Life of Don West* (Champaign: University of Illinois Press, 2007), 27; M. Horton, J. Kohl, and H. R. Kohl, *The Long Haul: An Autobiography* (New York: Teachers College Press, 1998).

38. Smith, "Myles Horton, Highlander Folk School, and the Wilder Coal Strike of 1932," 3.

39. Lorence, *A Hard Journey*, 24, 32.

40. Kester, "Radical Prophets," 10.

41. Howard Kester, "Religion—Priestly and Prophetic—in the South," *Radical Religion* 1, no. 4 (Autumn 1936): 28, Howard Kester Papers.

42. In 1931, while in New York on FOR business, Kester had dined with Norman Thomas, the Protestant preacher and leader of the Socialist Party. Thomas had encouraged the seminarian to read Marx, Engels, and Lenin. He made such an impression that in the fall of 1932, Kester ran for Congress as the Socialist candidate in Nashville. He was spectacularly unsuccessful, receiving only 677 votes and finishing in last place. Undeterred, Kester increasingly came to see the issues besetting the region as part of a complex constellation of problems inherent in capitalism. Real change could come only through the class struggle and the transformation of the socio-economic order. The Wilder Strike, with its starvation, violence, and murder, dramatically confirmed Kester's new worldview.

43. Howard Kester, "The Interracial Situation," 1932, Howard Kester Papers.

44. Kester, "Religion—Priestly and Prophetic—in the South," 28.

45. Kester, "Radical Prophets," 9.

46. Dunbar, *Against the Grain*, 10.

47. Kester, "Religion—Priestly and Prophetic—in the South," 28. In his writing about the funeral, Kester does not mention West at all, claiming "a mountain preacher and I preached the funeral sermon." Kester, "Early Life of Howard Kester," 9. Perhaps Kester removed him from the

narrative, as by 1940 the Fellowship of Southern Churchmen (FSC) had distanced itself from West, refusing him membership due to what they believed were his communist sympathies. Dunbar, *Against the Grain*, 197.

48. Kester, "Early Life of Howard Kester," 6.

49. Kester, "Religion—Priestly and Prophetic—in the South," 28.

50. Howard Kester, "A Brief History of the Wilder Strike," 1.

51. Kester, "Radical Prophets," 10; Egerton, *A Mind to Stay Here*, 79.

52. Egerton, *A Mind to Stay Here*, 80.

53. Annual Report of Howard Kester, Southern Secretary, Annual Conference of the Fellowship of Reconciliation, October 1933, Howard Kester Papers. This was left out of the printed version in the FOR newsletter.

54. Annual Report of Howard Kester, 1933.

55. Annual Report of Howard Kester, 1933.

56. "Annual Conference of the Fellowship of Reconciliation at Swarthmore, Pa." *The News Letter*, Fellowship of Reconciliation, November 1933.

57. Edmund B. Chaffee, "Why I Stay in the F.O.R.," *Christian Century*, January 3, 1934, 15.

58. Chaffee, "Why I Stay in the F.O.R.," 15; See also Joseph Kip Kosek, *Acts of Conscience: Christian Nonviolence and Modern American Democracy*, Columbia Studies in Contemporary American History (New York: Columbia University Press, 2009), 141.

59. Reinhold Niebuhr, "Why I Leave the F.O.R.," *Christian Century*, January 3, 1934, 19.

60. J. B. Mathews to Howard Kester, January 1934, Howard Kester Papers.

61. "Committee on Economic and Racial Justice," 1940, Howard Kester Papers.

62. Howard Kester, *The Lynching of Claude Neal* (New York: The National Association for the Advancement of Colored People, 1934), 3, Howard Kester Papers.

63. James R. McGovern, *Anatomy of a Lynching: The Killing of Claude Neal* (Baton Rouge: Louisiana State University Press, 1982), 74.

64. Walter White to Howard Kester, telegram, October 30, 1934, NAACP Papers, in Martin, *Howard Kester and the Struggle for Social Justice in the South, 1904-77*, 74.

65. Kester, "Radical Prophets," 33.

66. Howard Kester to Walter White, telegram, October 30, 1934, NAACP Papers, in Martin, *Howard Kester and the Struggle for Social Justice in the South, 1904-77*, 74.

67. H. L. Mitchell claims Kester stopped at Tuskegee on the way to Tallahassee to see his friend George Washington Carver. H. L. Mitchell and Michael Harrington, *Mean Things Happening in This Land: The Life and Times of H. L. Mitchell, Co-Founder of the Southern Tenant Farmers Union* (Norman: University of Oklahoma Press, 2008), 69. Mitchell gives this detail to add context to his story that Carver gave Kester a cyanide capsule on a chain to be used in the event of his capture by a lynch mob. Mitchell told McGovern of this gift in an interview in 1977, but at that time he indicated Carver gave it to Kester *after* the Marianna affair. McGovern, *Anatomy of a Lynching*, 127. Tuskegee would have been a good place to break the drive from Nashville to Tallahassee. At the same time, if the story of the cyanide capsule is true, it also seems likely that it was the publicity around Kester's report of the Claude Neal lynching that prompted Carver to make the gift. Mitchell is the only source I have found for this story.

68. Walter White to Leon Ransom, November 1, 1934. NAACP Papers, in McGovern, *Anatomy of a Lynching*, 126.

69. Kester, "Radical Prophets," 101.

70. Kester, "Radical Prophets," 102.

71. Interview with Howard Kester, July 22, 1974.

72. Interview with Howard Kester, July 22, 1974.

73. All the events in this description of Kester's investigations in Marianna are taken from Kester's own accounts. Kester does not give specific places for these events. I have been able to figure out with varying degrees of certainty the locations. In an interview, he describes the "nice hotel." Interview with Howard Kester, July 22, 1974. In his report, he includes details of wages of the employees at the Chipola Hotel (bellboys, maids, waitresses) that strongly suggests he was a guest there. Kester, *The Lynching of Claude Neal*, 7.

74. Dale Cox, "Jackson County May Not Own Courthouse Square," *Jackson County, Florida* (blog) June 5, 2016, http://twoegg.blogspot .com/2016/06/jackson-county-may-not-own-courthouse.html.

75. Kester, "Radical Prophets," 102; interview with Howard Kester, July 22, 1974; interview with Howard Kester by David Jones, March 5, 1976, F-0027, in the Southern Historical Collection, Lewis Round Wilson Special Collections Library, University of North Carolina at Chapel Hill.

76. Walter White to Gov. B. M. Miller, November 22, 1934, in Dale Cox, *The Claude Neal Lynching: The 1934 Murders of Claude Neal and Lola Cannidy* (Bascom, FL: Old Kitchen Books, 2012), Kindle location 1419 of 3826.

77. Kester, *The Lynching of Claude Neal*, 2. Based on his interview with

two of the lynching party in the 1980s, local historian Dale Cox disputes the possibility that Red was an eyewitness to the lynching. However, he concedes that the main features of the gruesome lynching are correct. Cox, *The Claude Neal Lynching*, Kindle location 1419 of 3826.

78. Howard Kester to Walter White, November 7, 1934, in NAACP Papers, in Martin, *Howard Kester and the Struggle for Social Justice in the South, 1904-77*, 74-75.

79. Kester, *The Lynching of Claude Neal*, 7.

80. Kester, *The Lynching of Claude Neal*, 7.

81. Joshua Youngblood, "'Haven't Quite Shaken the Horror': Howard Kester, the Lynching of Claude Neal, and Social Activism in the South During the 1930s," *Florida Historical Quarterly* 86, no. 1 (2007): 31-32.

82. Kester, "Radical Prophets," 102.

83. It is likely that the church in Kester's story is Saint Luke Baptist church. In the 1974 interview, Kester refers to it as "the Negro church in Marianna," and St. Luke's was the principle black church in town—other black congregations were located several miles outside of the town—more of a hike than an afternoon stroll. According to Kester's description, the church needs to be "up on a kind of a hill" next to "a ravine that led from the church down to Marianna." The historic marker at St. Luke says "The church is located on one of the highest points in central Marianna," http://www.hmdb.org/marker.asp?marker=74196. The ground drops steeply away from the church on its northern and eastern side down to what is now the four-lane Lafayette Street running back toward town. In the 1930s, what is now Lafayette Street was Highway 90 running into Main Street. Tantalizingly, the marker also lists the church's pastors responsible for completing its construction. Started in 1921, the construction was completed four pastors later by Rev. Dr. A. H. Parker (1907-1995). If Parker had been the pastor in 1934, he would have been twenty-seven years old—perhaps the young man Kester met in Tallahassee.

84. Kester, *Radical Prophets*, 102.

85. Kester, "Early Life of Howard Kester," 10; interview with Howard Kester, July 22, 1974.

86. Interview with Howard Kester, July 22, 1974.

87. Interview with Howard Kester, July 22, 1974.

88. Howard Kester to Claude Williams, November 18, 1934, Howard Kester Papers.

89. Howard Kester to H. L. Mitchell, November 23, 1934, Howard Kester Papers.

90. Walter White to Eleanor Roosevelt, November 20, 1934, Eleanor Roosevelt Papers, Series 100,1325, Roosevelt Library, in McGovern, *Anatomy of a Lynching*, 125.

91. Eleanor Roosevelt to Walter White, November 23, 1934, Eleanor Roosevelt Papers, Series 100,1325, Roosevelt Library, quoted in McGovern, *Anatomy of a Lynching*, 125.

92. McGovern, *Anatomy of a Lynching*, 129.

93. Kester, *The Lynching of Claude Neal*, 1.

94. "Howard Kester Luncheon," NAACP Papers in Youngblood, "'Haven't Quite Shaken the Horror,'" 31; Kester, "Radical Prophets," 103.

95. Grace Elizabeth Hale, *Making Whiteness: The Culture of Segregation in the South, 1890–1940* (New York: Pantheon Books, 1998), 222; McGovern, *Anatomy of a Lynching*, 2, 141.

96. Howard Kester to Claude Williams, November 18, 1934, Howard Kester Papers.

97. H. L. Mitchell to Howard Kester, November 24, 1934, Howard Kester Papers.

98. H. L. Mitchell recalls in his 1979 autobiography that he first met Kester when he "stopped by Tyronza" in November 1934. In 1940, Kester recalled his first visits to Arkansas as happening in the fall of 1934. Kester, "Early Life of Howard Kester," 10. If he did in fact visit Mitchell in the fall, it must have been brief. It also demonstrates Kester's packed itinerary. Mitchell had been expecting Kester on November 11—an appointment he had missed because he was in Florida. Kester wrote to Mitchell saying he hoped to see him (Howard Kester to H. L. Mitchell, November 23, 1934), and Mitchell wrote to Kester on November 24, 1934. However, on November 30, Kester was at a conference at Shaw University in North Carolina. Martin, *Howard Kester and the Struggle for Social Justice in the South, 1904–77*, 69.

99. Kester, "Radical Prophets," 33.

100. Howard Kester to Elizabeth Gilman, January 13, 1936, Howard Kester Papers.

101. Interview with Nancy Kester Neale by Dallas A. Blanchard, August 6, 1983, F-0036, in the Southern Oral History Program Collection #4007, Southern Historical Collection, Lewis Round Wilson Special Collections Library, University of North Carolina at Chapel Hill, http://docsouth.unc.edu/sohp/F-0036/F-0036.html.

102. Howard Kester to Alice Kester, December 14, 1936, Howard Kester Papers.

103. Kester, "Early Life of Howard Kester," 11; Kester, "Radical Prophets," 37.

104. Kester was one of a cadre of young white men that Carver called his "adopted boys." Being adopted into this "family" meant receiving a consistent stream of encouraging letters. Linda O. McMurry, *George Washington Carver: Scientist and Symbol* (New York: Oxford University Press, 1982), 203. Carver wrote regularly to Kester (as he did to many of his "family") addressing him as "my beloved boy Howard." George Washington Carver to Howard Kester, March 2, 1927, Howard Kester Papers. In 1940, Kester wrote, "I have spent hundreds of invaluable hours with this great but simple man who opened to me new vistas of a more abundant life here in the South, especially for those who till the soil. Among other things he taught me how to paint with pastels and later with water colors and oils from which I now get immeasurable satisfaction when I can spare time to paint." Kester, "Early Life of Howard Kester," 4.

105. Egerton, *A Mind to Stay Here*, 76.

106. Interview with Howard Kester, July 22, 1974.

107. Howard Kester to Alice Kester, October 6, 1933, Howard Kester Papers.

108. Kester, "Early Life of Howard Kester," 8. In an undated letter from his mother probably written near the end of her life (she died in 1963), she wrote to her son "This A.M. I read where a Negro married a white girl by a Congregationalist minister. I hope you will not come into contact with him. If I should read anything in the papers about you mixed with the negros [sic] I would comit [sic] suicide at once. I could not live under such a case." She signs off "Don't think I am nuts for writing this letter but you be careful about the Negros they are the worst enemies we have." Nannie Holt Kester to Howard Kester, no date, Howard Kester Papers.

109. Howard Kester to Elizabeth Gilman, January 13, 1936, Howard Kester Papers.

110. This is my own reconstruction of the conversation. It is based on the actual telegram (H. L. Mitchell to Norman Thomas, January 17, 1936, Howard Kester Papers) and the most likely sequence of events. The telegram sets the time of Kester's encounter with the mob as "THIS AFTERNOON," suggesting the telegram was sent in the evening. Though sent by Mitchell, it has clearly been composed after he has heard the story from Kester and learned of his "EXCELLENT HANDLING" of the situation. Mitchell and Kester had obviously done some considerable work before sending the telegram to Norman Thomas, including sending a telegram

to the White House and perhaps contacting the Associated Press (AP) as Mitchell remembers. The purpose of Mitchell's telegram to Norman was to prompt material support for the evicted tenant farmers. This, presumably, is why Thomas would have read it to guests at dinner. Kester's biographer, Robert Martin, relies too heavily on Kester's later accounts of the evening. Martin, *Howard Kester and the Struggle for Social Justice in the South, 1904–77*, 96. When Kester tells the story in 1940, he appears to have embellished it. People call Alice asking if Howard has "escaped in safety." Kester, "Early Life of Howard Kester," 11. By the 1970s Kester's story has changed and grown in the telling: the telegram is now sent by Mitchell to Thomas *before* Kester's return to Memphis and contains the news that Kester has been lynched. The phone calls to Alice are from people sending their condolences. Kester, "Radical Prophets," 107; Egerton, *A Mind to Stay Here*: 82. Mitchell, writing an account in 1979 has a different story. In his telling there is no telegram, it is his report to the AP that Kester and colleagues "had been kidnapped and were likely to be lynched" that Norman relays to his guests. Mitchell and Harrington, *Mean Things Happening in This Land*, 144.

111. Kester, "Radical Prophets," 107. This is Kester's recollection of the time of Alice's call. I believe this time is reasonably accurate as it is a possible start time for Kester's night drive to Nashville.

112. Kester and H. L. Mitchell, "For Immediate Release," January 18, 1936, Howard Kester Papers.

113. H. L. Mitchell to Norman Thomas, telegram, January 17, 1936, Howard Kester Papers #3834, courtesy of Southern Historical Collection, Louis Round Wilson Special Collections Library, University of North Carolina at Chapel Hill.

114. Kester, "Radical Prophets," 107.

115. For a description of the abduction of Kester, see Kester, "Radical Prophets," 105–7; Dunbar, *Against the Grain*, 111–13.

116. Kester, "Radical Prophets," 107.

117. Howard Kester to Alice Kester, January 30, 1936; Howard Kester to Alice Kester, January 31, 1936, Howard Kester Papers.

118. Henry C. Fleisher to Howard Kester, February 1, 1936, Howard Kester Papers.

119. Howard Kester to Alice Kester, January 26, 1936, Howard Kester Papers.

120. Howard Kester, *Revolt among the Sharecroppers* (New York: Covici, 1936), 21.

121. Kester, *Revolt among the Sharecroppers*, 96; for a good analysis of

Kester's religious hopes for the STFU see Robert H. Craig, *Religion and Radical Politics: An Alternative Christian Tradition in the United States* (Philadelphia: Temple University Press, 1992), 158–59.

122. Kester, *Revolt among the Sharecroppers*, 92.

123. Dorothea Lange photographed the farm for the Farm Security Administration in June 1937, http://www.loc.gov/pictures/collection /fsa/. For more on the Delta Cooperative Farm; also see Robert Hunt Ferguson, *Remaking the Rural South: Interracialism, Christian Socialism, and Cooperative Farming in Jim Crow Mississippi* (Athens, GA: University of Georgia Press, 2018); Will D. Campbell, *Providence* (Atlanta: Longstreet Press, 1992); Sam H. Franklin, *Early Years of the Delta Cooperative Farm and the Providence Cooperative Farm* (self-published, 1980), Southern Media Archive, University of Mississippi Libraries.

124. Kester, "Early Life of Howard Kester," 13.

125. Howard Kester to Elizabeth Gilman, January 12, 1936, Howard Kester Papers.

126. Reinhold Niebuhr to supporters of CERJ, November 16, 1936, Howard Kester Papers.

127. Kester, "Early Life of Howard Kester," 11; Kester, "Radical Prophets," 37.

128. Interview with Nancy Kester Neale.

129. Howard Kester to Alice Kester, December 14, 1936, Howard Kester Papers.

130. Howard Kester to Alice Kester, December 14, 1936, Howard Kester Papers.

131. Howard Kester to Alice Kester, December 14, 1936, Howard Kester Papers.

132. Howard Kester to Alice Kester, January 3, 1937; January 5, 1937; interview with Howard Kester, July 22, 1974; Ferguson, *Remaking the Rural South*, 55, 65, 72; Martin, *Howard Kester and the Struggle for Social Justice in the South, 1904-77*, 101.

133. Howard Kester to Alice Kester, January 11, 1937, Howard Kester Papers.

134. Robert L. Zangrando, *The N.A.A.C.P. Crusade against Lynching, 1909-1950* (Philadelphia: Temple University Press 1980), 141–43.

135. Howard Kester, "Lynching by Blow Torch: A Report upon the Double Lynching at Duck Hill, Miss., April 13, 1937 " (1937), Howard Kester Papers. In 1939, Kester explained to White, "Soon I shall have to give this sort of work up for it seems to produce emotional strain which in turn

brings on severe cases of asthma. However, I would like to have a chance to crack this thing wide open. God knows someone has got to do it!" Howard Kester to Walter White, October 10, 1939, Howard Kester Papers.

136. Kester, "Lynching by Blow Torch," 5.

137. Wayland, "Biography," 6.

138. Elizabeth Gilman to Howard Kester and Alice Kester, May 3, 1937; Elizabeth Gilman to Alice Kester, May 28, 1937, Howard Kester Papers. Gilman notes that Kester was only paid expenses by the NAACP for his investigation in Mississippi.

139. Dunbar, *Against the Grain*, 164–68; Martin, *Howard Kester and the Struggle for Social Justice in the South, 1904-77*, 106.

140. "Elijah and Elisha," *Prophetic Religion* 1, no. 3 (February 1938): 1, Howard Kester Papers. It was probably written by the editor of the Fellowship's newsletter Thomas Beveridge "Scotty" Cowan, a veteran of the First World War and Presbyterian minister in Chattanooga.

141. Egerton, *A Mind to Stay Here*, 84.

142. Kester, "The Fellowship of Southern Churchmen: A Religion for Today," 6. It is important to note that in this quote it is faith in Jesus that makes one a realist. While the FSC was influenced by Reinhold Niebuhr's Christian realism, Kester never argued for pragmatic action that was less than that preached by Christ in the Sermon on the Mount.

143. Sermon, "Dreamers and Doers" (text: Rev. 21:1), Howard Kester Papers. Kester gave this sermon, or one with the same title, at the biennial meeting of the General Council of the Congregational Christian Churches in Durham, New Hampshire, in 1942. "Religion at Work," *Portsmouth Herald*, June 20, 1942, Howard Kester Papers.

144. Kester, "Early Life of Howard Kester," 5.

145. Howard Kester to Alice Kester, December 14, 1936, Howard Kester Papers.

146. Leaflet, Chamber of Commerce, Black Mountain, North Carolina, n.d., Howard Kester Papers.

147. It was a long project. It took twenty years "to build a fairly satisfactory home." Kester, "Radical Prophets," 78.

148. Interview with Nancy Kester Neale, by Dallas A. Blanchard, August 6, 1983, F-0036, in the Southern Oral History Program Collection #4007, Southern Historical Collection, Lewis Round Wilson Special Collections Library, University of North Carolina at Chapel Hill.

149. Mitchell, *Roll the Union On*, 48; Mitchell and Harrington, *Mean Things Happening in This Land*, 183.

150. T. B. Cowan to Howard Kester, telegram, January 16, 1939; Howard Kester, "Along the Front," *Prophetic Religion*, 2, no. 1 (January 1939): 8; Dunbar, *Against the Grain*, 178.

151. Mitchell and Harrington, *Mean Things Happening in This Land*, 190; Dunbar, *Against the Grain*, 178.

152. Interview with Nancy Kester Neale.

ELLA BAKER

1. Sweet Honey in the Rock, "Ella's Song," recorded 1983 on *We All . . . Everyone of Us*, Spindrift SPIN 106, 33⅓ rpm.

2. Bernice Johnson Reagon, interview by Bill Moyers, *The Songs Are Free: Bernice Johnson Reagon and African American Music*, PBS, February 6, 1991.

3. Keri Day, *Unfinished Business: Black Women, the Black Church, and the Struggle to Thrive in America* (Maryknoll, NY: Orbis Books, 2012), 89. The Poor People's Campaign was inaugurated in 1963 as a movement for economic justice that promoted cooperation across racial and ethnic divides.

4. J. Todd Moye, *Ella Baker: Community Organizer of the Civil Rights Movement* (Lanham, MD: Rowman & Littlefield Publishers, 2013), 2.

5. Joanne Grant, *Fundi: The Story of Ella Baker* (Icarus Films, 1981), DVD.

6. Joanne Grant, *Ella Baker: Freedom Bound* (New York: John Wiley & Sons, 1998), 9.

7. Rosetta E. Ross, *Witnessing and Testifying: Black Women, Religion, and Civil Rights* (Minneapolis: Fortress, 2003), 35.

8. Ross, *Witnessing and Testifying*, 35.

9. Ross, *Witnessing and Testifying*, 33.

10. Moye, *Ella Baker*, 19.

11. Ross, *Witnessing and Testifying*, 17.

12. Moye, *Ella Baker*, 19.

13. Moye, *Ella Baker*, 20.

14. Moye, *Ella Baker*, 5.

15. Ross, *Witnessing and Testifying*, 38.

16. Ross, *Witnessing and Testifying*, 39.

17. Ella Baker and Marvel Cooke, "The Bronx Slave Market," *The Crisis*, November 1935, 330.

18. West, *Disruptive Christian Ethics*, 21.

19. West, *Disruptive Christian Ethics*, 25.

20. Ross, *Witnessing and Testifying*, 37.

21. Moye, *Ella Baker*, 4.

22. Mary King, *Freedom Song: A Personal Story of the 1960s Civil Rights Movement* (New York: William Morrow and Company, 1987), 43.

23. Moye, *Ella Baker*, 5.

24. Moye, *Ella Baker*, 6.

25. Moye, *Ella Baker*, 5.

26. Grant, *Ella Baker*, 7.

27. Ross, *Witnessing and Testifying*, 37.

28. Grant, *Ella Baker*, 129.

29. Grant, *Ella Baker*, 129.

30. King, *Freedom Song*, 45.

31. Grant, *Ella Baker*, 132.

32. *The Songs Are Free*.

33. Grant, *Ella Baker*, 163.

34. Grant, *Ella Baker*, 164.

35. Grant, *Ella Baker*, 165.

36. Josh Sanburn, "All the Ways Darren Wilson Described Being Afraid of Michael Brown," Time.com, November 25, 2014, http://time.com/3605346/darren-wilson-michael-brown-demon/.

37. John Eligon, "A Teenager Who Was Grappling with Problems and Promise," *New York Times*, August 25, 2014, Late edition, sec. National Desk.

DOROTHY DAY

1. Forest, *All Is Grace: A Biography of Dorothy Day* (Maryknoll, NY: Orbis Books, 2011), 18.

2. Robert Ellsburg, ed., *The Duty of Delight: The Diaries of Dorothy Day* (New York: Image Books, 2011), 629.

3. William D. Miller, *Dorothy Day: A Biography* (New York: Harper & Row, 1982), 25, 440–41; Ellsburg, *The Duty of Delight*, xxvii; Forest, *All Is Grace*, 124, 139, 203, 209, 243, 245.

4. Day, *The Long Loneliness* (San Francisco: Harper & Row, 1981), 25; Miller, *Dorothy Day*, 9.

5. Dorothy Day, *From Union Square to Rome* (Ossining, NY: Orbis Books, 2011), 33; Day, *The Long Loneliness*, 28.

6. Day, *The Long Loneliness*, 28–29; Day, *Union Square*, 33.

7. Day, *The Long Loneliness*, 160–61.

8. Day, *Union Square*, 37; James T. Fisher, *The Catholic Counterculture in America, 1933–1962* (Chapel Hill: University of North Carolina Press, 1989), 16, 47.

9. Day, *The Long Loneliness*, 25.

10. Day, *The Duty of Delight*, 463.

11. Dorothy Day, "A Reminiscence at 75," *Commonweal*, August 10, 1973, https://www.commonwealmagazine.org/reminiscence-75.

12. Day, *The Long Loneliness*, 25.

13. Day, *The Long Loneliness*, 24; Day, *The Duty of Delight*, 656, 661.

14. Day, *The Duty of Delight*, 458.

15. Miller, *Dorothy Day*, 28; Day, *The Long Loneliness*, 37.

16. Miller, *Dorothy Day*, 28; Day, *The Long Loneliness*, 36–37, 41.

17. Day, *The Long Loneliness*, 37.

18. Day, *The Duty of Delight*, 98.

19. Miller, *Dorothy Day*, 25; Day, *Union Square*, 34; Day, *The Long Loneliness*, 37.

20. Day, *Union Square*, 37.

21. Day, *The Long Loneliness*, 37; Forest, *All Is Grace*, 18–19.

22. Day, *The Long Loneliness*, 37.

23. Day, *Union Square*, 37; Miller, *Dorothy Day*, 29.

24. Miller, *Dorothy Day*, 47; Day, *Union Square*, 64.

25. Day, *Union Square*, 64; Miller, *Dorothy Day*, 54; Day, *The Long Loneliness*, 50.

26. Forest, *All Is Grace*, 59; Miller, *Dorothy Day*, 149.

27. Miller, *Dorothy Day*, 55; Day, *Union Square*, 71; Forest, *All Is Grace*, 28; Day, *The Long Loneliness*, 43.

28. Miller, *Dorothy Day*, 108–9; Day, *The Long Loneliness*, 84.

29. Day, *The Long Loneliness*, 84; Day, *Union Square*, 91; Miller, *Dorothy Day*, 113.

30. Day, *The Long Loneliness*, 87; Miller, *Dorothy Day*, 119.

31. Dorothy Day, *The Eleventh Virgin* (Lake Worth, FL: The Cottager Press, 2011), 252; Miller, *Dorothy Day*, 125; Kate Hennessy, *The World Will Be Saved by Beauty* (New York: Scribner, 2017), 23.

32. Miller, *Dorothy Day*, 126.

33. Miller, *Dorothy Day*, 133. Day, *The Eleventh Virgin*, 275; Hennessy, *The World Will Be Saved*, 25.

34. Day, *The Eleventh Virgin*, 288, 295; Hennessy, *The World Will Be Saved*, 25, 33; Miller, *Dorothy Day*, 127, 134.

35. Robert Ellsberg, ed., *All the Way to Heaven: The Selected Letters of Dorothy Day* (New York: Image Books, 2010), 510; Miller, *Dorothy Day*, 136; Forest, *All Is Grace*, 54.

36. Day, *The Eleventh Virgin*, 303; Miller, *Dorothy Day*, 138–40; Hennessy, *The World Will Be Saved*, 27.

37. Ellsberg, *All the Way to Heaven*, 510; Day, *The Eleventh Virgin*, 309; Miller, *Dorothy Day*, 140; Forest, *All Is Grace*, 55; Hennessy, *The World Will Be Saved*, 28.

38. Miller, *Dorothy Day*, 142; Forest, *All Is Grace* 55; Day, *The Eleventh Virgin*, 314.

39. Miller, *Dorothy Day*, 143–45; Hennessy, *The World Will Be Saved*, 29–30; Day, *Union Square*, 102; Day, *The Long Loneliness*, 94–95.

40. Rosalie Riegle Troester, *Voices from the Catholic Worker* (Philadelphia: Temple University Press, 1993), 95.

41. Miller, *Dorothy Day*, 147; Hennessy, *The World Will Be Saved*, 30.

42. Miller, *Dorothy Day*, 147; Day, *The Long Loneliness*, 95.

43. Miller, *Dorothy Day*, 149; Hennessy, *The World Will Be Saved*, 32.

44. Day, *Union Square*, 103; Day, *The Long Loneliness*, 98.

45. Miller, *Dorothy Day*, 148–49.

46. Day, *The Long Loneliness*, 98.

47. Day, *Union Square*, 103; Day, *The Long Loneliness*, 98.

48. Day, *The Long Loneliness*, 98–99.

49. *Encyclopedia Britannica*, s.v. "Palmer Raids," https://www.britannica.com/topic/Palmer-Raids; Day, *The Long Loneliness*, 99.

50. Day, *Union Square*, 109; Day, *The Long Loneliness*, 105.

51. Day, *Union Square*, 84–85; Day, *The Long Loneliness*, 73; Miller, *Dorothy Day*, 90–94.

52. Day, *The Long Loneliness*, 100.

53. Day, *The Long Loneliness*, 104.

54. Day, *The Duty of Delight*, 628.

55. Day, *The Eleventh Virgin*, 319.

56. Robert Ellsberg, ed., *Dorothy Day: Selected Writings* (Maryknoll, NY: Orbis Books, 2015), 305.

57. Agnes Boulton, *Part of a Long Story* (New York: Doubleday, 1958), 89; Miller, *Dorothy Day*, 116.

58. Day, *The Long Loneliness*, 84; Ellsberg, *The Duty of Delight*, 221.

59. Day, *The Long Loneliness*, 105.

60. Forest, *All Is Grace*, 61; Hennessy, *The World Will Be Saved*, 33.

61. Ellsberg, *The Duty of Delight*, 629; Day, *The Long Loneliness*, 107.

62. Day, *The Duty of Delight*, 629, 646.

63. Joris-Karl Huysmans, *En Route* (Boston: E. Dutton, 1920), 462.

64. Miller, *Dorothy Day*, 165–66.

65. Day, *The Long Loneliness*, 109; Miller, *Dorothy Day*, 163, 170.

66. Miller, *Dorothy Day*, 169.

67. Ellsberg, *All the Way to Heaven*, 8, 12.

68. Day, *Union Square*, 120.

69. Ellsberg, *The Duty of Delight*, 515.

70. Augustine, *De Catechizandis de Rudibus*, New Advent, http://www
.newadvent.org/fathers/1303.htm.

71. Day, *The Long Loneliness*, 116, 120, 136, 121.

72. Miller, *Dorothy Day*, 166; Day, *The Long Loneliness*, 113, 134.

73. Day, *The Long Loneliness*, 19; Ellsberg, *The Duty of Delight*, 515–16.

74. Ellsberg, *Selected Writings*, 305; Ellsberg, *The Duty of Delight*, 298, 329; Troester, *Voices from the Catholic Worker*, 93.

75. Ellsberg, *The Duty of Delight*, 165.

76. Day, *The Long Loneliness*, 30; Ellsberg, *The Duty of Delight*, 17, 20–21, 36, 106.

77. Ellsberg, *The Duty of Delight*, 299.

78. Ellsberg, *The Duty of Delight*, 29.

79. Miller, *Dorothy Day*, 166; Day, *The Long Loneliness*, 148.

80. Day, *The Long Loneliness*, 120–21.

81. Day, *The Long Loneliness*, 120, 134; Day, *Union Square*, 115; Hennessy, *The World Will Be Saved*, 44.

82. Day, *The Long Loneliness*, 133.

83. Day, *The Long Loneliness*, 136; Miller, *Dorothy Day*, 175.

84. Day, *The Long Loneliness*, 136; Miller, *Dorothy Day*, 179.

85. Forest, *All Is Grace*, 78; Day, *The Long Loneliness*, 136, 143; Day, *Union Square*, 131.

86. Day, *The Long Loneliness*, 142.

87. Day, *The Long Loneliness*, 144.

88. "Sacco and Vanzetti: Justice on Trial." The Official Website of the Massachusetts Judicial Branch, accessed November 2017, http://www
.mass.gov/courts/court-info/sjc/edu-res-center/saco-vanz/sacco-vanz
-2-gen.html.

89. Day, *The Long Loneliness*, 139.

90. Day, *The Long Loneliness*, 147.

91. Day, *Union Square*, 13.

92. Day, *The Long Loneliness*, 148.

93. Forest, *All Is Grace*, 84; Day, *The Long Loneliness*, 149; Day, *Union Square*, 146.

94. Fisher, *The Catholic Counterculture in America, 1933–1962*, 47.

95. Ellsberg, *The Duty of Delight*, 80.

96. Ellsberg, *The Duty of Delight*, 228.

97. Ellsberg, *The Duty of Delight*, 246, 365, 424, 547.

98. Ellsberg, *The Duty of Delight*, 109, 651.

99. Ellsberg, *The Duty of Delight*, 73.

100. Hennessy, *The World Will Be Saved*, ix; Ellsburg, *The Duty of Delight*, 302, 631, 638.

101. Miller, *Dorothy Day*, 314, 332–33.

JOHN A. RYAN

1. Washington Gladden, *Working People and Their Employers* (Boston: Lockwood, Brooks, and Company, 1876), 31–50.

2. Minnesota Minimum Wage Law, Section 3904–3923, Sec. 20(1).

3. Union membership did not drop, but the minimum wage did eventually become the maximum wage.

4. Patrick W. Gearty, *The Economic Thought of Monsignor John A. Ryan* (Washington, DC: The Catholic University of American Press, 1953), 33–34; Francis L. Broderick, *Right Reverend New Dealer, John A. Ryan* (New York: Macmillan, 1963), 81–84.

5. Mary Beth Norton et al., eds., *A People & a Nation: A History of the United States*, Brief Edition (Boston: Houghton Mifflin, 1984), 264–65.

6. James Patrick Byrne, Philip Colman, Jason King, eds., *Ireland and the Americas: Culture, Politics, and History: A Multidisciplinary Encyclopedia*, vol. 2 (Santa Barbara, CA: ABC-CLIO, 2008), 349; James P. Rodocheko, "An Irish American Journalist and Catholicism: Patrick Ford of *The Irish World*," *Church History* 39, no. 4 (December 1970): 527, 532.

7. Rt. Rev. Msgr. John A. Ryan, *Social Doctrine in Action: A Personal History* (New York and London: Harper & Brothers, 1941), 7–8.

8. Broderick, *Right Reverend New Dealer*, 9.

9. Ryan, *Social Doctrine in Action*, 3, 7.

10. Ryan, *Social Doctrine in Action*, 11–12. Years later he remarked that Donnelly's campaign and victory "exercised more influence upon my political and economic thinking than any other factor of those early years," *Social Doctrine in Action*, 12.

11. Ryan, *Social Doctrine in Action*, 21.

12. John Ireland, *The Church and Modern Society* (Chicago: D. H. Mc-Bride, 1896), i, 55, 71, 78–79, cited in Broderick, *Right Reverend New Dealer*, 15. Broderick noted that Ryan marked these particular sentences in his own copy of the book.

13. Ryan, *Social Doctrine in Action*, 44.

14. Mary Christine Athans, BVM, *"To Work for the Whole People": John Ireland's Seminary in St. Paul* (New York: Paulist Press, 2002), 84–86, 91; Ryan, *Social Doctrine in Action*, 58.

15. John A. Ryan, Journal, November 20, 1892, box 69, folder 22, p. 27, John A. Ryan Papers, the American Catholic History Research Center and University Archives, the Catholic University of America, Washington, DC (hereafter Ryan Papers, ACUA).

16. John A. Ryan, Journal, October 16, 1892, box 69, folder 22, p. 21, Ryan Papers, ACUA.

17. John A. Ryan, Journal, September 29, 1892, emphasis original, box 69, folder 22, p. 17, Ryan Papers, ACUA.

18. John A. Ryan, Journal, November 17, 1894, box 69, folder 22, pp. 43–44, Ryan Papers, ACUA.

19. John A. Ryan, Journal, November 21, 1894, box 69, folder 22, p. 44, Ryan Papers, ACUA.

20. Broderick, *Right Reverend New Dealer*, 25; *Manuale e Pontificale Romano: De Confirmandis, De Ordinibus Conferendis, De Consecratione Electi in Episcopum cum Missa et Precibus* (Rome: Society of Saint John the Evangelist, 1923), 54–74.

21. *Manuale e Pontificale Romano*, 60.

22. Broderick, *Right Reverend New Dealer*, 31.

23. Broderick, *Right Reverend New Dealer*, 36–38.

24. Broderick, *Right Reverend New Dealer*, 45.

25. Ryan, *A Living Wage: Its Ethical and Economic Aspects* (New York: Macmillan, 1906), xi–xii.

26. Ryan, *A Living Wage*, 67, 74, 324.

27. Ryan, *A Living Wage*, 44.

28. Ryan, *A Living Wage*, 73.

29. Ryan, *A Living Wage*, 100.

30. Ryan, *A Living Wage*, 239.

31. Ryan, *A Living Wage*, 250–51.

32. Ryan, *A Living Wage*, 252–53.

33. Ryan, *A Living Wage*, 301.

34. Ryan, *A Living Wage*, 302.

35. Ryan, *A Living Wage*, 319–21.

36. Ryan, *A Living Wage*, 323.

37. John A. Ryan, *A Program of Social Reform by Legislation* (New York: Catholic World Press, 1909).

38. John A. Ryan, *A Minimum Wage by Legislation* (St. Louis: Central Bureau of German Roman Central Verein, 1911).

39. Ryan, *Social Doctrine in Action*, 114.

40. Ryan, *Social Doctrine in Action*, 112–15.

41. Ryan, *Social Doctrine in Action*, 113.

42. Letter from Joseph H. McMahon to [indecipherable], September 10, 1913, box 74, folder 2, Ryan Papers, ACUA.

43. Morris Hillquit and John A. Ryan, DD, *Socialism: Promise or Menace?* (New York: Macmillan, 1914).

44. Francis L. Broderick interview with Francis J. Gilligan, April 26, 1958, and Raymond A. McGowan, winter 1958, cited in Broderick, *Right Reverend New Dealer*, 117.

45. Joseph M. McShane, *"Sufficiently Radical": Catholicism, Progressivism, and the Bishops' Program of 1919* (Washington DC: The Catholic University of America Press, 1986), 156–57; Broderick, *Right Reverend New Dealer*, 104–5; Ryan, *Social Doctrine in Action*, 144–45.

46. John O'Grady, unpublished autobiography, 30–31, National Conference of Catholic Charities Collection, ACUA, cited in McShane, *"Sufficiently Radical,"* 156.

47. "Bishops' Program of Social Reconstruction: A General Review of the Problems and Survey of Remedies" (National Catholic Welfare Conference, February 12, 1919, Washington, DC) (hereafter "Bishops' Program, 1919").

48. "Bishops' Program, 1919," 1.

49. "Bishops' Program, 1919," 5.

50. "Bishops' Program, 1919," 7–8.

51. "Bishops' Program, 1919," 7.

52. "Bishops' Program, 1919," 8.

53. "Bishops' Program, 1919," 15.

54. "Bishops' Program, 1919," 15 (emphasis added).

55. John A. Ryan, Journal, November 17, 1894, box 69, folder 22, pp. 43–44, Ryan Papers, ACUA.

56. In 1922, the NCWC changed its name to National Catholic Welfare *Conference* when the Vatican objected to any suggestion of a council that could be understood to rival its authority.

57. Archbishop William O'Connell to Archbishop Michael Curley, November 2, 1924, box 39, folder 24, Ryan Papers, ACUA.

58. Broderick, *Right Reverend New Dealer*, 212–14, 217.

59. Boris Stern to Ryan, November 4, 1933, cited in Broderick, *Right Reverend New Dealer*, 214.

60. Ryan hired McGowan as his assistant director in 1920. Beginning in the early 1920s, McGowan functioned as the de facto director of the Social Action Division of the Catholic Welfare Conference, because Ryan chose to exercise his directorship by publishing frequently, accepting numerous public speaking engagements, and serving on national committees—all at the expense of day-to-day and less politically exciting efforts. It is easy to imagine Ryan asking McGowan to send a slightly revised version of his *Social Reform by Legislation* (1909) and his "Bishops' Program, 1919" to Labor Secretary Perkins.

61. Broderick, *Right Reverend New Dealer*, 219; Executive Order, *Establishing the Committee on Economic Security and the Advisory Council on Economic Security*, December 1, 1934, https://www.ssa.gov/history /reports/ces/cesbookapen13.html.

62. John A. Ryan, "Americanism: The Counterfeit and the Genuine," in *Seven Troubled Years, 1930–1936: A Collection of Papers on the Depression and on the Problems of Recovery and Reform* (Ann Arbor, MI: Edwards Brothers, 1937), 227; also cited in Broderick, *Right Reverend New Dealer*, 221.

63. Alan Brinkley, *Voices of Protest: Huey Long, Father Coughlin, and the Great Depression* (New York: Alfred Knopf, 1982; New York: Vintage Books, 1983), 91–106, 254–61.

64. Arthur Meyerowitz to John A. Ryan, September 28, 1936, box 41, folder 15, Ryan Papers, ACUA.

65. Brinkley, *Voices of Protest*, 256.

66. John A. Ryan, "Roosevelt Safeguards America" (address of Rt. Rev. John a. Ryan, D.D., October 8, 1936; Hotel Biltmore, NY; The Democratic National Committee), Box 41, Folder 12. Ryan Papers, ACUA. 1. The DNC issued the text of the speech as a twelve-page pamphlet printed by union workers. See also John A. Ryan, "Roosevelt Safeguards America," October 8, 1936, audio recording, user CD, Box 80, Folder 1. Ryan Papers, ACUA.

67. Ryan, "Roosevelt Safeguards America," 4.

68. Ryan, "Roosevelt Safeguards America," 6.

69. Ryan, "Roosevelt Safeguards America," 12.

70. *Social Justice*, October 19, 1936, cited in Broderick, *Right Reverend New Dealer*, 227.

71. T. N. Stewart to John A. Ryan, October 8, 1936, box 74, folder 1, Ryan Papers, ACUA.

72. George Quitman Flynn, "Franklin D. Roosevelt and American Catholicism, 1932–1936" (PhD diss., Louisiana State University, 1966), 369–74.

73. Ryan did not deny the possibility that FDR's invitation for Ryan to give the benediction was a payoff for the speech. He remarked that if it was, he had "no reason to be ashamed nor [was] the honor thereby diminished." Ryan, *Social Doctrine in Action*, 271.

74. John A. Ryan, Journal, November 17, 1894; and November 21, 1894, box 69, folder 22, pp. 43–44, Ryan Papers ACUA.

FRANK WILLIAM STRINGFELLOW

1. William Stringfellow, *A Simplicity of Faith* (Ann Arbor, MI: Abington Press, 1982), 21.

2. William Stringfellow, *A Private and Public Faith* (Eugene, OR: Wipf and Stock, 1999), 78.

3. Stringfellow, *A Private and Public Faith*, 79.

4. Stringfellow, *A Private and Public Faith*, 79.

5. Stringfellow, *A Private and Public Faith*, 78.

6. Stringfellow, *A Private and Public Faith*, 80.

7. Over his lifetime, Berrigan was an antiwar activist, an opponent of the death penalty, a writer, and an ally of later protest movements such as the Occupy movement, protesting inequality around the world. Berrigan died in April of 2016. See the essay on Berrigan in this book for more on his life and witness.

8. William Stringfellow, *Suspect Tenderness: The Ethics of the Berrigan Witness* (New York: Holt, Rinehart and Winston, 1971), 8–9.

9. William Stringfellow and Anthony Towne, "An Indictment & a Reply," *New York Review of Books*, February 11, 1971, http://www.nybooks.com/articles/1971/02/11/an-indictment-a-reply/.

10. Stringfellow, *Dissenter in a Great Society: A Christian View of America in Crisis* (Eugene, OR: Wipf and Stock, 2006), 79.

11. Stringfellow, *A Simplicity of Faith*, 44.

12. William Stringfellow, *Imposters of God* (Dayton, OH: G. A. Pflaum, 1969), xxi–xxii.

13. William Stringfellow, *An Ethic for Christians and Other Aliens in a Strange Land* (Waco: World Books, 1973), back cover.

14. William Stringfellow, *A Private and Public Faith*, 77.

15. Jason M. Breslow, "By the Numbers: Childhood Poverty in the U.S.," PBS.org, *Frontline*, http://www.pbs.org/wgbh/frontline/article/by-the-numbers-childhood-poverty-in-the-u-s/.

16. Shared Hope International, "FAQs," http://sharedhope.org/the-problem/faqs/.

17. Stringfellow, *A Private and Public Faith*, 22.

18. Stringfellow, *A Private and Public Faith*, 46.

19. Stringfellow, *A Private and Public Faith*, 74.

20. William Stringfellow, *A Second Birthday* (Garden City, NY: Doubleday, 1970), 21.

21. William Stringfellow, *Count It All Joy: Reflections on Faith, Doubt, and Temptation as Seen through the Letter of James* (Grand Rapids: Eerdmans, 1967), 16.

22. Stringfellow, *Dissenter in a Great Society*, 28.

23. Stringfellow, *Dissenter in a Great Society*, 13–14.

24. Stringfellow, *A Simplicity of Faith*, 130.

25. Stringfellow, *A Simplicity of Faith*, 37.

26. Stringfellow, *A Simplicity of Faith*, 51.

27. Stringfellow, *A Second Birthday*, 52.

28. Stringfellow, *A Second Birthday*, 39.

29. Stringfellow, *Dissenter in a Great Society*, vii.

30. Stringfellow, *A Private and Public Faith*, 92.

MAHALIA JACKSON

1. Mahalia Jackson interview with Studs Terkel, 1953, WFMT Studs Terkel Radio Archive, Chicago Historical Society.

2. Mahalia Jackson interview with Studs Terkel, 1953.

3. Deborah Williams, "His Eye Is on the Sparrow," National Public Radio, September 3, 2000, http://www.npr.org/2000/09/03/1081503/his-eye-is-on-the-sparrow.

4. Mahalia Jackson interview with Studs Terkel.

5. Mahalia Jackson interview with Studs Terkel.

6. Jules Schwerin, *Got to Tell It: Mahalia Jackson, Queen of Gospel* (Oxford: Oxford University Press, 1992), 21.

7. Schwerin, *Got to Tell It*, 21.

8. Mahalia Jackson interview with Studs Terkel.

9. Schwerin, *Got to Tell It*, 30.

10. Richard Wright, *12 Million Black Voices*, reprint ed. (New York: Basic Books, 2002), 35.

11. Michael W. Harris, *The Rise of Gospel Blues*, reprint ed. (Oxford: Oxford University Press, 1994), 258.

12. Harris, *The Rise of Gospel Blues*, 258.

13. Lorraine Dixon, "Teach It, Sister: Mahalia Jackson as Theologian in Song," *Black Theology in Britain: A Journal of Contextual Praxis* 2 (April 1999): 77.

14. W. E. B. DuBois, *The Souls of Black Folk* (Oxford: Oxford University Press, 2007), 147.

15. David Levering Lewis, introduction, *The Souls of Black Folk* (New York: Random House, 2003), iv.

16. Harris, *The Rise of Gospel Blues*, 258.

17. Harris, *The Rise of Gospel Blues*, 259.

18. Harris, *The Rise of Gospel Blues*, 259.

19. Studs Terkel, "Hi-Fi Show," September 30, 1957.

20. Dixon, "Teach It, Sister," 79.

21. Deborah Williams, "His Eye Is on the Sparrow."

22. Keith Morris, "Jesus Steps Right in When I Need Him Most."

23. Schwerin, *Got to Tell It*, 65.

24. Alden Whitman, "Mahalia Jackson, Gospel Singer, and a Civil Rights Symbol, Dies," *New York Times*, January 28, 1972.

25. Mahalia Jackson with Evan McLeon Wylie, *Movin' on Up* (New York: Hawthorn Books, 1966), 91.

26. Horace Clarence Boyer, notes accompanying *Gospels, Spirituals, and Hymns*, Sony Legacy, 1998, compact discs.

27. Johiri Jabir, "On Conjuring Mahalia: Mahalia Jackson, New Orleans, and the Sanctified Swing," *American Quarterly* 61, no. 3 (September 2009): 666.

28. Schwerin, *Got to Tell It*, 77–78.

29. Mark Burford, "Mahalia Jackson Meets the Wise Men: Defining Jazz at the Music Inn," *Musical Quarterly* 97, no. 3 (December 2014): 439.

30. Schwerin, *Got to Tell It*, 76.

31. Schwerin, *Got to Tell It*, 112.

32. Edward R. Murrow, "Person-to-Person" interview with Mahalia Jackson, Season 5, episode 30, March 28, 1958.

33. Jabir, "On Conjuring Mahalia," 663.

34. Keith D. Miller, *Voice of Deliverance: The Language of Martin Luther King, Jr., and Its Sources* (Athens: University of Georgia Press, 1998), 170.

35. https://www.youtube.com/watch?v=rZck6OXR_wE

36. Jabir, "On Conjuring Mahalia," 664.

37. Dixon, "Teach It, Sister," 88.

LUCY RANDOLPH MASON

1. Lucy Randolph Mason, *To Win These Rights: A Personal Story of the CIO* (New York: Harper and Brothers, 1952), 114–17.

2. Encyclopedia.com, s.v. "Mason, Lucy Randolph (1882–1959)," http://www.encyclopedia.com/women/encyclopedias-almanacs-tran scripts-and-maps/mason-lucy-randolph-1882-1959.

3. John A. Salmond, *Miss Lucy of the CIO: The Life and Times of Lucy Randolph Mason, 1882–1959* (Athens: University of Georgia Press, 1988), 1–14. Salmond's work is invaluable for biographical information on Mason. See also Mason, *To Win These Rights*.

4. In the South, class worked in a variety of ways. While the status of groups or individuals was often based on affluence, it was not always economic worth or wealth that undergirded a privileged station. At times, a group or individual's status was based on lineage or past family hegemony rather than on monetary superiority. See Bertram Wyatt Brown, *Southern Honor: Ethics and Behavior in the Old South* (New York: Oxford University Press, 1982).

5. Mason, *To Win These Rights*, 1.

6. Salmond, *Miss Lucy of the CIO*, 6.

7. Mason, *To Win These Rights*, 22.

8. Lucy Randolph Mason, "I Turned to Social Action Right at Home," in *Labor's Relation to Church and Community*, ed. Liston Pope (New York: Harper & Brothers, 1947), 146.

9. Mason, *To Win These Rights*, 3.

10. Salmond, *Miss Lucy of the CIO*, 3.

11. Mason, "I Turned to Social Action."

12. Mason quoted in Landon R. Y. Storrs, "Civilizing Capitalism: The National Consumers League and the Politics of Fair Labor Standards in the New Deal Era" (PhD diss., University of Wisconsin, 1996), 97.

13. See Lucy Randolph Mason, "The Divine Discontent," circa 1914–

1917, Adele Clark Papers, Special Collections, James Branch Cabell Library, Virginia Commonwealth University, Richmond, Virginia.

14. Salmond, *Miss Lucy of the CIO*, 8. Salmond quotes early drafts of Mason's *To Win These Rights*.

15. Paul Harvey, *Freedom's Coming: Religious Culture and the Shaping of the South from the Civil War to the Civil Rights Era* (Chapel Hill: University of North Carolina Press, 2007), 82.

16. Mason, "I Turned to Social Action," 146–47. There is some historical debate about the presence and pervasiveness of the Social Gospel movement in the South. Samuel Hill has argued that the Social Gospel did not make a significant impact in the region. But others—namely John Lee Eighmy and Wayne Flynt—have dissented from that opinion. See John Lee Eighmy, *Churches in Cultural Captivity*; J. Wayne Flynt, *Poor but Proud: Alabama's Poor Whites* (Tuscaloosa: University of Alabama Press, 1989). For further discussion, see my (Susan's) thesis, "'Life in Scorn of the Consequences': Clarence Jordan and the Roots of Radicalism in the Southern Baptist Convention" (MA thesis, University of Mississippi, 1994). Suffice it to say that for Lucy Mason, who was a Southerner and who worked primarily in the South, the Social Gospel was of significant influence.

17. See Mason, *To Win These Rights*, 1–18; Salmond, *Miss Lucy of the CIO*, 8–14.

18. Salmond, *Miss Lucy of the CIO*, 9–18.

19. See Mason, *To Win These Rights*, 1–18; Salmond, *Miss Lucy of the CIO*, 8–14.

20. Mason, *To Win These Rights*, 5.

21. Mason, *To Win These Rights*, 4.

22. Emma Lindsay, "Why I Am Skeptical of White Liberals in the Black Lives Matter Movement," *Medium*, July 14, 2016, https://medium.com/@emmalindsay/why-i-am-skeptical-of-white-liberals-in-the-black-lives-matter-movement-42a2b6eb2b0f#.r4xn0mv63.

23. Margaret Lee Neustadt, "Miss Lucy of the CIO: Lucy Randolph Mason, 1882–1959" (MA thesis, University of North Carolina at Chapel Hill, 1969), 8.

24. Neustadt, "Miss Lucy of the CIO," 10.

25. A growing number of Richmond's white community supported Mason's beliefs, although perhaps not as stridently. Langston Hughes visited colleagues of Mason's in Richmond in 1926 and later wrote, "Richmond was certainly kind to me. And I discover that not all Southerners are as vile as Mr. Mencken of Baltimore and the Negro press make them out to

be. I want to come back there sometime." Letter from Langston Hughes to Hunter Stage, Hunter Stage Collection, James Branch Cadell Library, Virginia Commonwealth University, December 1, 1926.

26. Neustadt, "Miss Lucy of the CIO," 12.

27. Mason, *To Win These Rights*, 4.

28. Encyclopedia.com, "Mason, Lucy Randolph."

29. *New York Times*, December 14, 1932, Mason quoted in Neustadt, "Miss Lucy of the CIO," 12–13.

30. Letter to Mr. Henry P. Kendell, Boston, MA, from Lucy Randolph Mason, February 27, 1931, Lucy Randolph Mason Papers, Operation Dixie Collection, Duke University Library.

31. Encyclopedia.com, "Mason, Lucy Randolph."

32. Letter to Elizabeth Magee from Lucy Randolph Mason, November 15, 1944, reel 29, National Consumers League Papers, Library of Congress.

33. Lucy Randolph Mason, "The Divine Discontent," circa 1914–1917, Adele Clark Papers, Special Collections, James Branch Cabell Library, Virginia Commonwealth University, Richmond, Virginia.

34. Mason papers, Duke University, circular letter, August 31, 1937.

35. Mason, *To Win These Rights*, 16.

36. She explained her interest in the South: "Much of my time is spent working in the South because it is the most backward section." Letter to Robert Rivers Lamonte from Lucy Randolph Mason, June 23, 1936, reel 29, National Consumers League Papers, Library of Congress.

37. Hollinger F. Barnard, ed., *Outside the Magic Circle: The Autobiography of Virginia Foster Durr* (Tuscaloosa: University of Alabama Press, 1990), 118.

38. See Zieger's *The CIO* (Chapel Hill: University of North Carolina Press, 1997), 66–89; Steve Rosswurm, ed., *The CIO's Left-Led Unions* (New Brunswick, NJ: Rutgers University Press, 1992); Michael Kazin, *The Populist Persuasion: An American History* (New York: Basic Books, 1995).

39. Encyclopedia.com, "Mason, Lucy Randolph."

40. Encyclopedia.com, "Mason, Lucy Randolph."

41. Mason, *To Win These Rights*, 24, 26, 29–30.

42. Mason, *To Win These Rights*, 26. Mason does not report how she dealt with these cases; she only relates that she "reported the success of the mission in some detail to Mr. Bittner."

43. Zieger, *The CIO*, 75–76.

44. Letter to Franklin Delano Roosevelt from Lucy Randolph Mason,

August 12, 1937, reel 62, Lucy Randolph Mason Papers, Operation Dixie Collection, Duke University Library.

45. Letter to Eleanor Roosevelt from Lucy Randolph Mason, May 28, 1940, reel 62, Lucy Randolph Mason Papers, Operation Dixie Collection, Duke University Library.

46. Letter to Lucy Mason from Franklin D. Roosevelt, October 7, 1940, reel 62, Lucy Randolph Mason Papers, Operation Dixie Collection, Duke University Library.

47. Lucy Randolph Mason, circular letter to ministers for Labor Day, August 25, 1937, reel 62, Lucy Randolph Mason Papers, Operation Dixie Collection, Duke University Library.

48. Salmond, *Miss Lucy of the CIO*, 82–83.

49. Lucy Randolph Mason, circular letter, February 24, 1938, quoted in Neustadt, "Miss Lucy of the CIO," 34.

50. See Mason correspondence to Eleanor and Franklin Roosevelt, John E. Rankin, and the FBI, April 15, 1938, reel 62, Lucy Randolph Mason Papers, Operation Dixie Collection, Duke University Library. See also Mason, *To Win These Rights*, 50–53; Neustadt, "Miss Lucy of the CIO," 38–41; Salmond, *Miss Lucy of the CIO*, 82–83.

51. See Letter to Lucy Randolph Mason from J. Edgar Hoover regarding his assignment of the case to "Joseph B. Keenan, The Assistant to the Attorney General, U.S. Department of Justice, Washington, DC, for such attention as he may deem appropriate," July 16, 1938.

52. Salmond, *Miss Lucy of the CIO*, 82–83.

53. Mason, *To Win These Rights*, 75.

54. Letter to Lucy Mason from Jonathan Daniels, September 9, 1937, reel 62, Lucy Randolph Mason Papers, Operation Dixie Collection, Duke University Library. Daniels's letters reveal an editor sensitive to the effects of race on labor in the South. This same note asks Mason for information on hotel employment. He noticed that in many large urban Southern hotels "white girls have been substituted almost entirely for Negro waiters. I wonder if anyone has made a study of the extent to which this has taken place, where these girls come from, and how much they make—also what happens to the Negroes." He knew of Mason that "if anybody can give [the information] to me you can." Mason referred Daniels to the NAACP and the National Urban League, both of whose boards she was a member. Mason to Jonathan Daniels, September 11, 1937, reel 62, Lucy Randolph Mason Papers, Operation Dixie Collection, Duke University Library.

55. John Egerton, phone interview by author, notes in Glisson's possession, July 29, 1999.

56. Letter to Lucy Mason from Grover C. Hall, January 18, 1938, reel 65, Lucy Randolph Mason Papers, Operation Dixie Collection, Duke University Library.

57. Mason, *To Win These Rights*, 39–40.

58. She listed three areas which required prison reform in South Carolina: "(1) there should be no sale of prison-made goods; (2) the state should employ its own personnel to direct the prison industry rather than hiring private business to direct it; and (3) the state should pass an act prohibiting the sale of prison-made goods from other states." Neustadt, "Miss Lucy of the CIO," 60. See also letter to W. R. Harley from Lucy Randolph Mason, September 22, 1939; letter to James C. Derieux from Lucy Randolph Mason, September 1939, reel 62, Lucy Randolph Mason Papers, Operation Dixie Collection, Duke University Library.

59. Neustadt, "Miss Lucy of the CIO," 60–62.

60. Letter to Eleanor Roosevelt from Lucy Randolph Mason, January 20, 1940, reel 62, Lucy Randolph Mason Papers, Operation Dixie Collection, Duke University Library.

61. Margaret Neustadt's thesis records this attempt by Mason to secure federal intervention through Mrs. Roosevelt. The thesis does not show Roosevelt's response, and there is no corresponding record in Mason's papers.

62. See Neustadt, "Miss Lucy of the CIO," 117, 126.

63. Letter to William R. Moody from Lucy Randolph Mason, October, 25, 1951, reel 62, Lucy Randolph Mason Papers, Operation Dixie Collection, Duke University Library.

64. Neustadt, "Miss Lucy of the CIO," 131.

65. Address by Mason, circa 1951, reel 65, Lucy Randolph Mason Papers, Operation Dixie Collection, Duke University Library.

Richard Twiss

1. Terry LeBlanc, "In Memoriam: Richard Leo Twiss," in Richard Twiss, *Rescuing the Gospel from the Cowboys* (Downers Grove, IL: IVP Books, 2015), 9.

2. "Rosebud Sioux Reservation," Atka Lakota Museum and Cultural Center website, http://aktalakota.stjo.org/site/News2?page=NewsArticle &id=8658.

3. James B. LaGrand, *Indian Metropolis: Native Americans in Chicago, 1945-75* (Chicago: University of Illinois Press, 2002), 18.

4. Richard Twiss, 2011 plenary session talk, Christian Community Development Association (CCDA) 2011 National Conference, https://www.youtube.com/watch?v=fGw7AU6VDOs (hereafter 2011 CCDA talk).

5. Richard Twiss, *One Church, Many Tribes* (Ventura, CA: Regal Books, 2000), 17.

6. Willie James Jennings, *The Christian Imagination* (New Haven: Yale University Press, 2010), 6.

7. Twiss, *One Church, Many Tribes*, 39-40.

8. Twiss, 2011 CCDA talk.

9. Twiss, 2011 CCDA talk.

10. Twiss, *One Church, Many Tribes*, 27.

11. LaGrand, *Indian Metropolis*, 206-7.

12. LaGrand, *Indian Metropolis*, 211.

13. Twiss, *One Church, Many Tribes*, 37.

14. Twiss, 2011 CCDA talk.

15. Twiss, *One Church, Many Tribes*, 30.

16. Twiss, *One Church, Many Tribes*, 31.

17. "Disparities," Indian Health Service, https://www.ihs.gov/newsroom/factsheets/disparities/.

18. Twiss, *One Church, Many Tribes*, 31.

19. Twiss, *One Church, Many Tribes*, 32.

20. Twiss, *One Church, Many Tribes*, 33.

21. Twiss, 2011 CCDA talk.

22. Richard Twiss, *Rescuing the Gospel from the Cowboys*, 37.

23. Richard Twiss, *Dancing Our Prayers* (Vancouver, WA: Wiconi Press, 1998), 10.

24. Twiss, 2011 CCDA talk.

25. Twiss, *Dancing Our Prayers*, 33.

26. Twiss, *Rescuing the Gospel from the Cowboys*, 12.

27. "A Brief History of NAIITS," NAIITS website, https://www.naiits.com/history/.

28. See Soong-Chan Rah, "The Power of Personal Story," chap. 1 in *Return to Justice* (Grand Rapids: Brazos, 2016).

29. Twiss, 2011 CCDA talk.

30. Twiss, 2011 CCDA talk.

31. Twiss, 2011 CCDA talk.

DANIEL BERRIGAN

1. Daniel Berrigan, *Prayer for the Morning Headlines: On the Sanctity of Life and Death* (Baltimore: Apprentice House, 2007), on the cover.

2. Berrigan, *To Dwell in Peace: An Autobiography* (San Francisco: Harper & Row, 1987), 47.

3. Daniel Cosacchi and Eric Martin, eds., *The Berrigan Letters: Personal Correspondence between Daniel and Philip Berrigan* (Maryknoll, NY: Orbis Books, 2016), 7.

4. Berrigan, *To Dwell in Peace*, 108-9.

5. Berrigan, *To Dwell in Peace*, 121.

6. Berrigan, *Selected & New Poems* (New York: Doubleday, 1973), 9.

7. Berrigan, *Consequences: Truth and . . .* (New York: Macmillan, 1967), 17.

8. Cosacchi and Martin, *The Berrigan Letters*, 29.

9. Daniel Berrigan, *Night Flight: War Diary with 11 Poems* (New York: Macmillan, 1968), 40.

10. Daniel Berrigan, *Testimony: The Word Made Flesh* (Maryknoll, NY: Orbis Books, 2004), 124.

11. Quoted in Walter B. Kalaidjian, *Languages of Liberation: The Social Text in Contemporary American Poetry* (New York: Columbia University Press, 1989), 164.

12. Berrigan, *To Dwell in Peace*, 181.

13. Martin Luther King Jr., "Beyond Vietnam" (speech, Riverside Church, New York, April 4, 1967).

14. Cosacchi and Martin, *The Berrigan Letters*, 30.

15. Berrigan, *To Dwell in Peace*, 180.

16. Sharon Erickson Nepstad, *Religion and War Resistance in the Plowshares Movement* (Cambridge: Cambridge University Press, 2008), 47-48.

17. Paul G. Pierpaoli Jr., "Balitmore Four," *The Encyclopedia of the Vietnam War: A Political, Social, and Military History*, ed. Spencer C. Tucker (Oxford: Oxford University Press, 2001), 92.

18. Cosacchi and Martin, *The Berrigan Letters*, 39.

19. Cosacchi and Martin, *The Berrigan Letters*, 43.

20. Daniel Berrigan, *Lamentations: From New York to Kabul and Beyond* (Chicago: Sheed and Ward, 2002), 13.

21. Berrigan, *To Dwell in Peace*, 200-201.

22. Patrick Henry, "New Biography of Jesuit Fr. Daniel Berrigan Outlines His Activism, Exile," *National Catholic Reporter*, May 7, 2018, https://

www.ncronline.org/news/people/new-biography-jesuit-fr-daniel-berri
gan-outlines-his-activism-exile.

23. Daniel Berrigan, "Our Apologies, Good Friends," in *Daniel Berrigan: Essential Writings,* ed. John Dear (Maryknoll, NY: Orbis Books, 2016), 105.

24. Berrigan, *To Dwell in Peace,* 219.

25. Berrigan, *To Dwell in Peace,* 217–20.

26. Cosacchi and Martin, *The Berrigan Letters,* 47.

27. Cosacchi and Martin, *The Berrigan Letters,* 63.

28. *Investigation of a Flame,* documentary directed by Lynn Sachs (New York: Icarus Films, 2003), DVD.

29. Daniel Berrigan, *America Is Hard to Find: Notes from the Underground and Letters from Danbury Prison* (Doubleday: New York, 1972), 96.

30. Daniel Berrigan and Robert Coles, *Geography of Faith: Conversations between Daniel Berrigan When Underground, and Robert Coles* (Boston: Beacon, 1971), 25.

31. Anthony Towne and William Stringfellow, "On Sheltering Criminal Priests," in *Suspect Tenderness: The Ethics of the Berrigan Witness* (Eugene, OR: Wipf and Stock, 2006), 22.

32. Towne and Stringfellow, "On Sheltering Criminal Priests," 31.

33. Towne and Stringfellow, "On Sheltering Criminal Priests," 48.

34. Berrigan, "Trial of the Catonsville Nine" in *Poetry, Drama, Prose,* (Maryknoll, NY: Orbis Books, 1988), 240–41.

35. Daniel Berrigan, *And the Risen Bread: Selected Poems,* ed. John Dear (New York: Fordham, 1998), 230, used with permission of the Daniel Berrigan Literary Trust, 2018.

36. Berrigan, *Testimony,* 5–6.

37. "Jeremy Scahill Remembers His Longtime Friend Daniel Berrigan," Jeremy Scahill, interview by Amy Goodman, *Democracy Now!,* May 3, 2016, https://www.youtube.com/watch?v=Jc28QfybR34.

38. Daniel Berrigan, *We Die Before We Live: Talking with the Very Ill* (Seabury: New York, 1980), 23.

39. Berrigan, *We Die Before We Live,* 41.

40. Berrigan, *Lamentations,* 31.

41. Berrigan, *Testimony,* 203.

42. Berrigan, *Testimony,* 220–21.

43. Daniel Berrigan, The Mission*: A Film Journal* (San Francisco: Harper & Row, 1986), 149.

44. Chris Hedges, "Daniel Berrigan: Forty Years after Catonsville," *The Nation,* May 20, 2008, http://www.thenation.com/doc/20080602/hedges.

MARY STELLA SIMPSON

1. Sr. Mary Stella Simpson, *Sister Stella's Babies: Days in the Practice of a Nurse-Midwife* (New York: American Journal of Nursing Company, 1978), 20. This book, one of the few sources about Sister Mary Stella Simpson, contains excerpts from letters she wrote to her Sisters at St. Mary's Hospital in Evansville, Indiana, during her first year in Mound Bayou. Excerpts from this book will be noted with the date of the letter.

2. Unless otherwise noted, the quotes from Sr. Mary Stella in this section have been taken from a short autobiography she wrote for the Daughters of Charity: "Sr. Mary Stella Simpson, August 27, 1910–April 19, 2004," in *Memories, Vol. 8: Daughters of Charity, East Central Province, 2003–2005* (Evansville, IN: Mater Dei Provincialate, n.d.), 99–111. I would like to thank the Daughters of Charity who made this autobiography available to me through their Provincial Archives and for their assistance with this project. Additional material, including quotations, is taken from a three-hour interview with Sr. Mary Stella conducted by Irene Matousek for the American College of Nurse-Midwives Oral History Project. Citations from that interview will simply be noted with "Matousek interview." See Irene Matousek, "Interview with Mary Stella Simpson, 1993-10-30," University of Kentucky Special Collections Research Center, Oral History Collection: ACNM001, Transaction Number: 6100, https://kentuckyoral history.org/catalog/xt7k3j393148. Additional background information provided by Suzy Farren, "Sr. Mary Stella's Babies," *Catholic Digest* (October 1992): 45–50.

3. See the Daughters of Charity, "Early History," http://daughtersof charity.org/about-us/early-history/, and "Who We Are," http://daughters ofcharity.org/about-us/the-daughters-of-charity/.

4. The largest Catholic health system today, Ascension Health, was formed through a merger of the Daughters of Charity National Health System and the Sisters of St. Joseph Health System in 1999. At that time, the DCNHS included nearly eighty hospitals, nursing homes, outpatient clinics, and other health care facilities in fifteen states. See http://ascen sion.org/about/history. Catholic Sisters began arriving in America in 1728 to care for the poor sick, often invited by local bishops or physicians. Almost three hundred years later, the Catholic health ministry comprises the largest group of nonprofit health care providers in the US with more than 600 hospitals and 1,400 long-term-care health facilities in all fifty states, representing approximately 15 percent of all hospital admissions

and outpatient visits annually. This history is recounted in careful and comprehensive detail in Christopher Kauffman, *Ministry and Meaning: A Religious History of Catholic Health Care in the United States* (New York: Crossroad, 1995). For information on the scope of Catholic health care in the US see Catholic Health Association, "Catholic Health Care in the United States: Fact Sheet January 2017," https://www.chausa.org/docs /default-source/default-document-library/cha_2017_miniprofile.pdf ?sfvrsn=0.

5. St. Vincent Medical Center, "About Us: History of St. Vincent Medical Center," https://stvincent.verity.org/about-us/.

6. Sr. M. Theophane Shoemaker, *History of Nurse-Midwifery in the United States* (Washington, DC: Catholic University of America Press, 1947).

7. Anne Z. Cockerham and Arlene W. Keeling, "Faith and Finance at the Catholic Maternity Institute, Santa Fe, New Mexico, 1944–1969," *Nursing History Review* 18 (2010): 152–53, https://doi.org/10.1891/1062 -8061.18.151.

8. For the novelty of this, see the 1972 article about Sr. Mary Stella: "'Dad's Lib' Is Urged in Maternity Wards," *Chicago Tribune*, November 26, 1972, http://archives.chicagotribune.com/1972/11/26/page/368 /article/dads-lib-is-urged-in-maternity-wards.

9. "In Remembrance: Sister Mary Stella Simpson, ACNM's Fifth President," *Journal of Midwifery & Women's Health* 49, no. 5 (September–October 2004): 469, https://doi.org/10.1016/j.jmwh.2004.06.006.

10. Eventually the organization had six certified nurse-midwives and covered five counties.

11. Mound Bayou was recently visited by Melissa Block, a correspondent for National Public Radio, as part of its Our Land series. See "Here's What's Become of a Historic All-Black Town in the Mississippi Delta," *NPR*, March 8, 2017, http://www.npr.org/2017/03/08/515814287/heres -whats-become-of-a-historic-all-black-town-in-the-mississippi-delta.

12. Charles Stringer Jr., "Jewel of the Delta: Mound Bayou, Mississippi" (capstone project, California State University Monterey Bay, May 2002), http://digitalcommons.csumb.edu/cgi/viewcontent.cgi?article =1257&context=caps_thes.

13. The material in this section about Mound Bayou was drawn from the two previous sources as well as the following. Please consult these to learn more about the important and vibrant history of Mound Bayou: *The Mound Bayou, Mississippi, Story*, The Delta Center for Culture and Learn-

ing, Delta State University, https://ia801408.us.archive.org/7/items /moundbayoumissisootext/moundbayoumissisootext.pdf; Jon Ross and John H. Rodgers III, *Mound Bayou: Jewel of the Delta* (Chicago: JR2 Films, 2012), https://vimeo.com/34941038; "Portrait of a Black Town: Mound Bayou—Past, Present, and Future," *Mound Bayou's "The Voice"* 4, no. 8 (July 1971): 1–40; Booker T. Washington, "A Town Owned by Negroes: Mound Bayou, Miss., an Example of Thrift and Self-Government," in *Booker T. Washington Rediscovered, Supplemental Materials*, ed. Michael Scott Bieze and Marybeth Gasman (Baltimore: Johns Hopkins University Press, 2012), originally published in *World's Work*, July 1907; Norman L. Crockett, *The Black Towns* (Lawrence: Regents Press of Kansas, 1979).

14. Rev. Dr. Otis Moss III, "The Genius of African People" (sermon, Trinity United Church of Christ, Chicago, Illinois, February 28, 2016).

15. Simpson, *Memories*, 5.

16. The information on the Tufts-Delta Health Center is drawn from the following sources: Jennifer Nelson, "Medicine May Be the Way We Got in the Door: Social Justice and Community Health in the Mid-1960s," in *More Than Medicine: A History of the Feminist Women's Health Movement* (New York: New York University Press, 2015), 15–56; Jennifer Nelson, "'Hold Your Head Up and Stick Out Your Chin': Community Health and Women's Health in Mound Bayou, Mississippi," *NWSA Journal* 17, no. 1 (Spring 2005): 99–118; Greta de Jong, "Plantation Politics: The Tufts-Delta Health Center and Interracial Class Conflict in Mississippi: 1956–1972," in *The War on Poverty: A New Grassroots History, 1964–1980*, ed. Annelise Orleck and Lisa Gayle Hazirjian (Athens: University of Georgia Press, 2011), 256–79; John Dittmer, "Interview with Dr. H. Jack Geiger," Civil Rights History Project, Southern Oral History Program, Smithsonian Institution's National Museum of African American History and Culture and the Library of Congress, March 16, 2013, video and transcript available at https://www.loc.gov/item/afc2010039_crhp0076/; and Thomas Ward Jr., *Out in the Rural: A Mississippi Health Center and Its War on Poverty* (Oxford: Oxford University Press, 2016).

17. The median annual income of Mound Bayou was less than $1,000 per family per year, the unemployment rate was over 50 percent, 90 percent of the dwellings were unfit for human habitation, and the infant mortality rate was 59 percent. Malnutrition, particularly among children, was widespread, and Geiger found himself writing prescriptions for food. Most rural African Americans at the time had never seen a doctor due to a dearth of African American physicians. Many hospitals that would admit

African Americans turned away patients who could not pay, though health insurance was largely unavailable to blacks due to discrimination in the insurance industry.

18. The NHC network expanded quickly, and today there are more than thirteen hundred community health centers in the US, providing care at over nine thousand sites of clinical service, serving more than twenty-five million low-income patients. H. Jack Geiger, "The First Community Health Center in Mississippi: Communities Empowering Themselves," *American Journal of Public Health* 106, no. 10 (October 2016): 1740. These sites are now referred to as Federally Qualified Health Centers (FQHC), and the TDHC—now the Delta Health Center—has the distinction of being the first FQHC in the US.

19. Suzy Farren, *A Call to Care: The Women Who Built Catholic Healthcare in America* (St. Louis: Catholic Health Association, 1996), DVD.

20. Mary Stella Simpson, "Walking with Wise Women," *Charity Connections* 38 (Spring 2009): 4.

21. County Health Rankings and Roadmaps, http://www.county healthrankings.org/app/mississippi/2017/rankings/bolivar/county/out comes/overall/snapshot.

22. Mississippi Department of Health, "Infant Mortality Report, 2016," http://msdh.ms.gov/msdhsite/_static/resources/7027.pdf.

Index

Page numbers in *italics* represent photographs.